SHEPHERDS SPEAK

SHEPHERDS SPEAK

AMERICAN BISHOPS CONFRONT THE SOCIAL AND MORAL ISSUES THAT CHALLENGE CHRISTIANS TODAY

Edited by Dennis M. Corrado
and James F. Hinchey

CROSSROAD · NEW YORK

The Crossroad Publishing Company
370 Lexington Avenue, New York, N.Y. 10017

Printed in the United States of America

Library of Congress Cataloging in Publication Data

Shepherds speak.
   1. Catholic Church—United States.   2. Catholic
Church—United States—Bishops.   3. United States—
Social conditions—1980-   4. United States—Moral
conditions.   I. Corrado, Dennis M.   II. Hinchey, James F.
BX1406.2.S53 1986   282'.73   86-8967
ISBN 0-8245-0737-1

To Francis J. Mugavero, D.D., Bishop of Brooklyn,
whose unfailing support gives testimony
to the encouraging ways shepherds speak.

Contents

Foreword

> They will not ask his help unless they believe in him,
> and they will not hear of him unless they get a preacher,
> and they will never have a preacher unless one is sent.
> ... So faith comes from what is preached, and what is
> preached comes from the word of Christ. (Rom. 10:
> 14–17)

Such was St. Paul's practical interpretation of the word of Christ who, bidding farewell to the apostles at the appointed meeting place in Galilee, had given the mandate, "Go, therefore, make disciples of all nations" (Matt. 28:19). Thus has it been through the nearly twenty centuries of the Church's history, and thus will it remain in one form or another until the end of time.

Nor was it different at the birth of the organized Catholic community in the United States when John Carroll, founder of the American hierarchy, as Bishop of Baltimore addressed the first pastoral letter to his far-flung flock in May, 1792. If he could not enjoy the consolation of seeing them all, he said, at least he could leave them, "according to the nature of my duty some words of exhortation, by which you may be strengthened in faith and encouraged in the exercises of a Christian life."[1] That in essence has continued to be the duty of all Carroll's successors down to the present day as the approximately 400 American bishops approach their bicentennial year of 1989.

"Shepherds speak" in a variety of ways. If the pastoral letter of an individual bishop, such as Carroll's of 1792, has been a favorite device of American prelates for fulfilling their obligation as moral teachers to their clergy, religious, and laity, they have employed the same medium when gathered in council with their fellow bishops. At each of the seven provincial and three plenary councils held in Baltimore between 1829 and 1884, the bishops "spoke" through the canons or decrees they enacted for the guidance of their people. Likewise at the close of these ten assemblies they issued a joint pastoral letter wherein they combined moral directives with both positive and negative comments on the current national scene that related to doctrinal and moral issues. As societal trends changed, so too did the content and emphasis of the bishops' comments, and thus their pronouncements constituted an extended commentary on American life as it touched the Church and her members. For example, when the abuse of lay trusteeism was an acute problem for certain congregations the pastoral letter of the First Provincial Council in October, 1829—the first and only time that the laity were addressed directly—the latter were warned:

> We feel it to be our duty to declare to you, that in no part of the Catholic Church does the right of instituting or dismissing a clergyman to or from any benefice or mission, with or without the care of souls, exist in any one, save the ordinary prelate of the diocese or district in which such benefice or mission is found.[2]

With the gradual elimination of lay intrusion of this kind the bishops returned to the subject only one more time (1837), after which it was heard of no more.

Thus has it been throughout the American Catholic past for problems that either found a solution or for one reason or another ceased to be a serious concern. It has been otherwise in the case of persistent problems that not only perdured but have grown more serious with the passage of time. Here divorce offers a prime example. The Fifth Provincial Council of Baltimore in the spring of 1843 condemned divorce with a severity that reflected the general reprobation with which it was then viewed, and the practice was repeatedly condemned in episcopal pronouncements thereafter.

If bishops are compelled on occasion to speak on unpopular themes that give rise to dissent, and that not only from outside the Church but at times from Catholics themselves—here abortion offers an example of what is meant—they have solid precedent for continuing to affirm the Church's teaching in the face of opposition. Thus when Jesus spoke in the synagogue of Capernaum and said, "He who eats my flesh and drinks my blood lives in me and I live in him," he met immediate resistance, for Saint John tells us, "After this, many of his disciples left him and stopped going with him" (John 6:56, 66). Yet opposition did not cause the Master either to alter his teaching or to lapse into silence on the basic truth embodied in the Eucharist. As authentic spokesmen of the Church, bishops have no alternative in circumstances of this kind and must be reconciled to paying the price that the enunciation of Christian truths demands of them. This is especially the case in an age such as our own where the pervasive and extreme individualism has taken a heavy toll on the concept of authority in general, a situation quite unknown to the immigrant ancestors of American Catholics.

There have, indeed, been occasions of that kind in the history of the Catholic Church in the United States, for example, in November, 1943, when the bishops spoke in behalf of the rights of the blacks, and initiated a policy of integration in St. Louis, Washington, and Raleigh that led to vociferous opposition from many Catholics in those dioceses, not to mention the resistance shown in solidly Catholic neighborhoods in Chicago, Milwaukee, New Orleans, and Boston on the same score. The bishops in question continued, nonetheless, to speak on the evils of racism, as they did at length in their statement, *Discrimination and Christian Conscience* of November, 1958.[3] On this subject the bishops were far in advance of large segments of their clergy and laity, and their consistent and persistent teaching ultimately contributed to the full integration of Catholic churches, schools, hospitals, and other institutions, abetted as they were by the national drive of those years for racial justice. In a word, initial resistance to what bishops speak can with patient persistence give way to acceptance.

Historically speaking, the circumstances of each succeeding period of the American past have accounted in large measure for what the United States bishops have said and what they have not said. Even though Catholics had become by 1850 the largest religious denomination in the Republic, they continued for more than a century thereafter to be regarded by many of their fellow citizens as a "foreign" people out of tune with the national ethos. By 1950, however, that situation had begun to change in a radical way with an increasingly prominent role being played by Catholics in politics—their original breakthrough—the professions, and the world of business and finance. With these gains came a wave of confidence hitherto unknown in Catholic ranks, a confidence felt by bishops as well as by Catholic laymen and laywomen. The point can be illustrated by what the bishops did not say in a more timid age when the United States waged unjust wars against Mexico in the 1840's and against Spain in 1898. The historical record yields nothing by way of episcopal pronouncements that called in question those unjustified resorts to armed conflict.

Mutatis mutandis, the same can be said for American interventions in Central America and Vietnam in the present century. Only in 1971 did the bishops speak out strongly on the Vietnam War and urge that the United States withdraw its armed forces from Southeast Asia. But the intervening years witnessed a marked change in that regard with a confident approach that not only found expression in repeated statements condemning armed intervention in Central America but also in the detailed pastoral letter on nuclear warfare, *The Challenge of Peace: God's Promise and Our Response*, voted by an overwhelming majority of the bishops in May, 1983. This striking challenge to many positions held by the American government drew criticism, to be sure, but it also prompted notable approval from one of the ranking authorities on international relations when George F. Kennan, former ambassador to Russia and professor emeritus at the Institute for Advanced Study at Princeton characterized the pastoral letter as

> the most profound and searching inquiry yet conducted by any responsible collective body into the relations of nuclear weaponry, and indeed of modern war in general, to moral philosophy, to politics and to the conscience of the national state.[4]

If in this instance the bishops spoke in a manner to evoke such praise from so distinguished a source, it was due as well to their exhaustive consultation that enriched the document with the opinions of a wide spectrum of experts from various walks of life. In fine, the pastoral of 1983 made history in more ways than one, and the same widespread consultation has been followed in the hierarchy's pastoral letter on the United States economy which is scheduled for final action in 1986. Here, then, is the voice of American bishops speaking with a sophistication and professional approach that illustrates the new-found confidence mentioned above, an approach that has gained them not only a national audience but international attention as well.

Meanwhile, conscious as they have been that like Newman's gentleman they must "have their eyes on all their company," forty-two bishops have responded to the invitation of the co-pastors of Brooklyn's Cathedral of St. James to address themselves to a wide variety of topics, all of which have relevance for the People of God in the 1980's. The eighteen papers presented in this book range all the way from the highly pertinent subject, "Theological Diversity and Dissent within the Church," of Richard J. Sklba, Auxiliary Bishop of Milwaukee, to a complementary theme, "Bishops and Theologians in the American Church: Their Mutual Contributions," by John S. Cummins, Bishop of Oakland. That is to cite only two examples from the rich fare this book affords. All eighteen are well worth a reader's careful perusal. Mention of the Sklba and Cummins contributions is meant to call attention to two aspects of what in the judgment of many observers is at the moment the single most troublesome problem in American Catholic circles, namely, the pervasive divisiveness within this religious community. If that has been markedly true among theologians, they are by no means unique in that regard, nor have the bishops themselves remained untouched by the swirling currents of ideological controversy. These differences are, of course, nothing new in the Church's history, the record of which demonstrates that if held within reasonable limits diverse opinions can redound to the general good. By the same token, however, if differing opinions are carried to excess with no room left for legitimate and contrasting views, they can—and have—inflicted serious injury on the unity of the Christian cause.

Here, then, are shepherds speaking on a variety of subjects that relate to the American Catholic scene as it unfolds in these closing years of the twentieth century, a scene that has grown both more enriched and more complicated by Catholics' acceptance in the national mainstream. The original mandate of Jesus mentioned above remains the same, the approach and style change with the new cultural patterns of these postconciliar years. Thus are these

bishops fulfilling the duty incumbent on all who bear public witness to the Master, a duty which Pope John Paul II described in
1982 when he spoke to the representatives of the major seminaries
of Italy in words that can be applied as well to bishops. John Paul
declared:

> It is necessary in particular that knowledge of the movements
> of philosophical thought and of literature, the reading of the
> events of history and of the cultural and social formation of
> peoples, and the whole humanistic formation in general should
> give the future pastor of souls that capacity of interpreting
> the outstanding stages of human civilization in a Christian
> key, in order to be truly a spiritual guide for his contempo-
> raries, especially for youth.[5]

JOHN TRACY ELLIS
Professorial Lecturer in Church History
The Catholic University of America

NOTES

1. Hugh J. Nolan ed., *Pastoral Letters of the United States Catholic Bishops*
   (Washington: United States Catholic Conference, 1984), I, 16.
2. Ibid., I, 46.
3. Ibid., II, 201–206.
4. *The New York Times*, Sunday, May 1, 1983, p. E 21.
5. *L'Osservatore Romano* (English weekly edition), February 15, 1982, p. 8.

Introduction

Those readers old enough to remember the preconciliar Church (now that more than twenty years have elapsed since the end of the Second Vatican Council) would probably agree that there were few memorable public voices among U.S. Catholic bishops of that period. For years, before the National Conference of Catholic Bishops was reorganized following Vatican II, American Catholics were apt to know who their local bishop was and knew something about the handful of cardinal-archbishops whose pronouncements and activities created headlines in major newspapers. But other than this, most contact with bishops tended to be primarily ceremonial, and one would be hard-pressed to recall occasions when individual bishops came to national attention for expressing vigorous or prophetic views. In fact, many Catholics grew up knowing virtually nothing about what their own bishops thought concerning important social, moral, political, or spiritual matters.

Certainly, this had not always been true about bishops in America. One has only to think of some of the more colorful and outspoken nineteenth-century bishops, such as John Carroll, John Ireland, "Dagger" John Hughes, James Cardinal Gibbons, and John England, to be reminded that the postmodernist appearance of episcopal uniformity of voice and viewpoint represents more of a detour in American Church history than its most authentic traditions.

During the past several years, more than forty bishops and archbishops from every region of the United States have participated in an historic series of talks sponsored by the Cathedral-Basilica of St. James in the Diocese of Brooklyn. This present volume—a collection of eighteen of those presentations on issues as diverse as capital punishment, racism, disarmament, religion and politics, capitalism, women in the Church, poverty in America, theological diversity and dissent—represents a return to the best traditions of Church leadership with bishops who are both teachers and listeners, shepherds who speak with courage and insight, with vigor and compassion. These spokesmen for the Roman Catholic community in our country are boldly confronting some of the thorniest, most complex issues that now challenge Roman Catholics, Christians of different ecclesial traditions, and men and women of conscience everywhere. The cross-section of topics chosen for inclusion in this volume are refreshingly diverse, but are, at the same time, unified by a common thread of concern for the sacredness of life and the dignity of all human persons.

In addition to clarifying major issues, *Shepherds Speak* is also meant to be a source of encouragement and hope for those searching, hungering, struggling Catholics who have often bemoaned the scarcity of bishops who were more forthcoming, daring, willing to stand alone, capable of pursuing a more prophetic course, more open to diversity, less afraid of dialogue and consultation, less prone to equate unity with uniformity. *Shepherds Speak* dramatically demonstrates that a still-growing number of bishops across this land are emerging from a cloud of relative anonymity to respond to the challenges that the Gospel poses for people of every age.

The variety found in this volume is ideal for parish leadership teams, lay and religious ministers, adult-education programs, ecumenical discussion groups, peace and justice committees, R.C.I.A. programs, the ongoing formation of parish councils, and religious studies programs in high schools and colleges. Directors of religious education will also welcome this volume as an authentic teaching instrument. It provides contemporary and concise answers to the often heard question: "But what does the Church teach?"

For the baby-boom generation of Catholics who are looking again at active membership in the Catholic Church, *Shepherds Speak* is a succinct guide to reentry into a Church rekindled by the spirit of Vatican II. These reflections are for all those interested in knowing what *aggiornamento* and "opening the windows" mean for the Catholic Church, especially as it seeks dialogue and loving relationships with other religious traditions and modern cultures.

It is encouraging to observe that several of the topics originally addressed in *Shepherds Speak* at St. James Cathedral in Brooklyn subsequently became agenda items for the National Conference of Catholic Bishops. Clearly, it has been helpful to create an environment wherein bishops might speak out. They did speak out, and their brother bishops began to listen to them and act. In these articles, and in the pastoral letters of the last several years, the American Catholic shepherds have begun to exhibit a healthy vitality, a publicly expressed desire to become the teachers they were ordained to be. They are actively seeking to understand and to be understood. We can only hope that by becoming more accessible to us, more forthright with us, more courageous for us, they will learn more deeply how to know and serve all those who listen when shepherds speak.

DENNIS M. CORRADO
JAMES F. HINCHEY
Co-Rectors
Cathedral-Basilica of St. James
Brooklyn, New York

Part I

Ecclesia Semper Reformanda:
The Life of the Church Itself

The Church as a Community of Conscience

CARROLL T. DOZIER
Retired Bishop of Memphis

"Silver and gold I have none; but what I have, that I give thee. In the name of Jesus Christ of Nazareth, arise and walk." (Acts 3:6)

This series of talks has a timely and distinct message to bring to all of us. It is important now, more than ever, that we reveal to our moment of history and give to this our country the only thing we have—the gift of our faith. "In the name of Jesus Christ of Nazareth," and in his name we must say to all, "arise and walk."

But first you and I have an assessment to make. Have we been faithful to the trust that the Second Vatican Council handed to us? It is now eighteen years since the great Pope John XXIII opened the Council. It is now fifteen years since Pope Paul VI closed the Council. Now is the time for reflection. What happened?

John XXIII's faith was apparent in his opening talk to the Council:

We feel we must disagree with those prophets of gloom, who are always forecasting disaster, as though the end of the world were at hand.

In the present order of things, Divine Providence is leading us to a new order of human relations which, by men's own

Delivered at the Cathedral-Basilica of St. James in Brooklyn on April 11, 1980.

efforts and even beyond their very expectations, are directed toward the fulfillment of God's superior and inscrutable designs. And everything, even human differences, leads to the greater good of the Church.

Pope John XXIII's faith was built upon the good and gracious God and on the dignity of the human person. He saw the linkage in creation and in redemption that placed the interaction between God and the person as the area toward which truth must be directed. He explained that there was no need to emphasize one article of faith or another in the Council, since the continuity of doctrine was secure, but he added:

> The Christian, Catholic, and apostolic spirit of the whole world expects a step forward toward a doctrinal penetration and a formation of consciousness in faithful and perfect conformity to the authentic doctrine, which, however, should be studied and expounded through the methods of research and through the literary forms of modern thought. The substance of the ancient doctrine of the deposit of faith is one thing, and the way in which it is presented is another. And it is the latter that must be taken into great consideration with patience if necessary, everything being measured in the forms and proportions of a magisterium which is predominately pastoral in character.

This vision is absolutely necessary so that we can keep clearly in mind the intentions for which the Council was opened. Otherwise we will not be faithful to its message. As time goes by our reference to the message of the Council becomes academic and abstract. As it becomes mere book learning, the Council loses the freshness of the air that prevailed when John threw open the windows. All through the world a new spirit seemed to come alive. There was a vibrance in religious life; there was an awakening of interest in the hearts of men and women, not all of whom were religious. If a poll had been taken a few months after John's death the whole world would have proclaimed John XXIII a saint of God.

Paul VI carried this Council through its tasks and brought it to a finish on December 8, 1965. It was a glorious concluding liturgy. But on the previous day he had spoken to the Fathers of the Council in these words which I am going to quote for you. The quotation is from the Latin translation which uses the general word for a human being, *homo*, rather than the specific word for a male, *vir*. However, the common translation uses the term *man*; the intent includes all persons.

> Yes, the Church of the Council has been concerned not just with herself and with her relationship of union with God, but with man—man as he really is today; living man, man all wrapped up in himself, man who makes himself not only the center of his every interest but dares to claim that he is the principle and explanation of all reality. Every perceptible element in man, every one of the countless guises in which he appears has, in a sense, been displayed in full view of the Council Fathers who, in their turn, are mere men, and yet all of them are pastors and brothers whose position accordingly fills them with solicitude and love. Among these guises we may cite man as a tragic actor of his own plays; man as the superman of yesterday and today, ever frail, unreal, selfish and savage; man unhappy with himself as he laughs and cries; man the versatile actor ready to perform any part; man the narrow devotee of nothing but scientific reality; man as he is, a creature who thinks and loves and toils and is always waiting for something; man sacred because of the innocence of his childhood, because of the mystery of his poverty, because of the dedication of his suffering; man as an individual and man in society; man who lives in the glories of the past and dreams of those of the future; man the sinner and man the saint.

While the quotation is long, it does relate to us the comprehensiveness of Paul VI's grasp of the person and his ability to describe the object of the Church and the Council. It is phrased in this fashion because the Council renewed the Church as the People of God and charted anew its mission as servant of the People of God. We will not understand the message of the pope if we restrict the image of the human person in any manner whatsoever. But while we may be abstract in our talking and in our thinking, so that we may be comfortable in our approach to the concept of people, the pope destroys this temptation and brings us face to face with actual reality in our living out of our life as the People of God.

Paul VI ended his talk with the following words, and I must quote him again so that the force of this truth will come from him and not from me:

> If we remember how in everyone we can and must recognize the countenance of Christ, the Son of Man, especially when tears and sorrow make it plain to see, and if we can and must recognize in Christ's countenance the countenance of our heavenly Father—"He who sees me," our Lord said, "sees also the Father"—our humanism becomes Christianity; our Christianity becomes centered on God; in such sort that we may say, to put it differently, a knowledge of man is a prerequisite for a knowledge of God.

Our problem in the last few years is that we begin to question whether this is orthodoxy or not. These words do not sound like religious words, nor do they sound as if they have to do with God Himself. Where are those sounds with which the ear was familiar? Have they been stolen? Has an enemy entered the Holy of Holies and destroyed or defamed the deposit of faith? We have become almost silent again.

The emphasis of these two popes and the Council reechoed the very beginning of the Sacred Scripture where Genesis tells us something about God and something about the human person whom God was fashioning.

> Then God said: Let us make man in our image, after our likeness. God created man in his image, in the divine image He created him, male and female he created them. (Gen. 1: 26–27)

Have we thought about God's creation sufficiently to have made it a guide in our daily lives? Do we treat one another with the preciousness due to a creation of God, one in His own image and likeness? Our answer has to be negative.

The image of God is the key to understanding the action of Jesus in Nazareth when he began his mission of teaching. That was the day he was handed the scroll of Isaiah; he unrolled it and read:

The spirit of the Lord is upon me
therefore He has anointed me
He has sent me to bring glad tidings
to the poor
to proclaim liberty to captives
recovery of sight to the blind
and release to prisoners
to announce a year of favor from the Lord.

Then he began by saying to them: "Today this scripture is fulfilled in your hearing." (Luke 4:18–21)

Who is to repeat these words today? It is at this point that we slip off into dreamland. It is someone else who must keep alive "the image of the God idea" and keep alive the mission to those fashioned in God's image. It is the bishop's task or the priest's or the religious' or the missionary's. Do we dare ask, "Is it I, Lord?" for fear the answer will be "yes"? The Council, working out of its pastoral format, was making much more practical the answer to that question. Its answer was an emphatic "yes!"

> The Church carries it on in various ways through all her members. "For by its very nature the Christian vocation is also a vocation to the apostolate.... Incorporated into Christ's Mystical Body through baptism and strengthened by the power of the Holy Spirit through confirmation, they are assigned to the apostolate by the Lord himself" (*Decree on the Apostolate of the Laity*, nos. 2 and 3).

The Church, the People of God, the baptized, yes, you and I, are called to this kind of proclamation of the Good News. We need to proclaim the work of God in each of us; we need to proclaim the saving mission of Jesus Christ in each of us. But we have received only to give to others.

Baptism inserted us into the life, death, and resurrection of Jesus. We become related to the Just One in a new way and take our pattern of living from the preaching and ministry of Jesus. The image of God that relates all of us as human persons now has the power of baptism, relating all of us in Jesus. The call to call others to tenderness and forgiving, to gentleness and healing, to vindication of the oppressed can be stated in a new way. Christians are called to be the conscience of the human community. In a positive sense this means that Christians are called to be the advocates of human dignity and development and to collaborate in such a mutually self-dedicating way as to act in favor of that dignity and development. In a negative sense it means that Christians must dare to critique all those aspects of life in the human community that go counter to the dignity and development that are each person's right in the light of the image of God present in the person.

In establishing the Christian's call to be the conscience of the human community, I have left out the word "Church" because it is a word that allows us to slip out from under obligations and transfers those obligations to someone else. Too long has baptism been forgotten in our particular examination of conscience. Right relationships are not at the head of our list when we examine our own conscience. Unless we begin to form a conscience building upon baptism and its call, we will fail in the Good News.

When Christians collaborate, they begin to form the Christian community and this then becomes the Church, and while we have been wasting time since the Council, now seems to be the time, when the needs of human dignity are so apparent, that we must begin the appointed task. Voice of conscience, an awesome responsibility, is the task of the Christian community.

While baptism calls the community of conscience together and empowers it to act for the liberation of the human community, there is another sacrament, confirmation, which affirms that power of conscience and calls us to the responsibility of developing the critical understanding so crucial to conscience. The demand for that constant critical development is not unrealistic. It is not without a continuing strength and nutrition.

The community gathered in Eucharist mutually empowers the development of this conscience by experiencing the saving memorial of Christ, the recollection of the saving death and resurrection. This death and resurrection are the actions of Jesus Christ as the conscience of his people, for which cause they, the people, exacted their penalty. But it is into that saving mission that we are called in baptism. It is from the Eucharist that we gain the courage to follow the pathway of the Lord.

The parable of the Good Samaritan tells us much about the way we live in isolation, away from the "images of God." We pass by. The person of conscience stops, helps, and ministers.

The woman in adultery is forever a scene that shames our reaction to the sinners in our midst. Jesus asked, "Where are they who accuse you?" They had fled. "Neither shall I accuse you."

Jesus was putting into practice the orthodoxy of the mercy and love of God to all those fashioned in God's image.

Is there any wonder, then, that human rights have come forward as the critical point of human relationships if we are to be the conscience that proclaims the Good News? If we have been hesitant in the past, now we are called to step forward throughout our land in the cause of justice and of love.

The formation of our conscience must develop from the creation story of Genesis and our apostolate from the words of Jesus quoting from the text of Isaiah. Freedom and liberty—these are words of meaning for us.

But from the basic principles there flow imperatives that are made upon the Christian community of conscience. That community must speak out:

1. By doing the truth:
   a. This calls for constant metanoia.
   b. This calls for mutual respect and mutual self-dedication.
   c. This calls for "paying one's dues"—sacrifice.
2. By articulating the truth:
   a. This calls for critical reflection.
   b. This calls for personal discipline of quiet and solitude in order to reflect prayerfully.
   c. This calls for naming that truth for the sake of transforming activity.

Did these notes characterize the work of the martyred Archbishop Oscar Romero? He was on the side of the poor; he decried the violence of the oppressors; he spoke of healing and peace. Like his Master, his dues were assassination.

April 4 is a sad day in Memphis for it brings before us the memory of the late Dr. Martin Luther King, Jr. He was on the side of the oppressed; he was against the violence of the oppressor. He was critical of the injustice toward the blacks. His pathway in the footsteps of his Master allowed him to prophesy his death on the evening before it occurred.

That we are indeed a community of conscience for the sake of the dignity and development of humankind calls us and strengthens us. We have the gift and the challenge of critiquing present modes of life among ourselves in our land, and in the international community. In a word, the community of conscience is a self-critical as well as a world-critical reality. We answer that call only by actually doing in the present, and critically articulating that doing, so that our doing in the future will be better.

Dr. King used the following image in one of his sermons: "The Church must be a beacon for the human community. How many times have we been a taillight? How many times have we been no light at all?"

It is the whole People of God that must grow spiritually, and all of them, in proportion to the gifts they have received, must help one another in the building up of the Christian community. The task is not exclusively assigned to anyone, but to all together.

Since the call is given us in freedom and the work of the Lord is accomplished only in freedom, we must be free so as not to resist the call. Let us reinforce these words with those of Paul to the Ephesians:

> It is he who gave apostles, prophets, evangelists, pastors and teachers in roles of service for all the faithful to build up the body of Christ, till we become one in faith and in the knowledge of God's Son and form that perfect man who is Christ come to full stature. (4:11–13)

2

The Role of the Bishop
as Teacher and Listener

JAMES W. MALONE
Bishop of Youngstown

We are told of a battered and bruised knight who returned to the castle after a hard day's battle. He limped up to the lord of the castle to report:

"Sire, I have followed your orders dutifully. I have plundered all of your enemies to the west."

"The west? I said the east, not the west, I have no enemies to the west."

The knight thought about this for a moment, and replied, "Well, you do now."

We may presume that the man was sent back to school—knight school naturally—for a crash course in listening.

In this paper we will try to accomplish four things:

1. We will look at some of the factors that I think have caused bishops to become better listeners since Vatican II.

2. We will try to build a theological model of the Church where those factors are more comfortable.

3. We will survey the many constituencies that a listening and teaching bishop serves.

4. We will attempt to pinpoint what this means for the Church in our time.

Delivered at the Cathedral-Basilica of St. James in Brooklyn on April 24, 1981.

First of all, let us begin with an ending—the conclusion of a document published in 1977 by Pro Mundi Vita, the Catholic International Information and Research Center based in Belgium. That paper was on pastoral approaches to a bishop's leadership. It concludes with this:

> So many talents have always been needed . . . to acquit oneself well in the episcopal ministry that no one can fully reach this ideal. In addition to great faith, love for every member of the flock, and trust that God is the future and shapes it, there is need for humility, for wisdom that comes from realism, for a gospel-inspired serenity and liberty vis-à-vis those who wield power (even in one's own country and one's own Church), and a need for courage to face suffering without breaking down under the strain of many tensions.

And the last few lines then say:

> Without such qualities, a bishop will have great difficulty in accompanying his people along their pilgrim way. It is only from this attitude of faith and this mixture of human ingredients that new models for guiding the Church will emerge, and in these models, following the example of the Lord, the emphasis will be not on directing but rather on listening and serving.

That conclusion is significant, I think: listening and serving.

The foreword of that same paper notes that several factors have helped shape demand for a new style of Church leadership on the part of us bishops.

One of these factors is a combination of political, economic, educational, and scientific developments that have challenged the Church's monarchial model of government. The increased emphasis on the need for a bishop to listen is one response to this challenge.

Other factors that have helped us to see the value in listening have come from Vatican II.

At the Council, we stressed the importance of local churches, that is, dioceses such as Brooklyn or Youngstown. We made a commitment to shift from highly centralized decision making to a more collegial form. This collegiality, or shared decision making, was seen by the Council Fathers to be an ideal, both within the Church and for those in other faith communities.

Vatican II also gave new life to the theological concept of the People of God, with the result that there are new opportunities available now for participation in ministry, including sharing some management decisions in some places.

Two Council documents, *The Constitution on the Church* and *The Constitution on the Church in the Modern World,* see the local bishop as a bridge-builder between the Church and the world.

All of these factors have called bishops to become better listeners, as they meet their mandate to be teachers. I believe that in the process of listening, a bishop becomes a better teacher. I also believe that others in the faith community are also becoming better listeners—to each other, and yes, even to their bishops. The days of expecting lay persons to "pray, pay, and obey" without question are history and behind us. Our people are listening, however, sometimes quite intently, and they expect the same attentiveness from those of us who are called to serve them as bishops.

Let us now turn our attention to my second point, namely: We will try to sketch a model of the Church that takes Vatican II into special account.

I have found the ideas of a Canadian theologian, J. M. Tillard, helpful in putting this model of the Church into perspective. Tillard, and many others, has observed that there were two different theologies of Church involved in the process that produced the documents of Vatican II. The contrast is very familiar to those of us who took part in that process.

Simplistically put, one theology placed a heavy emphasis on teaching as a unilateral experience—the hierarchy pronounced, and all others listened and obeyed. The other theology, more communal in nature, based more on a response to Scripture, placed a high premium on teaching as dialogue—where both parties listen and learn from each other. Both models, the hierarchial and the communal, were present at the Council; however, Tillard points out that most often the first model was favored by a minority of Council Fathers, while the latter model was clearly favored by the majority. If you have any doubts, I will tell you that I align myself with the majority, whose principles and beliefs Tillard described with a Latin word—*communio.*

Those of us who communicate in English may have some trouble translating *communio* into an acceptable one-word equivalent in our native tongue. There is of course "communion," but that word perhaps means too many things to be useful in this context. It could also be translated "community" or "union." But neither of those words fully encompasses what Tillard has in mind.

Tillard used the term *communio* to describe the unique effect of our interaction with God. It is a mystical but real coming together with Christ in the spirit. Because of this, we become one with all humankind.

We would all agree that the central event in the life of the Church is the Eucharist. Eucharist demonstrates that *communio* which is the essence of the Church's life. Eucharist forms that oneness because it brings us together (even though we have other differences), brings us together—with the Lord, in the Spirit, under the ordained ministry of the bishop.

We call this gathering the local church—our diocese. It is a form of *communio* but it is not the fullness of it. Each local church is called to be one with all other local faith communities. Together we are the universal Church, gathered around the bishop of Rome. This is central to our Catholic concept of Church.

To belong to the Church is to belong to the risen Body of Christ. We are incorporated into the Body of Christ through the Spirit, who at the same time makes us one with each other.

Now, we might think of this communion as both vertical—with God, and as horizontal—with each other. But the reality is a single action—we are one with Christ's Body, with the Church.

The fact, that the Church is a communion with God—that it belongs to God, and lives a life according to God's ways—is primary in any discussion of bishop as listener and teacher.

All of us are bound to each other through faith and charity, as well as in our call to mission. We all receive gifts—charisms to carry out our mission. We all receive the graces of reconciliation and hope, which help to make us one.

Furthermore, we all have a bond with those believers who came before us. We extend back to the first apostolic community, but we do not jump over the ages that are between ours and those of the apostles. We realize our kinship with the generations of believers who have gone before us. It is an important part of what we call tradition. It is an essential part of our oneness in the Church.

Another bond of unity that we have with each other comes from our gifts of ministry, which include that of a bishop but do not end with the bishop. The local church cannot come fully alive except through the combined action of all of the gifts that are given to all of us by the Spirit.

A bishop serves as coordinator for the various charisms—to bring them into unity, to allow the Spirit to make us one.

Again, I say, a bishop serves by coordinating the various gifts— to bring them to unity, to allow the Spirit to make us one.

Just as we all have a bond to the past, we also forge one for the future. It is especially true that we forge a bond with those who are Catholic, but it is also true for those who are not formally a part of the Catholic Church. Somehow these other Christian communities must be embraced by us who are the local church, even as we wait for the formal ties that will bind us.

Let us now move to our third point, which is: A listening and teaching bishop must be aware of the variety of people and opinions that make up his constituency.

A pre-Vatican II caricature of the local church might depict it as a pyramid. The bishop had only to listen to the pope above, while everyone else in the Church, presumably, listened to the bishop.

The bishop neither had nor desired much contact with those outside the Church. Speaking for myself as a bishop who was ordained—it was called "consecrated" in those days—a few years before Vatican II, I can assure you that life was not really that simple. But the picture is true enough for our purposes of contrast with today's Church.

A bishop's first school of both listening and teaching is really his own prayer. If this prayer element is missing, a bishop's effort to be a catalyst for Church community is doomed to failure. Like all members of the faith community, a bishop is called to be first and foremost a disciple. He can learn this only from the Master, by listening to his Lord. Until he does this, neither a bishop nor anyone else has anything of value to teach the People of God.

In contrast with the pyramid, our post-Vatican II diagram of the local church might be drawn as a circle with the bishop in the center, so that he may both listen and teach in various directions. The bishop must be listening—listening to what the pope and his brother bishops have to say, and yes, the bishop must be willing to "teach" them as well—to contribute his experience and that of his people for the good of the whole Church.

You might consider what Cardinal Suenens has done in this regard—becoming open to the charismatic movement and interpreting it to the Church universal—integrating that movement into the larger Church community.

Or, in Latin America, consider the example of Helder Camara and the martyred Oscar Romero, bishops who put themselves in jeopardy in order to bring to the attention of the whole Church the need for justice as an integral part of our mission.

Not all of us bishops fulfill our role as listeners and teachers as well as these men, but we know that is part of our job description. It has always been there, but now, perhaps, we are more conscious of it.

A listening bishop must also have an ear for the past, he must listen to and speak for tradition, just as he does for the Church in our time. A bishop is not, however, a tape recorder for the past; the bishop must encourage his community to value the tradition received, as well as the tradition being lived, so that which is handed on will be a living tradition.

In this regard, a bishop must be willing to listen to and to share his experiences with theologians. It is not an easy task to define the precise relationship of theologians to bishops as teachers. This very issue continues to heat up the Church kitchen in our time. It is, however, important that bishops listen to theologians while also teaching them. It is also important that theologians listen to bishops. Theologians offer bishops a perspective on Church thought through the ages, and also on the life we experience today. Bishops offer theologians what we have learned of God through our ministry and experience with His people.

I have found theologians quite willing to do this. As a participant in the dialogues between U.S. bishops and theologians on more than one occasion, I have not failed to gain from their experience. Their willingness to listen to me and my brother bishops has never failed to add to my admiration for theologians.

Of course a bishop must also listen, so that he will be more sensitive to the people whom he serves. The bishop must listen to priests, to deacons, to women religious, to religious brothers, and to laymen and laywomen. He will likely do a lot of listening in structured ways: through priests' senates, councils of religious, diocesan and pastoral councils, and a host of other special advisory committees and commissions. But that will not limit his listening. The bishop will listen at confirmation ceremonies and receptions, but also on the street, while in the barbershop, and at his supper table.

A bishop will listen to the events that affect his peoples' lives, through newspapers, through TV and radio, and through other media that reflect the world in which he finds himself.

The bishop will adapt as his motto the early Church dictum, *nihil humanum mihi alienum est*: Nothing human is alien to me.

The bishop will listen not to measure what he hears by some hidden standard that comes with ordination to the episcopacy. Nor need he react to everything he hears with some profound observation. He should listen in order to be human, to learn, to give sympathy, to grow, and to become a better person.

Let us now look at point four: namely, to try to pinpoint what some of my earlier observations can mean for the contemporary Church. In this connection, I suggest that a listening bishop must also contribute to the dialogue. The bishop is not just a sounding board for the local community—echoing the people's voice. The bishop must teach. He has the responsibility to challenge his people, to assist them to grow spiritually, to help them meet their obligations to others. A stanceless silence will not meet those needs. A bishop may disagree with his people, but both he and they will know with what he is in disagreement.

It is in dialogue that a bishop can best teach. It is in the exchange of ideas, in listening and in responding, that he can be most effective as teacher. We bishops have few formal opportunities to teach others. And that is probably just as well. Some of my best "teaching moments" have come in those settings where I am also listening. Once a mutual listening atmosphere is achieved, I have found that people pay more attention to what I have to offer.

Moreover, in today's Church, a bishop's co-workers must also be good listeners. Often it is the bishop's close associates, those with whom he works on a day-to-day basis, in the chancery, in central services, who are the conduit for both the varied voices of the people to him, as well as for the response that the bishop wishes to make to them.

A listening bishop in the 1980's must also have an ear for those who are outside the circle of the Church—certainly an ear for other Christians and other believers, but also for the nonbeliever. And within the Church community of our day, it is important for us, both bishop and people, to remember that there is a close link between listening and teaching.

The late Father Charles Curran, the psychologist at Loyola University in Chicago, demonstrated that those who feel listened to and understood are more willing to be taught than those who are not listened to. People who do not feel they are being listened to (Father Curran's research has proven) either don't learn much or quickly forget what they do learn.

The application to the life of the Church is evident. If bishops hope to help bring their people to communion—to oneness with God and with one another—they must provide encouragement and extensive support through their own attentive listening.

But a point is reached in the relationship where the people must also develop an "active-listening-attitude" if bishops are to lead them to full communion. A local church that believes that it has learned all that its bishop can teach is a church that will stagnate —that will cease to grow. It is also true that a bishop who imagines that he has learned all that he can from his people will hardly be able to offer them the quality of leadership that leads to community.

Perhaps we can now see why the Pro Mundi Vita study, which I quoted earlier, insists that the emphasis in a bishop's ministry in the coming years "will be not on directing but rather on listening and serving."

The fundamental role of the bishop in the local church has not changed, but the emphasis of the role has changed dramatically. The bishop has always been charged to carry out Christ's priestly, prophetic, and kingly mission by teaching, sanctifying, and governing. Today, both bishop and people are recognized as sharing the prophetic, priestly, and kingly characteristics of Christ. Consequently, the bishop is not so much above the people—directing them, teaching them, and dispensing grace to them—as he is among them, teaching by listening, directing by service, and sanctifying by ministering with them. That shift of emphasis implies that the bishop must in some sense allow himself to be taught if he is to teach effectively, and he must be ministered to if he is to sanctify effectively. In John's Gospel we read: "'Lord,' Simon Peter said to Jesus, 'do you wash my feet?' 'If I do not wash you,' Jesus answered, 'you have no part in me.'" No fellowship, no *communio*. Peter replied, "'Lord, not my feet only but also my hands and my head'" (13:6–9).

In today's Church, I affirm that a bishop is part of God's pilgrim people, rather than apart from them. The bishop plays a central role in their achievement of *communio*, but he himself achieves it better both by listening and by receptive interaction with his people. Without that, the bishop has no part with them and there is no Church. On the other hand, without him and his teaching, there is no point at which, or for which, to gather. One can understand afresh Augustine's words: "With you I am a Christian, for you I am a priest. What I am for you alarms me; what I am with you comforts me."

In my opinion, the bishop's role today requires a delicate balance. I have explored the dynamics of that balance in terms of the special relationship that prevails between the bishop's responsibilities to teach and to listen.

I cannot imagine myself as an effective bishop-teacher of the Gospel to this generation of God's people without attentively listening to them. The meaning of the Word and the movement of the Spirit can neither be discovered nor made clear to others by bishops except through an intensive listening process. By the same token, believers need to listen to bishops and allow themselves to be influenced by what we say. *Communio* is built up by the Spirit through the interaction of the gifts God gives His people, including those that are peculiarly vested in the teaching and listening office of bishop.

3

Theological Diversity and Dissent within the Church

RICHARD J. SKLBA
Auxiliary Bishop of Milwaukee

I would like to begin this paper with a story about two balloon-ists who were floating around in the air. After some difficulty in maneuvering, they finally landed in a tree. Looking out of the bas-ket, they saw two people down below walking beneath the tree. The balloonists shouted, "Hello," and the people below said, "Hello. Where are we?" "You're up in a tree!" "Are you bishops?" the balloonists asked. "Yes," those below replied, "but how did you know?" "What you say is true," answered the balloonists, "but it doesn't mean a darn thing."

I write from the standpoint of a biblicist. While I acknowledge vast areas of limited knowledge, I do know something about scrip-ture, and that supplies the basic categories out of which I choose to think and write.

It seems appropriate to begin with an exploration of terms, be-cause our discussion will be confused and confusing if we bring different understandings when we talk about diversity and dis-sent. If by "dissent" we mean contentious behavior or some type of stubborn, possibly arrogant insistence on our own point of view, or if we mean a lack of willingness to listen to any other voice, or a self-centered clinging to a personal opinion that is dis-

Delivered at the Cathedral-Basilica of St. James in Brooklyn on May 8, 1981.

ruptive and disrespectful, then there is no place for "dissent" in the Church. That is not the topic of this exploration. At least, that is not what I am talking about.

When St. Paul writes to the Galatians, he concludes with a statement about all the works, the *erga*, of the flesh (5:19–21). His list of such includes "feuds, wrangling, jealousy, bad temper, quarrels, disagreements, factions" and similar breakdowns of human relationship. We are not talking about "dissent" in that sense. When Paul complains in his first letter to the Corinthians that there is so much wrangling and jealousy among them that they clearly must be fleshly and not spiritual people (3:3), he thus indicates that such behavior or underlying attitude does not belong in the Church. Finally, when Paul writes to the Romans, what does he mention in the very first chapter? Again, he lists strife and disruptive activities (1:29).

So, if contention is what we mean by "dissent," there is no place for that in the Church. But it is curious that it is precisely Paul who gets himself embroiled in discussions and controversies. He is described as being rightfully buried outside the walls of Rome because it is from that location that he continues to speak the truth to the whole Church.

On the other hand, if in our exploration of terms we mean that assuming a different approach, choosing a new perspective, or expressing a different opinion is all part of one's search for the truth, then there must be a place for that in the Church. The Spirit gives many gifts, and when the New Testament lists the primary historical forms of the gifts that existed in the early Church, we find apostles, prophets, evangelists, pastors, and teachers (Eph. 4:11). Each of these has a distinctive contribution to make and a perspective that will inevitably be very different.

If we refer to different conclusions about the will of God in a specific situation or to different judgments about the rightness or opportuneness of a given action, if we refer to a minority view that tries to establish its legitimacy even against the prevailing opinion of religious authority, then there must be a place for that in the Church. There has been a long tradition of prophets in Israel and in the Church. They were minority voices. They were, in fact, not accepted. But history proved them correct and thus they were "canonized," that is, called the "norm" for later generations of believers. Prophets fit into the second definition of dissent and disagreement in the Church.

So does Jesus. At the end of the first chapter of Mark's Gospel, we read that a leper came up to him and said, "If you will, you can make me clean" (1:40). Jesus looked around and saw a group of professional religious people who were watching him very carefully and who believed, on the basis of Leviticus 14, that it was very clearly against God's will to touch a leper. Jesus realized that his whole human career was on the line, yet he touched the leper, "and immediately the leprosy left him." That action merits our thinking about for a long time.

Peter also stood in that tradition at times. We are told, for example, that Peter preferred to obey God rather than the supreme religious authority, the Sanhedrin (Acts 5:29). Later, in that famous confrontation between Paul and Peter, Peter was faced with the very delicate but foundational question of table fellowship (Gal. 2:11–14). All we have in the text is from Paul's standpoint. Maybe a case could be made to justify Peter's approach. It was a pastoral approach to people who were faced with practical questions and problems, but nevertheless, because of the principle involved, Paul had to confront Peter to his face then and there. That confrontation is canonized, preserved in scripture. Therefore, if there isn't a place for that kind of disagreement in the Church, that kind of sorting out to discover the proper attitude or action in a given situation, then our Church is not biblical, it is not Catholic, it is not truly universal.

Unfortunately, not all disagreements are so clear to us or so noble. Moreover, when a disagreement is right on our doorstep, when we are forced to take some action or make a decision, then where do we stand? How do we decide? Do we choose to live with the tension? Perhaps living with that kind of tension and with those kinds of disagreements may be awkward, but where there is genuine life and creativity, tension always exists.

The issue of dissent and pluralism is an enormous topic. I recognize that we could approach it from any number of standpoints and that we could be at it for a long time. What I would like to do is to impose some discipline on myself and consider the image of the Church as a circle of dialogue. Such an approach may spell out some of the circumstances that are peculiar to our age, and may indicate that dialogue is more necessary today than ever. Finally, I shall highlight two classical cases of diversity and dissent; namely, making personal conscience decisions and stating a theological position.

When I started thinking about this topic several months ago, I recalled Paul VI's first encyclical, *Ecclesiam Suam* (the English title usually used is *Paths of the Church*). Curiously enough, the first encyclical of any papal ministry is often the best or at least offers a unique insight into the new pope's way of thinking and area of concerns. It is the encyclical that makes a clear, fresh contribution. It states things newly. Pope Paul's statement was for me very, very useful, because he talked about different images of the Church and suggested that probably the most useful one (remember the Council was still going on) was the Church as a "concentric circle of dialogue."

Pope Paul refers to several circles of dialogue. He states that there is a type of dialogue that exists because we are all human beings. Thus one level of dialogue proceeds out of that richness of our common humanity. There is another circle that exists when we add to our common humanity the fact that there are many of us on this planet who believe in one God. Monotheism adds a new element to the dialogue. Then there is the specific dialogue that exists among Christians, for whom the one God took human flesh in order to die and rise again. The pope went on to say that the Catholic Church can also be described as a circle of dialogue. He has some strong things to say about that. I wish everybody in the Church would read them, including those who might happen to be in Rome at a later date.

> It is our ardent desire that the dialogue within the Church should take on further new themes and speakers so that the holiness and vitality of the Mystical Body of Christ in each may be increased. We bless and encourage all those who, under the guidance of competent authority, take part in the life-giving dialogue of the Church. (*Ecclesiam Suam*, no. 116)

Considering the Church as a circle of dialogue, we note, first of all, that there are things that destroy dialogue or at least disrupt it on any level within this dialogue of "faith seeking understanding." When, for example, we take a position in the dialogue merely to obtain greater power or authority, or when we take a position not to seek truth, our action destroys genuine dialogue.

Or again, there is no true dialogue when we make a unilateral claim on the truth as if the entire field and the last word is ours. In that case, dialogue does not exist, it is finished, it is a monologue, and monologues are usually neither enjoyable nor illuminating. I've gone home as quickly as possible whenever I've been subjected to such treatment.

Dialogue may also be impeded when there is an immediate resorting to threats or sanctions. In my experience at least, power does not serve the truth; it does not seek the truth which should have its own kind of power.

Or again, if a person resorts to pressure or to some type of publicity to orchestrate public opinion, or tries to avoid the effort to seek testimony from the larger Church's conviction (which might also, at times, be a legitimate way of obtaining due process), but looks for public pressure and publicity in order to force the dialogue in a certain direction, then once again true dialogue does not take place.

According to the 1976 statement of the International Theological Commission, there are characteristics of a good dialogue, and these might include the attempt to be clear and precise. A good dialogue says, "let's be clear." A good dialogue seeks an accurate statement of one another's opinion. A good dialogue includes an effort to achieve comprehensiveness. It includes genuine humility before the truth, not bitterness or arrogance but meekness, not about the truth, but about the way in which we recognize that we have only a partial grasp of the truth, all of us. It includes a mutual trust and respect for other people's right to stand up and state a position. Without respectfulness and trust, there is no dialogue. Certainly, there should be no sense of arrogant superiority; all involved should be looking for the intellectual and cultural communication necessary for the flow of discussion.

Such are the characteristics of the type of dialogue that must take place in the Church if it is to be truly a dialogue. If we begin to speak about dissent and disagreements and pluralities from the standpoint of the Church as a circle of people in dialogue with differences of perspective or opinion, then the characteristics just mentioned must be present.

In particular, there are certain circumstances today that force our age to indulge in dialogue as never before. I have six reasons for this, reasons why our age requires more dialogue, more listening, more speaking than ever. The consequence is that we open ourselves to differences of opinion in new ways.

First of all is the shift in the self-consciousness of the Church. Today we try very hard to identify the Church with *all* the people who are called together to worship and extend the Kingdom and the mission of Christ. The Church is not identified with the hierarchy alone. The Church is not the building. The Church is us. If that is the case, then the Church is the baptized people of God whom some people are ordained to serve. If that is the case, we must look toward coresponsibility, toward collegial action that tries to develop the skills of listening, of gathering consensus in faith and charity. If anything requires dialogue, that does!

For a long time we presumed that the teaching authority of the Church is exclusively equated with episcopal ministry in the Church. That may have made sense when the Church was viewed primarily as a hierarchy; it does not make sense when one broadens the total teaching function of the Church to encompass all the ministries involved in evangelization and catechesis. I prefer to say that there is a type of teaching authority from experience which results from baptism and which is the fruit of the struggle between grace and sin in our lives. There is a kind of authority that is found in all who struggle with some degree of success to live the life of grace. This is the teaching authority of saints in the church.

There is another type of teaching authority that comes from competence, skill, or learning, an authority that comes from long exposure to the intricacies and history of any given problem. Therefore, one is able to speak out of knowledge. That represents a second type of teaching authority. Finally, there is the type of authority that comes from delegation.

These three types of authority are found in everyday experience. Someone might know all the reasons why a person should stop smoking, but still continue to smoke. Someone else may have struggles with the problem and decide to quit. That represents an experiential authority beyond the purely intellectual. Someone else may have the authority to make sure that there is no smoking in a particular building. These are three quite different types of authorities. The same kinds of diversification of authority exist in the Church. One of the roles of the bishop is not merely to represent the delegated responsibility for tradition but rather to make sure that the Church community experiences a healthy balance between those three kinds of teaching authorities. The bishop ensures that knowledge, experience, and delegation are speaking to one another. Although I am not sure of the technical term, I can take an example from stereophonic radio where fine tuning and balance of sound is required. In the Church someone has to make sure that all the richness of the different tones and harmony is present. No single instrument may be arbitrarily singled out from the harmony of the entire tradition.

A second reason for the importance of dialogue in the Church is the fact that at this point in the history of Catholicism, we can no longer identify Christianity with Western civilization. The civilizations and cultures of Africa or Asia must be allowed to speak their own understanding of the Christian message and to put it in categories that make sense to them. Karl Rahner claims we are at a moment of transition in the history of the Church that is at least as important as the transition that occurred in the second century, when the Church experienced transition from Judaism to Hellenism. Today we are moving from identifying the Church with Western civilization to accepting the possibility that Christianity and indeed Catholicism must be expressed in a variety of cultures, and that these cultures must thus enter into dialogue with one another. That is a second reason why the dialogue within the Church with possible disagreement at times is more necessary today than it has been in hundreds of years. It is a rare opportunity; it is not something to be afraid of. At least I am not afraid of it.

A third reason can be found in the marvelous discoveries of science and the explosion of knowledge that has occurred in our time. Science raises questions we never thought of before. There is the realization, because of our knowledge of history, that we learn only now why we did things the way we did, and we must be open to the possible discovery that some of those reasons were not as strong as we thought. We must ask the same questions over again. Because of the knowledge explosion—theological, philosophical, historical, and scientific—there is a new level of interdisciplinary dialogue coming, and one has to listen. We must be reflective and critical, in the best sense of the word, in the face of our own tradition. A theologian thinks backward in a sense, looks at the tradition of faith, constantly reviews it, sorting out the assumptions.

Consider some of the reasons why Marian devotions were given their forms. As indicated earlier, I am a biblicist, a student of scripture, and I know that the ways in which scripture was used for Marian devotion have not always been faithful to the original intent of scripture and have not always been helpful to the true image of Mary in the Church. So we as a Church go back not to reconstruct but to reclaim. I do not wish to downplay the role of Mary as model of faith and model of the Church, but I think we must speak about this tradition more correctly and more forcefully. That is another reason for the need for dialogue today.

A fourth reason stems from the fact that there is always the possibility that some persons in the Church may be more acutely aware of a given problem than others. There is always the possibility that someone has painfully struggled with a question of conscience and achieved a sensitivity that I do not have. In this whole world of experience there is always the possibility that one individual or a group has agonized over an issue and experienced a new sense of sinfulness in an area that I have not. Precisely because there are different levels of conscience, some consciences in the Church are more sensitive than others. As pro-life issues and peace issues are explored, different responses may be elicited from different people. The result is a need for dialogue, and perhaps dissent, calling us all to grow in response to challenges of conscience. Episcopal or papal teaching as well as the heroic convictions of the baptized may be the source of this level of dialogue.

A fifth reason why dialogue is more necessary today than ever is found in the fact that we are summoned to be adult Christians; we are summoned to take some measure of responsibility for our own lives, and not all of us are equally mature at any given time. We may be forty-five years old or we may be an adolescent. It is not a matter of chronological age but of maturity in faith. What does one do when there are people at different maturity levels except explore the issues? Sometimes there are different responses that are, in fact, in disagreement. In a family, for example, one encourages people to grow up, to make decisions, to pay the price for that kind of responsibility. One must live with the resulting tension. We must do the same in the Church.

Lastly, there is always the possibility for someone living in a new age that new questions will be asked. Someone may ask, Why do you do that? and we may respond as if we had never heard the question before. That's the sixth reason.

Children always provide delightful stories, and I heard one recently that perfectly illustrates this point. I was in Milwaukee, preparing for a Eucharist which was going to close a session of parish commitment to the Renew Program. I was in the sacristy; my associate was in church preparing the altar. Two little girls came into the church; they had never been in that church before. The girls were probably four or five years old, six at most. They said, "Hello," and my associate said, "Hello." They looked at her and pointed to the altar. With the strange association of ideas that children have, they asked, "Is that where you put the dead bodies?" "No. That's where we pray." One of the little girls looked at my associate and asked, "Why are you whispering?" My associate replied, "Because, this is God's house." And the little girl said, "Oh. Does he sleep a lot?" I will never speak softly in a church again without thinking of that little girl. She asked the kind of question that nobody asked quite that way before. It went to the heart of the matter. We must be prepared for these kinds of questions, which can be very unsettling to practices we take for granted.

Those are six reasons why I think that in this day and age circle of dialogue is an appropriate model for the Church. But there is something else we should bear in mind, a seventh reason, one that is grounded in the Gospels. The first words of Jesus in his public ministry, as recorded in Matthew's Gospel, were: "Change your mind," "have a change of heart," more poorly translated, "repent" (4:17). The word really means, "change your mind about something." If the Gospel directs us to the constantly enduring imperative to change our minds, then we had best become agents and partners of dialogue. The possibility always remains that there may be differences of approach and differences of opinion and different stances about which we are all called to change our minds in the on-going process of conversion.

The norm in the Church and the goal of all our efforts is unity in faith and charity. The unity willed by God and inaugurated by the Holy Spirit is a gift that only reaches perfection at the end of time. That one faith may be experienced and expressed in many ways because of the diversity of cultures, practices, and historical contexts. Unity rooted in baptism and visibly expressed in the Eucharist is the norm, with the College of Bishops sustaining that unity together with the Bishop of Rome. Dissent is the exception, present because of our weak human condition and because of the historical unfolding of all our efforts.

There are two major types of dissent, two quasi classic cases of diversity and dissent and pluralism in the Church today. In the history of the Church they have been dealt with differently in various centuries, but I want to offer some observations about each of them here.

The first type of dissent is what I describe as a personal, private decision in some area of moral practice that is at variance with the general teaching of the Church. For example, an economist once came to me and said, "I am really struggling with *Pacem in Terris* because I understand the economic school out of which it comes. I want to know to what degree I must assent to the economics of that?" Other examples: Some in the peace movement genuinely felt that naming a nuclear submarine *Corpus Christi* was blasphemous. Although I personally was troubled by that naming, I also felt that those persons saw things more seriously perhaps than the traditional moral teaching. Or the person who says, "My second marriage is not objectively seriously disruptive of my relationship with God." Or the person who disagrees with Church teaching in some area of sexual morality. Those are examples of personal, private decisions in some area of moral practice that are at variance with the teaching of the Church.

As a bishop, as someone with a helping responsibility in the Church, I have some observations about such cases. Yes, the Church does possess a teaching authority that at times must say that certain actions or attitudes are not consistent with struggling for the Kingdom or enfleshing a sign of the Kingdom present. The Church does have a type of teaching authority to continue to speak about the Kingdom of God and to continue the mission of Christ. Nevertheless, while stating our convictions clearly, we must not lose our historical perspective. Not all things are equally serious, and we must keep in mind that there was a time in the Church when there were only three major areas which were viewed as completely disrupting the relationship between us and God: murder, idolatry, and adultery; other things may have been deeply sinful, but not so radically evil. Such was the penitential practice of the early Church even though they were familiar with the text of Paul which listed the sins which prevented a person from inheriting the Kingdom (1 Cor. 6:9–10). Not all things are equally serious even in matters at variance with the proclamation of the Gospel and the establishment of the Kingdom. Moreover, in the last analysis, I am convinced of the primacy of the informed conscience; whenever the informed conscience takes a position or makes a judgment, that is to be respected, even by the Church that teaches differently.

Furthermore, there are circumstances that will be judged and evaluated differently in the vortex of each unique human experience. I am not suggesting that we move into some kind of situation ethic, but I am saying that circumstances do alter the situation. Perceptions vary. When there is a conflict of values, persons may evaluate the values differently and may choose one over the other in different situations. Within the Church we acknowledge that, allow it to take place, and respect it.

Our basic stance toward people ought to be one of trust. Trust can be abused, but I remain convinced that we have to trust that people are trying to make the right decision, one that is not dishonest or totally self-serving. If we have to start from that standpoint, we will create a healthy climate in which people can grow and mature.

Finally, I note that the Church is a group of people in the process of conversion, and we live in that context. That suggests that all of us are called to make ever more refined moral decisions. All of us are constantly asked to explore the motivations and ramifications of any decision we make. We learn—at least I can say from my own experience—that there are times when in retrospect we have done the right thing for the wrong reason. And we also discover that we have done the wrong thing for the right reason. It is important that we acknowledge such insights candidly as a Church called to conversion. It is crucial that we explore the ramifications of conversion, and that we see ourselves as constantly willing to grow as human beings and as Catholic Christians. Evil is never good, but not all evils are equal. That is also part of the reality within which we live. If we are a Church in the process of conversion, supportive encouragement as well as challenge and confrontation are needed.

Secondly, there is a type of dissent, a classic case of diversity in the Church, in which a theological position is taken that seems to be at variance with the conviction of the Church's teaching authority. Some examples refer to the attempt to express an old truth in new words. For example, what does the incarnation really mean when we say Jesus is both God and human? How does one speak about the profound truth of the incarnation in a way that can be understood today? Others examples express a new truth that old answers do not adequately resolve, for example, genetic engineering. Traditional moral principles may not deal with such topics. Even I, knowing as little as I do about this area, understand that such maxims leave much unanswered. Thus, an answer to a problem in this area might be at variance with the Church's teaching because it really is a new question.

What kind of assent must be given to an old teaching now seen from a challenging new perspective? I come back to some of the Marian dogmas. In light of solid scripture studies, one must take a new look at such dogmas and traditions and ask again where do they come from and what do they mean. Do they reflect a solid evangelical base focusing on Christ the one Lord? What are the historical circumstances that condition them? What are they saying to us? It is very interesting to me that Our Lady always seems to address the concerns of the age in which she speaks; each appearance addresses very concrete contemporary issues. Her role as a model for the Church seems reaffirmed by the messages preached at each major Marian shrine.

The Church has the obligation and the ability to pass on the mystery of faith, the tradition, the *paradosis*. Consider for a moment the quotation from Paul to the Corinthians: "I hand on to you what I myself received, that Jesus suffered, died, was buried, rose again and appeared" (1 Cor 15:3–4). That is a creed; it is perhaps the oldest part of the New Testament. This ancient text goes on to speak of Christ appearing to a series of different groups: to 500 brethren, to the apostles, to James, to Peter. The text suggests a Church that is already socially complex.

The first conclusion I draw is that from the very beginning there was some type of structuring and diversification of function within the Christian community. Thence follows the understanding that specific individuals may have the responsibility for teaching and for preserving the tradition. By way of an aside, something I find intriguing is that the same word for "tradition" in Greek, *parado-sis*, also means a handing over in the sense of betrayal. That fact serves as a reminder that there are times when the handing over of something blindly, unquestioningly, without any kind of attempt to say it again in a language truly understood by the people to whom one is speaking can be a betrayal, a *paradosis*.

In the Church theologians have a distinctive role to play, which is not the task of proclaiming the good news but that of exploring the good news, delving into the deeper significance and interrelations of that message. In the phrase of the Jesuit poet Gerard Manley Hopkins, the theologian searches the "inscape" of each truth, the deepest pattern which reveals the whole of God's world. That is why we see a pro-life issue in the question of the beginning of life, in the question of armaments, in the question of the Church's statements on human rights. In each case, there is some kind of consistent concern for life. A serious concern for life in one area must also exist in all areas. A theologian's function in the Church is to critique a process, to say what was valid or what was, in fact, more problematic than first realized.

Undoubtedly, there is a need to define more carefully those different types of authorities that I mentioned earlier. But I feel very strongly about the fact that there isn't only one kind of authority in the Church. Experience, competence, and delegation all exist as authority forms. We must find a new way to bring them into consort and harmony. We haven't always done that very well. Whenever there is a theological position at variance with what is understood as the common opinion and conviction of the Church's traditional teaching authority, we must first be open to the judgment and discernment of peers in some kind of collegial fashion. That is where differences should be initially ironed out, among peers and colleagues in the theological field. Time must be allowed for those things to be sorted out, in spite of the pressures resulting from the immediacy of our communication media. Only afterwards does the episcopal teaching authority enter to resolve difficult or pressing questions.

In conclusion, I ask: What makes a Catholic? That we take seriously everything in the New Testament is what makes a Christian. Without respect for the New Testament, we are not Catholic Christians. But, then, what is the distinctiveness of Catholicism within the family of Christians? That we respect our traditions, take them seriously, and understand that while there is a primacy of conscience, we as Catholics believe that somehow as individuals we do not possess the last word on what is right or wrong. That last word is a collegial, an ecclesial reality. This fundamental stance distinguishes a Catholic.

Because Catholicism is sacramental in its nature, because we feel strongly about the sacraments, and because the sacraments unfold in life, as they illuminate it, we perceive a sort of gradualism that is behind our sacramental system. This also distinguishes Catholicism, a gradualism that is not content to say we are saved once and for all, or that we have the truth once and for all. The very fact that we are Catholics means that we take the sacramental system seriously. The very fact that we are Catholics means that we are universal, that we have to take diversity seriously and make space for it. To the degree that those characteristics are not present, to that degree proponents of any theological opinion are not Catholic. To that degree they place themselves on the margins of the Church.

The Gospel, which repeatedly describes the care of the Lord for those on the margins of his world, calls us to listen to diverse opinions. It is not to say what is wrong about them first but what is right about them. The call of the Gospel is a summons to say that this or that is of value, and to say all of that first. If there is a need to point out what is wrong about diverse opinions, we can do that in dialogue and discussion. But it is primarily what is right and noble and true that we want to affirm and encourage because we are pro-life people. Those are some of the things I wanted to say in order to initiate dialogue about theological diversity, dissent, and pluralism in the Church. I believe mine cannot be the last word, because that would be against my premise.

4

Assessing the Shortage of Priests: Nonclerical Alternatives to Ordained Ministry

RAYMOND A. LUCKER
Bishop of New Ulm

When I was first ordained, in almost every rectory there was a map of the United States, sent out by the Glenmary Fathers, that represented in color all of the counties in the United States that were without a priest. And I remember that there were only a few scattered counties, here and there, mostly in the South, which were without priests.

I look around the world today, and I see that there are many areas where there are no priests, and I am convinced that this condition will spread. In the Diocese of New Ulm, we now have seven parishes that are under the pastoral care of nonordained people. At the present time they are all women religious. The first one was appointed almost five years ago and we anticipate that there will be twenty-five such parishes in the next decade. In light of our experience with pastoral administrators, I would like to begin with three assumptions, three ideas that are very important to me and which color the directions we have taken in this and in many areas of ministry in our diocese.

My first assumption is that the greatest need in the Church in the United States is for *adult* faith, *adult* conversion, a continual turning to the Lord on the part of the *adult* members of the Church.

Delivered at the Cathedral-Basilica of St. James in Brooklyn on May 19, 1985.

Now, when I say that this is the greatest need, I am pointing not only to the laity, but also to priests, bishops, and religious. We are all in constant need of growth in faith, of conversion, of spiritual renewal. I see so many members of our Church who have been instructed but have never been converted, who have been sacramentalized but have not been evangelized. At the same time, there are so many members of our Church who, in recent years, have gone through incredible conversion experiences, so many people who are crying out for spiritual direction, for help in prayer, with a deep desire to grow in the spiritual life.

My second assumption is that so many members of our Church (and again I do not just mean lay people; I am including priests and religious—all of us) do not have a living awareness of what it means to be Church. When people are asked the question: "Where is the Church?" they tend to point to a building, to an institution, or perhaps even to priests, bishops, or maybe a few select others. But we do not have a deep awareness—a living awareness—that we are the Church. We forget that *we* are the Church in our families, in our work, in our society, and that, as the Church, we are called to build up the Kingdom of God.

My third assumption is that every single member of the Church is called to an active role in the life and mission of the Church. This is one of the great teachings of the Second Vatican Council. And we have not yet begun to realize the full implication of this teaching for every one of us.

Not long ago, only priests were looked upon as ministers in the Church. In fact, Catholics didn't even use the word "minister." That was a Protestant term. Then, gradually we allowed the term to be extended to Sisters, to members of religious communities, to a few extraordinary people in the Church. Now there is a veritable explosion in ministry. Every single member is called to an active part in the life and mission of the Church, and this means that every member of the Church is a teacher. Every member of the Church is a witness. Every member of the Church is called to respond in faith. There is no such thing as being just a passive onlooker. Every member, without exception, is called to participate actively in the liturgy, to be swept up in worship, to celebrate. There is no such thing anymore in the Church as just attending Mass, just hearing Mass. We are all invited to participate more fully in the life and mission of the Church. Everyone is to serve as everyone is served.

Additionally, everyone is to participate in the governance of the Church in some way. Everyone is invited to express themselves, to speak out, to be consulted. And there is no turning back. There is no turning back to the days when the Church was (either in theory or in practice) a clerical institution—when Father did it all, when Father made all the decisions, when Father had all the questions and knew all the answers, when Father paid all the bills and built all the churches, and, Lord help us, when Father had all the privileges. Those days are gone.

So these are my presumptions when I begin to talk about non-ordained pastoral administrators in the Diocese of New Ulm. Also it is important to see the context in which these appointments take place. The same kind of practice might not work in other kinds of dioceses. But I don't see why not. The Diocese of New Ulm is very small. There are seventy thousand Catholics in ninety-three parishes, all rural. The largest town in the diocese has a population of sixteen thousand people, with many parishes of 100, 200, and 300 families. The distances between towns are not very great.

We are also speaking, however, of a diocese in which there is a very strong sense of community. In our parishes everyone knows everyone else. As a child grows up, she knows her uncles and aunts, her cousins and grandparents. It is customary for grandparents to participate in their grandchildren's religious education. The whole extended family is part of a child's growth in faith. This is a very important reality in the Diocese of New Ulm. There is still a sense of neighborhood, a sense of community. When people gather together for liturgy, the liturgy doesn't have the burden of creating a community, but rather begins with a natural community that needs to be strengthened, needs to be filled with the Spirit, needs to be continually lifted up.

I want to tell you, also, that in the Diocese of New Ulm I live in a community myself that is not just a town community, but a small community of colleagues. For eight years now, I have lived with my staff. Right now there are three priests and five sisters. We have also had lay men and women as part of our community at different times. Over these years, we have grown in community. We pray together every morning. We read, share, and pray the Scriptures.

We gather for liturgy each noon. We pray vespers each evening. We share experiences after various meetings and conventions, and we have special community nights. This is an important part of the context out of which pastoral administrators are called forth in the Diocese of New Ulm. We are one staff. All of the diocesan staff operate out of one building. We have all agreed on a common mission statement for the diocese, and we exist as a diocesan staff to help and to support parish communities.

There is no such thing in our diocese as a "diocesan program." Everything that we do, we do to be of service to parishes in calling for, validating, and training people in ministry. We have the usual consultative bodies, the usual pastoral offices, but we are committed as a diocesan staff and by diocesan goals and objectives to the calling forth of people to ministry.

We have been committed for seven or eight years to a constant program of diocesan pastoral planning. We have just gone through an extensive consultative process of revising our goals and developing new objectives for the next five years. Out of the first round of planning we experienced a call for deepened spiritual renewal, and that has led us into a renewal process. We were one of the first dioceses to follow the "Renew" program after the Archdiocese of Newark started it. Now we are following up on that program, planning to continue what was done with Renew, and we are developing further formation opportunities in ministry, built on a conversion model.

Besides being a small rural diocese with a strong sense of community, we also have a shortage of priests. In 1976, the year I arrived as bishop of New Ulm, there was one priest ordained. In 1977 there was also one priest ordained. Then, for the next six years, there were none. In ten years there were only four priests ordained. Today, there is a growing number of students in the seminary, and we now usually ordain two or three priests a year.

So we had to move in the direction of yoking parishes. That is, one priest serving two parishes. We now have forty "yoked" parishes. We also thought about giving a number of parishes a mission status, which would mean that they would have the services of a priest only on an irregular basis. We were also faced with the prospect of closing some parishes, but when you consider the people who have been bound together by their faith, by their families, by their communities for a hundred years, it becomes very important to keep their parish structures alive if at all possible. All of this is background to the development of what we call pastoral administrators.

A pastoral administrator is a person who has not been ordained but is responsible, nevertheless, for the pastoral care of a parish. A pastoral administrator is in charge of a parish. The term is ours. We were the first, as far as I know, to use that term. And we developed that term since we did not feel that we could call them pastors or administrators because of canonical implications. We didn't want to call them pastoral associates or pastoral workers; so we conceived the term pastoral administrators.

As an aside, our diocese has a mission in Guatemala. We have been there for some twenty-three years. The little Diocese of New Ulm contributes to that mission in Guatemala about $350,000 a year. About one-third of our total diocesan budget goes to the poor and to the mission. And that is because of our commitment to the Church in Guatemala. I visited six or seven years ago, and heard that there were Sisters in one of the dioceses of Guatemala who were in charge of parishes, and that gave me the idea. If in Guatemala, why not in the United States?

We were in the process of developing all kinds of ministries; people were involved in educational ministries, school ministries, liturgical ministries, youth ministries, spirituality ministries, social concerns ministries. All of these people were trained as ministers in parishes, but what really moved us finally into appointing pastoral administrators was a statistical report required by Rome every year. One of the first questions was, How many parishes in the diocese are in the charge of diocesan priests? How many parishes are in the charge of religious priests? How many parishes are in the charge of religious women? How many parishes are in the charge of lay people?

If Rome was asking how many there are, certainly there was no reason why it couldn't be done. And so, in 1981, I appointed a Sister as pastoral administrator in charge of a parish. She became administrator of the goods of the church, responsible to see that the Word of God is announced, that religious education programs are developed, that adults are helped to grow in their faith, that catechumens are recruited, that records are kept, that the sick and the needy and the dying and the anxious and the troubled are visited, that people are prepared for the sacraments, that people are called to ministries as the spirit moves them.

Now, after almost five years, we have seven pastoral administrators. In the new Code of Canon Law, Canon 517, paragraph 2 says: "Where there is a pastoral need, a person may be appointed by the bishop who is in charge of a parish community to provide for the ordinary day-to-day pastoral, spiritual and administrative care of the parish."

The process we used is this. A candidate for pastoral administrator is first hired to work in that parish as a pastoral associate, as a pastoral worker, as a youth minister, or in some other capacity —long enough for that person to build up a relationship with the parish community and to be accepted by that parish community as a leader. The parish community, through the parish council, agrees to such an appointment.

Generally speaking, when there is a parish where there is no resident pastor, someone is hired by that parish to be their coordinator of religious education or their pastoral visitor. Then after a period of months, or maybe even a year or two, when the parish is ready, when that person is ready, when the religious community in this case is ready, then I appoint that person as pastoral administrator.

The pastoral administrators need to have competence in parish work, as well as some experience and training in ministry. They need to have the support of their own religious community, and they need to have a priest in the next parish or so who will agree to be the sacramental minister of that parish. This means that the priest comes for Mass and the sacraments, but it is the pastoral administrator who is in charge.

How has it worked? It has been simply amazing how well it has worked. Recently, I called all of the pastoral administrators to ask them about the response of the parishes. All of them have been received with joy, with acceptance. The people know that their parish can continue as a parish community, that they have an identifiable leader. All of the pastoral administrators indicated to me that they have received wonderful support.

Recently, in one of the parishes where there is a pastoral administrator, the sacramental minister—the priest—was not able to get there because of a snow storm. The few people who succeeded in getting to church that day were on hand. The pastoral administrator was there. She said: "Well, we will have to carry on alone. We're here. Let's go." Parishes with pastoral administrators regularly have services during the week when people will gather for the Liturgy of the Word, for praise of God, for reception of Holy Communion, for exchange of the Word of God. The people have indicated how important it is to have a leadership person present, to have a sign that calls them to community.

During my conversation, I kept pressing the pastoral administrators. I said: "You mean, you have never, ever heard any negative remarks?" And they all said: "No. Never. None." I asked about the people who are generally anti-feminist and could be expected to make some critical remarks. No such remarks were made, and in those small towns usually if comments are passed, you hear about them. The only negative reaction would be the disappointment on the part of a few people over not having a resident priest, but the pastoral administrators told me that they are convinced that even more people have accepted responsibilities in the parish, in ministry, with the part-time sacramental minister present, than when there was a priest present full-time. They said that once you enter into the lives of families through baptisms, through marriages, through sickness, through death, you become very special to them, and, of course, we know that as priests too. One of the pastoral administrators told me these have been the best years of her ministry.

What we have found is something really remarkable. The subtitle of this paper is "Nonclerical Alternatives to Ordained Ministry." Is it really an alternative to an ordained ministry? In one sense, no. There never can be an alternative to ordained ministry. We will need ordained ministers for the sacraments, to lead the Eucharist. Has it helped the shortage of priests? Yes. But what we have found is that a new ministry has become identified, and we find that there will continue to be a need for pastoral administrators whether we have enough priests or not. That is what has happened in our experience.

We have come to see and to recognize that this is a special call from God. There is a shortage of priests, yes. To some extent that is relative. Our shortage is much different from your shortage.

Our shortage is that we have far too many parishes for the number of people in the diocese. Your shortage is that you have far too many people for the number of parishes in your diocese. The sociological differences are there.

I believe that the appointment of nonordained pastoral administrators has been for us an occasion, an opportunity to recognize the gifts that God is giving to the Church in calling all people of faith to ministry.

5

Religious Life in the United States: Crisis and Challenge after Vatican II

THOMAS P. KELLY, O.P.
Archbishop of Louisville

From the outset let me make it clear that I am approaching the topic of "Religious Life in the U.S.: Crisis and Challenge after Vatican II" as a Dominican and a religious. It's not that I used to be one: I am one and hope that my life as a religious is the reason that I have been called to the episcopacy. I am a religious, like many others who have been called to the diaconate or to the priesthood or to the episcopacy, to be a pastor. And, in the same way, I feel that as a Dominican I have been called to serve as one whose life remains connected to my Dominican roots. So I am proud of being a religious and happy also to be on Archbishop Quinn's commission which is now bringing together—in a new kind of harmony and relationship—the bishops and the religious of the United States.

As you may know from the history of religious life, going back to the time of the early monks, the relationship between bishops and religious was not infrequently somewhat strained. Over the years Church law evolved to maintain the independence of religious so that they could go about their life and their work with a certain degree of guaranteed freedom and fidelity to the charism of their founder.

Only since the Second Vatican Council have we realized that

Delivered at the Cathedral-Basilica of St. James in Brooklyn on April 14, 1985.

the gulf between bishops and religious had really grown too great, and that the time had come for them to move toward one another, so that the very great gifts which religious have to contribute to the life of the Church may now be more perfectly assimilated. The Second Vatican Council did not really complete that work. There has been a series of postconciliar documents that have encouraged the bishops and religious to come together. Our current Holy Father, John Paul II, has given a special mandate to the bishops of the United States to work more closely in collaboration with religious so that we may promote, encourage, and support religious life in this country.

In order to achieve this, the Holy Father set up a commission, familiarly known as the "Quinn Commission," which is meant to facilitate this coming together. I welcome the opportunity to serve on the commission. As poor a religious as I may be, the fact is that I come to this work with the greatest love and respect. I feel that I have something to bring by way of sentiment, if not intellect. In the past couple of years, since we have begun working on this question, the bishops of the United States have—in a process developed by our pontifical commission—held hearings with a large number of religious in the United States. I come from a diocese in which there are four motherhouses and 1,600 religious. I didn't know how many would come to our three local hearings on the current state of religious life. Over 1,000 showed up! I was much impressed by their level of interest and by their willingness to get on with the work which the Holy Father has given to us.

The bishops will meet again in Collegeville, Minnesota, in June 1985 to discuss some of the more difficult theological questions that go into the make-up of religious life. Additional meetings are planned for the future. We go step by step, and I don't wish to make any predictions about what will happen next. I wish only to share some reflections about what we have already discovered through this process.

What we have discovered is very revealing, and it is very much related to our present topic about religious life—crisis and challenge. As we listen to the religious of the United States, we have sought to discover the things that were deepest and most important to them in an effort to build for the future. There is, since the Second Vatican Council and the period of renewal within religious life mandated by the Council, a new sense of identity. There is a far deeper awareness among religious than heretofore of their call to holiness in the Church and of the public character of that call.

In the seventh chapter of the *Dogmatic Constitution on the Church* of the Second Vatican Council there is a long and glorious exposition of this concept of the public response to the call to holiness that is extended to every Christian. The public character involves witness. It is witness to an identity perceived within oneself—a consecration that is made by God in response to a religious making vows through the mediation of the Church which approves a rule and constitution based on the charism of a founder as absolutely consistent with the Gospel of Jesus Christ and with consecrated life as we have understood it over the centuries.

Religious life is not in itself of divine origin, but our most recent Holy Fathers have called it a divine gift—a gift that has come to the Church from a God who loves us and draws out of us, through the influence of the Spirit, the best that is within us. The religious life must primarily be seen as a response to the call to holiness. "Be holy," the Lord Jesus has said to us, "as your heavenly Father is holy." Some within the Church answer that call in a public way, and by their lives and ministry they intend to proclaim that call to holiness and to give witness to it in their own lives.

That renewed awareness of who religious are has led, of course, to a lot of difficulties because, before they entered into that period of critical re-examination of their identity, many religious discovered themselves on a kind of pedestal not of their own making. Religious found themselves romanticized, sentimentalized, not properly understood. The call to holiness involves not an aggrandizement but an awareness of humble service, of following in the footsteps of the Lord Jesus who went first to the poor and was present to them. Religious have not always been understood in that way. In searching out their own identity in this recent period of renewal, religious have come to grips with their identity in the Church. As they have done this, they have moved to follow in the footsteps of the Lord Jesus with a deeper awareness of being present to the poor.

Thus, there is a whole new awareness of ministry to the poor —a more deinstitutionalized ministry, perhaps. We have always been present through our schools and hospitals, and in every other way we possibly could, but service to the poor had been taken for granted. Now there is a new awareness that the Lord Jesus not only ministered to the poor but was present to them in an intimate and mysterious way. The Lord Jesus walked among them, spoke to them, and was holy in their midst.

For us, it is also a case of learning from the poor, of seeing the face of the poor. In Louisville I live in the cathedral rectory. We have a bread line, and, too rarely, I work on it. I stand there and hand out bologna sandwiches to those who come to our door, or offer a cup of coffee, or shelter for the night. It is so important to see the face of the poor. Religious are beginning to be present to them in new ways, with a new sense of commitment, of presence. There is a new intimacy with the poor. From this has developed a new sense of awareness of the laity in general as religious tend to be more and more present to them and to assume different forms of ministry. There is concern. Above all, there is presence. And these things can contribute to the transformation of a community of religious.

May I tell a story? I went to South Africa in August of 1984 at the request of the bishops' conference there. Everything that is appearing almost daily in the papers about apartheid is perfectly true. It is a land where oppression has been institutionalized in a way that is virtually inconceivable to us. But in South Africa it was the religious women who broke the rules of the government first by renting a house in a part of the city where they were not legally permitted to live. White religious went to live with the so-called coloreds. They could not go to live among the blacks, but they did go to the coloreds where it was also forbidden for them to be. Their house was stoned; it was splashed with paint; the Sisters were vilified in different ways, but they stayed. That was presence. That was witness.

Much the same thing, if far less dramatic, is happening in our own country today. And this has required a new sense of what it means to be separate from the world. "Separate from the world" no longer means to American religious that they must live in a convent and be inside after five o'clock in the afternoon. It no longer means that they have to have an horarium or must be together for spiritual exercises during the day. Separation from the world is now taking a new expression as religious define it in terms of interior life, of their special gifts, of their need for one another, as well as of the need to be present to express the concern of Christ for others. So there has been a new development of "separation" as religious reach out for new ministerial opportunities.

We are now going through a great evolution with ministerial opportunities for religious in the United States. There have been a lot of developments—in parishes, in religious education, in ministry to the elderly and the disabled. In my own diocese, Sisters went out to work in Appalachia and rural areas of Kentucky where the poor have never seen anyone who could come to them and talk to them the way religious do. One area was served for fifty years by priests, and they hardly made a dent at all. They reached only the Catholics in a very strong non-Catholic territory. Then five religious women went into thirteen counties, and within a year they were received by these people in a way that priests had never been received—and then the priests were able to begin to do their work. It was a whole new opportunity for ministry. This evangelistic outreach is most welcome.

Another development in religious life that has been a source of both tension and grace concerns the far different way in which authority is exercised today in religious communities by comparison with the past. In the process of discernment by which religious seek out their ministries, they work together with superiors, with pastors, and with people who know them well and appreciate their gifts and their limitations. Religious are beginning to seek out those assignments where the needs of the Church can best be met by their gifts and talents. That certainly is a far cry from what we experienced before the Second Vatican Council. I can remember my own first assignment. Never had anyone asked me what I wanted to do. And I think that that must be the case for many religious as well. I am glad that there is beginning to be some kind of an inquiry. I think we will have better ministry. We will have better identity in the Church. We will have better awareness that people are answering the call to holiness if they pursue their ministry where they are best suited. And I believe that there is a new awareness of the needs of the Church as well.

In our pastoral letter on peace, we bishops identified at the very beginning three signs of our times: (1) The world wants peace;

(2) the arms race imposes an intolerable burden on the poor; and (3) we are confronted with new problems for which there must be new solutions. Religious are dealing with those signs of the times. Their presence as peacemakers and peace workers demonstrates this, as does their solidarity with the poor—decrying the disadvantages that are heaped upon them by economic and armament systems that despoil them; they are looking for new solutions to new problems.

With all of this, as they have gone through some uncharted ways, religious in our country have developed a new confidence in themselves, a new groundedness in their vocation, a new sense of reconciliation. They have faced, as it were, the old and the new and have managed to bring them together. In the midst of that, feeling and knowing themselves to be the hands of Jesus reconciling the world to God, as Pope John Paul II has called us, they have developed a new sense of prayer, a new sense of belonging to the Lord Jesus, of communicating through him to the Father, of accepting and receiving, and of being themselves the instruments of God's grace. This is new. This is the challenge. This is, in a time of crisis, a solid new beginning, a new way of realizing who they are and what they wish to be.

I do not see improvement as implying a greater institutionalization. However, there are some problems, and this is the "crisis" part of the question before us. There are some problems, and I would be foolish if I did not say that there are tensions. The very instruments that were set up to promote religious life are now misperceived as sources of opposition and confrontation. I deplore that, but I believe that the situation can be ameliorated with patience and mutual respect.

There are other problems. Among religious themselves there is anger, much anger, and there are some things to be angry about. Sometimes that anger expresses itself in rhetoric other members of the Church find almost impossible to listen to: for example, terms like sexism, paternalism, patriarchism, clericalism. That anger has got to be worked out. It needs to be addressed. It needs to be comforted and healed.

There is sometimes a sense of powerlessness. Language and methodology get in our way. Europeans and Anglo-Saxons write and interpret documents differently. Methodology and language problems are going to continue to exist. There is also loneliness and frustration. Our communities are aging. Some of them are dying. That is certainly part of the crisis that affects us. Many religious feel overworked and underpaid, and many *are* overworked and underpaid.

Religious want to give witness to poverty, and yet feel the tension of being themselves too middle class. It is very difficult to bear witness to poverty in a middle-class society. It is not like South Africa or South America, where poverty is present and you can embrace it. American poverty is hidden away. It is difficult to find. This is a problem that is not easily solved. That, too, is part of our crisis.

All of us have been demoralized by the departures. All of us have been hurt. The question I hear most often when I talk to religious is this: "What more could we have done to have kept our way of life attractive to and viable for those who left our ranks? What more could we have done?" The burden of response continues to be on us who remain.

The decline in vocations is certainly part of the crisis. For many it *is* the crisis. Somehow, we are not drawing others to us any more. A life that gave and gives us such joy—how can others not want to come and be part of that? A witness, a ministry, an identity that means so much to us—how is it that others are not coming? What are we doing wrong?

The tensions are with us. The crisis is here. I believe that it can and will be resolved. I believe that at the turn of the century, we will be alive and as well as we can be. But we may look a little different. We can stand that. Any community of religious in the United States that has survived the last twenty years has got plenty going for it. Note, though, that the realization of the opportunities must always be grounded in the thirst for holiness, and holiness itself requires a commitment to old concepts with, perhaps, new names. We are not going to get far away from such realities as humility and obedience. They are part of the very spirituality of the Lord Jesus. Some may think that I am looking at all of these difficult questions through rose-colored glasses and not facing stark realities. But it is the human spirit uplifted by the Lord Jesus through his salvific death that makes it possible for us to continue to hope that this divine gift of religious life will face its crises, accept its challenges, grow and be strong.

6

Bishops and Theologians in the American Church: Their Mutual Contributions

JOHN S. CUMMINS
Bishop of Oakland

I want to say a good word for theologians and, as you might expect from the way I make my living, for bishops as well. This topic is both appropriate and timely because I believe we are in an era of relationship between bishops and theologians that will be quickly seen as a new stage of cooperation and interdependence. At the same time, the years up to now have been prelude to this collaboration because they do not represent a history of opposition but of positive relationship, perhaps—in the words of a friend of mine—"notoriously so."

Let me illustrate my proposal, first, by three things I know of bishops and theologians from my own experience; secondly, by three things I know from reading and reflection; and, thirdly, by an elaboration of what I see to be the significant change in the present relationships of bishops and theologians in the United States.

Three Things from My Experience

First, I want to speak of theologians. Like many priests, I was taught and formed in substantial part by theologians who were

Delivered at the Cathedral-Basilica of St. James in Brooklyn on May 23, 1982.

members of the Society of St. Sulpice and who taught in the seminary of the Archdiocese of San Francisco. I am aware of the lingering and far-reaching effects of writings by theologians. I recall Abbot Columba Marmion's *Christ in His Mysteries* from seminary days and Yves Congar's *Lay People in the Church* from the period immediately preceding the Second Vatican Council. I remain grateful to many theologians in Berkeley, which is in our own backyard, or perhaps more properly, front yard of the Diocese of Oakland: theologians like Father Joseph Powers, S.J., whose book *Eucharistic Theology* gave me a good sense of moorings in those uncertain times a decade and more ago; or Sister Sandra Schneiders, I.H.M., whose recent probing of the contemporary problematic of religious obedience has been a helpful contribution and analysis.

I am obliged to acknowledge publicly the breadth of service done in our diocese by the schools of theology at the Graduate Theological Union in Berkeley and by the seminary of the Archdiocese of San Francisco as well. The faculty, and indeed students also, are generous to parishes, to clergy, and to adult-education programs as well as to religious-education congresses, diocesan committees, and that convenient but definitely mixed blessing, the telephone.

My second experience has to do with bishops. I want to note the blessing they have brought to my life. I think of the writings of Emanuel Cardinal Suhard of Paris, influential in our seminary days and whose letter, or really book, on the priesthood has been worth frequent rereadings. I think, too, of more concrete benefits from our first bishop in Oakland, Floyd L. Begin, who led or dragged us beyond the line of comfort in ecumenical affairs and whetted a startlingly ready appetite for the *Decree on Ecumenism* from the Second Vatican Council. I would pay tribute to the bishop of Sacramento, now in his retirement, whose association I treasure, a man who illustrated in troubled times "grace under pressure" and an imperturbable openness, tending the whole flock in which the Holy Spirit placed him to shepherd the Church of God.

A third point of reminiscing relates to a particular experience of collaboration between bishops and theologians. For six years I was secretary to the bishops of the California Catholic Conference in Sacramento, the arm of the California hierarchy for interdiocesan cooperation and for relations with the legislature and the governor's office.

Ours was an ongoing, changing, and, appropriately for the gold-dust trails of northern California, pioneering work. One decision in 1975 had to do with the repeal of the law governing private sexual conduct of consenting adults. We consulted legal experts, parents, law-enforcement people, the English hierarchy's history with a similar demand fifteen years earlier, and our moral theologians in California who were seven in number.

A studied decision ended up unanimously that the bishops should not oppose the repeal but should stand aside from any authoritative declaration over this uncertain question of civil law. It was not an easy or well-received judgment on the part of some in the Catholic community in California.

We had in contrast another case a year later. This concerned the law on death and dying, just at the high point of argument over the Karen Quinlan case. Our prejudgment was that the law was not needed, it could spawn more issues than it would settle, and it was alive with uncertain implications. Our moral theologians, by now eight in number, were clear on the moral evaluation of the proposed legislation. The political judgments, however, were divided. They remained so, even to the end when we had to make a decided but tentative decision. It was not so secure or supported that we did not earn the criticisms of some Catholic legislators, some dismayed pro-life people, and a spokesperson for a department of the United States Catholic Conference.

What was consoling and enduring was the gracious relation of theologians and bishops all those years. Though our judgments were toilsome and at times inconclusive, the respectful common pursuit of wise decision-making brought a mutual and appreciated satisfaction.

Three Things from My Study

The personal history of bishops and theologians is important to the discussion, and I do not apologize for beginning with it. I believe that my experience coincides with the desirable in the Church and even more reflects in great part the reality of ecclesiastical life in our time.

First of all, with regard to theologians, the office is a respected one in the Church and is well defined and described. I believe, too, that the theologian's task today is met with a good deal, not just of understanding, but of sympathy from various sectors of the Catholic community. This is largely because people can grasp the complexity of the theologian's responsibilities today, holding to old questions, moving to new ones, and maintaining equilibrium in an interdisciplinary world of learning and in a pluralistic society.

The International Commission of Theologians that was established by Pope Paul VI outlined in 1976 a succinct and manageable description of the theologian's work covering academic responsibility, freedom of inquiry, and pastoral sensitivity.[1] That described position or predicament of the theologian is also well defined and well documented in official statements of the Church. Even from some minor documents of Vatican II such as the *Declaration on Christian Education* come warm compliments and expectations for the theological enterprise.[2]

There are frequent references to the popular remark of Pope John XXIII that the deposit of faith is one thing, but its manner of presentation is another. Such a statement found its way into Council documents and into the apostolic constitution *Sapientia Christiana*, issued in 1979 by Pope John Paul II on ecclesiastical universities and faculties.[3]

There is a harder question, but one equally treated, from similar sources as those above. The *Declaration on Christian Education*, again, talks about "solutions . . . found for problems raised by the development of doctrine."[4] *Gaudium et Spes* specifies the matter even more clearly. "Science, history, and philosophy raise new questions which influence life and demand new theological investigations."[5] With the serene sense of understatement that should characterize the believer, the same document says that it is "sometimes difficult to harmonize culture with Christian teaching."[6] Pope John Paul II, during his recent visit to the United States, referred at Catholic University to the same theme, the need for theologians in this time and age that is "so profoundly marked by deep changes in all areas of life and society."[7]

The nature of this responsibility demands a quality that is universally conceded to the theologian, that of legitimate freedom.

Cardinal Newman, one and a quarter centuries ago remarked that "Great minds need elbow room, not indeed in the domain of faith, but of thought. And so indeed do lesser minds, and all minds."[8] *Gaudium et Spes* pursues that truth. All the faithful possess lawful freedom of inquiry and "the freedom to express their minds humbly and courageously about those matters in which they enjoy competence."[9] Pope John Paul II, speaking in Cologne Cathedral, November 15, 1980, expressed the wish of the Church for independent theological research.[10] That same week an article in the *Osservatore Romano* by an Italian priest, Father Battista Mondini, said, "It seems to me that after the heated disputes that have taken place since the end of the Council to the present time, the following truth is now established . . . that the theologian enjoys the utmost autonomy and freedom in his and her specific sphere of competence, which is the intelligibility and scientific character of the Christian message."[11]

Secondly, I turn to those who bear pastoral leadership responsibility in the Church, the bishops. Let me say that I do not think the satisfactions of the bishop's life center on power and authority. *Lumen Gentium* speaks of other attractive and enriching parts of the bishop's responsibility, the charity and unity of the Mystical Body that are manifested in any community existing around an altar under the sacred ministry of the bishop.[12] It speaks, too, of the joyful experience of anyone in the apostolate, including the bishop, preaching the faith that brings new disciples to Christ.[3]

The same document, however, deals directly and clearly with authority, stating that bishops are authentic teachers, that bishops teaching in communion with the Roman pontiff are to be respected by all as witnesses to divine and Catholic truth.

> In matters of faith and morals, the bishops speak in the name of Christ and the faithful are to accept their teaching and adhere to it with a religious assent of soul. This religious submission of will and of mind must be shown in a special way to the authentic teaching authority of the Roman Pontiff, even when he is not speaking *ex cathedra*. That is, it must be shown in such a way that his supreme magisterium is acknowledged with reverence, the judgments made by him are sincerely adhered to, according to his manifest mind and will.[14]

We can labor, and are indeed obliged to struggle, over the application and implication of this lengthy paragraph. But its clarity is evident. The episcopal office is the traditional locus of the magisterium or teaching authority. Though it is only part of the life of the bishop, it is a responsibility he must take seriously.

Thirdly, bishops and theologians with their identifiably different responsibilities in the Church are to be in relationship to one another. Specialized intellectual competence is the mark of one, and extensive pastoral authority is possessed by the other. Pope John Paul II said at the Cologne Cathedral, "It cannot be ignored that tension and even conflicts can arise."[15] I suppose one could say that conflict is built in. We could all nostalgically reminisce about the glorious early centuries of the Church with men like St. Augustine, St. Gregory Nazianzen, and St. Basil when the role of the theologian and bishop was conjoined in one person. We are, however, no longer in such simple times, and the demands of full-time pastoral leadership and specialized scholarship will not allow the combination.

We can then speak of conflict. Theologians can take stands explicitly or implicitly in disagreement with accepted Church positions. I do not mean arguments against defined doctrines of faith but postures of policy, direction, or offical teaching. The bishop may feel the tension of loyalty to the Church's pastoral authority. At the same time, he has in his own memory the conflicts on biblical scholarly approaches and the testings on the question of religious liberty, troubled investigations that eventually were blessed by the Second Vatican Council. Managing the responsibility of authority while remaining open to the guidance of the Spirit, all the while aware of the possibility of error, is a delicate and often enough difficult experience.

At this point, however, I would say that conflict is not to be exaggerated. I furthermore raise doubts that clash is the inevitable mark of the relationship of bishop and theologian. Father Raymond Brown's 1978 assessment coincides both with my experience and my reflection that theologians and the magisterium are not the main opponents in the matter of doctrine, and that disagreement between them is not the prevailing relationship.[16] I say this well aware of the danger of wrongly stating the case. I remember a well-intentioned prelate years ago speaking to a clergy he thought were unduly troubled, "I don't think things are really as bad as they are."

I turn now to an experience of my own. At the second session of the Second Vatican Council in 1963 I was present as secretary to our own bishop. I became acquainted with a gracious and personable gentleman who often sat with me at the morning gatherings. "He wrote *Pacem in Terris* for John XXIII," a friend told me. I mentioned that hearsay to the priest, who was Father Pietro Pavan, and he answered with just a smile. Since then the truth of that statement has been corroborated on a number of occasions. I have no trouble believing it because it seems very much part of a pattern. Leo XIII's encyclical on Thomism, *Aeterni Patris*, evidently was written by the German theologian Joseph Kleutgen. I read, too, the touching memoirs of Oswald von Nell-Breuning, S.J., forty years after he drafted *Quadragesimo Anno* for Pope Pius XI. With the breadth of vision that comes from age, he looked back with some misgivings about his having written so much that was not precisely the mind and intended meaning of the pope.[17]

Evidence from the last three general Councils supports what I believe to be the relationship between bishops and theologians. Jesuit Father T. Howland Sanks from Berkeley, in an article touching on the Second Vatican Council, found it "a high point in the collaboration of the magisterium and theologians."[18] That, I am quite sure, is the assessment of most people.

Father Sanks also finds an illustration, though a limited one, of such cooperation in Vatican I. The declarations of faith and revelation (*Dei Filius*) and of papal infallibility (*Pastor Aeternus*) "are the clearest examples of the cooperation of some theologians with the magisterium." Then he says with less than a compliment, "Indeed it is perhaps more than cooperation; it is coalescence."[19]

Father Yves Congar, the French Dominican, elsewhere has remarked on the active participation of theologians at the Council of Trent. "The Church," he said, "needs both *inquisitio* and *auctoritas*, that is, research and authority, two different but complementary roles and charisms which exist in the Church. Distinction between the two must be kept, even within the parameters of their necessary and felicitous collaboration." He goes on, "A synthesis of the two was fairly well realized at Trent." To the question, "Did Trent then provide a moment of balance?" Congar answers, "Yes."[20]

I recall some years ago the installation of a classmate of mine as pastor of one of our older parishes. The time was the late sixties and we were feeling the early disillusionment from the euphoric days of the Council. Standing in the hallway of the rectory waiting to go home, looking up at the single, naked light bulb that hung from a twisted cord, one local clerical pundit said with great, but mock gravity, "What went wrong, John?"

In response, let me attempt to say that not much went wrong. I think of so much collaboration of bishops and theologians. There are promising structures like the International Theological Commission of Pope Paul VI. One must take note of the abundant efforts by theologians and bishops in our country, both in formal dialogue and in studied articles, to establish an optimum mutual relationship. I think of the committees of our national bishops, such as those that drafted the pastoral letter on the health apostolate in 1981, the statement on moral values in 1976, the committee on women in society and the Church, and the committee under Archbishop Bernardin that developed the pastoral letter on war and peace. All of these had or have the active participation of theologians. Additionally, my own neighbor, Bishop Roger Mahony of Stockton, in completing a pastoral letter for his diocese in January 1982 on the question of nuclear arms, listed with thanks the theologians who prepared the document with him.[21] I am sure that these instances represent the general experience. Collaboration of bishops and theologians is a pattern, not an occasional event in the life of the Church, even in these most recent years.

A New Stage of Relationship

Collaboration of bishops and theologians is an appreciated heritage. Our gratitude also has to be extended to those who have engaged in the dialogue over the past several years and who have contributed to the present scene.

One of our Berkeley theologians pointed out to me that the relation of bishop and theologian has changed and has become a more demanding one, largely because of one factor, the development of the teaching role of the American bishop.

The phenomenon represents a growth in appreciation of an idea recovered in Vatican II, namely, the local church. Its evidence is in the large number of pastoral letters written by different bishops on the subject of nuclear arms that do not coincide either in detail or in resolution. There are other illustrations, such as statements on women in the Church, the pastoral care of homosexuals, and the matter of dissent within the Church.

These subjects come from local initiative and are not direct outflows of documents from the Holy See or from widely deliberated U. S. trends. Furthermore these depart from the character of the era or decade that we are just leaving. These recent years were marked by changes in theology produced by theologians and given impetus by the forces that were sprung from Vatican II. They brought major change in liturgy, in interest in Scripture, the place of Scripture in theology, its incorporation into the liturgy and into the everyday faith-life of our people. It brought different emphases and reflections to such dogmatic questions as the nature of the Church and led to the expression that has become commonplace, "We have different ecclesiologies" (with the all-too-human implied understanding, of course, that mine is the better one).

The present change has developed a different agenda. It furthermore has three identifiable dimensions.

First of all, bishops are speaking on topics of immediate and widespread awareness. The office of teaching, therefore, has taken on a force and an authenticity that have been much more the heritage of Europe than of North America.

Secondly, the issues are specifically American and represent an inculturation of the American Church that has not been so clearly evident before. Again, the war/peace questions are pertinent. So are the roles of women in the Church and economic justice. More topics will surely be opened up. John Courtney Murray in his 1960 work, *We Hold These Truths*, set up an agenda that included the Church as a community in a pluralistic society, a philosophy of foreign aid, and the matter of censorship.

One item of Murray's that appears to be ripening, an issue with theological dimensions as well as political ones, is the matter of schooling in America. I wish to make a digression here for a moment because I believe in its significance. The present agitation over the range of issues concerning quality of education, the place

58 · John S. Cummins

of values, the means of financing both public and private education, and tax credits represents not merely a contemporary
debate. Father Murray would portray these as evidence of a genuine malaise, a pattern of the failure to serve real needs in a country neither vaguely secular nor vaguely Protestant. The approach
to education must be diversified. "There is an increasing disposi-
tion to recognize," he says, "that the State laws which forbid all
manner of public aid to Church-affiliated schools are both out of
date and at variance with justice... and they realize that
nineteenth-century legislation does not solve the problem as it appears in mid-twentieth century." Father Murray points out the
relationship of education and spiritual needs and invites the country to pick up this unfinished agenda of relating schools to spiritual aspirations and provide a system at once more effective and
more just.[22]

The third dimension of the present change goes beyond specifically domestic needs. There has been a growth in the consciousness of American international responsibilities. The statement by
the bishops on the Panama Canal in 1978 was an object of criticism, and at times derision, by opponents of the bishops' position.
The Central American statement, however, of November 1981
was received much more seriously, as have been the testimonies of
United States bishops before Congress questioning foreign policy
toward Central American countries. The time given by the bishops at their annual meeting in 1980 to Bishop Mark McGrath of
Panama, as well as the delegations of bishops sent to Chile, El Salvador, Africa, and Asia in recent years represent a new outreach.
Not surprisingly, a Central American rector visiting us recently
remarked that the United States bishops are the avenue for the
Third World to reach the conscience of the American people.

I believe that bishops take intellectual competence seriously
and respect the directive of Lumen Gentium that the officially appointed teachers of the Church have to apply the appropriate
human means to arrive at the truth.[23] We can expect therefore
that bishops will be drawing more and more on theologians for
the writing of pastoral letters, for analyzing the American scene,
and for synthesizing the dialogue between U. S. theologians and
Latin American liberation theologians. The association of bishops
and theologians will, by necessity, be more interdependent, even

as one has called it "organic." I believe, too, that we bishops will be wise enough to consult not just those theologians with whom we are intellectually comfortable, but even a wider group so that we will have the sense of the broader reflection and experience of the community.

From one point of view, bishops and theologians are independent. Our Holy Father, Pope John Paul II, has said, "The magisterium and theology have two different tasks to perform, that is why neither can be reduced to the other. Yet they serve the one whole, but precisely on account of this configuration they must remain in consultation with one another."[24]

Father Joseph Fitzmyer, S.J., writing in *America* magazine, expressed the matter differently.

> As I have often liked to put it, the theologian and the exegete need the magisterium and the faithful to buzz about them like gadflies to make them reflect on "their dedication to intellectual honesty" and "responsible scholarship." But the magisterium and the faithful also need the theologians and the exegetes to buzz about them like gadflies to make them reflect on their need of "constant updating" and respect for "the deepest and noblest aspiration of the human spirit." This is the role of mutual stimulation, not confrontation.[25]

Respectful mutuality may be a softer and happier description. This leads to one more important point. Whether independent or interdependent, theologians and bishops operate within the Church. The echo of St. Paul's words surrounds all of our discussion.[26] Bishops are the gift of the Spirit of the Church; theologians are the gift of the Spirit of the Church. I believe it is true to say that neither forms the community. Rather, they exist within that community of believers and are meaningful only in relation to it. Pope John Paul II, in addressing theologians in Washington, D.C., made the point that they should be sensitive to the role of bishops and to the rights of the faithful.[27] That directive applies equally to all of us and is understood by people like Yves Congar who says with significance, "I seek no other mandate as a theologian for my duty and my desire to speak of God than my being a friar-preacher in the Church . . . I have said advisedly: in the Church."[28]

The relationship of bishops and theologians is in one sense prayerful as well as supportive. The atmosphere is a respectful family trust, not antagonism that divides the community which both are responsible to serve.

What we can be grateful for is the long history of collaboration and cooperation that has been immensely fruitful for the Church over the years. In line with this, I recall an observation made by the director of the bishops' study on the renewal of the parish that has gone on for the last three years. It has come from his research, he indicated, that if one separates out groups from the Church, one will experience in that conversation a feeling of isolation, of somberness, and a tendency to complain. Put them together and one will sense with excitement the vitality of our Catholic community as it is today. The relationship of bishops and theologians is lively enough at the moment. It promises to be more vital in the years ahead.

NOTES

1. International Theological Commission, 1976, summary of "Twelve Theses on the Relationship between Ecclesial Magisterium and Theology," quoted in Archbishop John R. Quinn, "The Magisterium and the Field of Theology," *Origins* 7, no. 22.

2. *Gravissimum Educationis*, in *The Documents of Vatican II*, ed. Walter M. Abbot (New York: 1966), no. 11, p. 650. All further references to conciliar documents and speeches will be to this edition.

3. Cf. John XXIII, "Opening Speech to the Council," p. 715; *Gaudium et Spes*, no. 62, p. 268; *Sapientia Christiana*, in *Crux of the News*, June 18, 1979, p. 1.

4. *Gravissimum Educationis*, no. 11, p. 650.

5. *Gaudium et Spes*, no. 62, p. 268.

6. Ibid.

7. John Paul II, *U.S.A.: The Message of Justice, Peace and Love* (Boston: St. Paul Editions, 1979), p. 260.

8. John Henry Newman, *The Idea of a University* (Garden City, N.Y.: Image Books, 1959), p.429.

9. *Gaudium et Spes*, no. 62, p. 270.

10. John Paul II, *L'Osservatore Romano*, November 24, 1980, p. 12.

11. Battista Mondini, *L'Osservatore Romano*, November 17, 1980, p. 11.

12. *Lumen Gentium*, no. 26, p. 50.

13. Ibid., no. 26, p. 51.

14. Ibid., no. 25, p. 48.

15. John Paul II, *L'Osservatore Romano*, November 24, 1980, p. 12.

16. Raymond Brown, "The Magisterium vs. the Theologian—Debunking Some Fictions," *Origins* 7 (April 13, 1978), pp. 673–82.

17. Oswald von Nell-Breuning, "The Drafting of *Quadragesimo Anno*," translated from *Stimmen der Zeit*, 1971, by John Doebie.

18. T. Howland Sanks, "Co-operation, Co-optation, Condemnation: Theologians and the Magisterium 1870–1978," *Chicago Studies* 17, no. 2 (Summer 1978), p. 223.

19. Ibid., p. 245.

20. Yves Congar, "Theologians and the Magisterium in the West: From the Gregorian Reform to the Council of Trent," *Chicago Studies* 17, no. 2 (Summer 1978), p. 223.

21. Roger Mahony, *Pastoral Letter on Nuclear Arms*, January 1, 1982.

22. John Courtney Murray, *We Hold These Truths* (New York: Sheed & Ward, 1960), p. 148.

23. *Lumen Gentium*, no. 25, p. 49.

24. John Paul II, *L'Osservatore Romano*, November 24, 1980, p. 12.

25. Joseph A. Fitzmyer, "John Paul II, Academic Freedom and the Magisterium," *America* 141, no. 13 (November 3, 1979), p. 249.

26. Cf. Ephesians 4:11.

27. John Paul II, *U.S.A.: The Message of Justice, Peace and Love*, p. 262.

28. Yves Congar, quoted in *Overview* (April 1982), p. 1. Original quotation appears in *New Blackfriars* (October 1981).

7

Getting Our House in Order:
Economic Justice within the Church

WILLIAM E. McMANUS, D.D.
Retired Bishop of Fort Wayne–South Bend, Indiana

When a retired bishop talks about economic justice within the Church, he lacks some credibility because he no longer has the responsibility of putting the principles he recommends into practice. Let me say, therefore, that this reflection was prepared while I was still the active bishop of Fort Wayne-South Bend, Indiana, and agonizing for the last time over such matters as fundraising, investments, the probable economic trends in northern Indiana, and the pressing need to provide higher salaries for all the people employed by the diocese, particularly the largest group among them, the teachers in Catholic schools. Before I retired, the diocesan board of directors accepted my plan for an 8 to 10 percent increase in all salaries and stipends during the fiscal year that began July 1, 1985.

Preliminary reports from my former diocese for the first quarter of the 1985–86 fiscal year indicate that parishioners' response to my appeals for increased contributions to cover the salary increases will be more than enough to pay the additional expense. However, a $250 increase in annual high-school tuition was not very popular. Enrollment dropped about 7 percent, but there is no evidence that most parents who transferred their children to public schools were unable to afford the additional tuition; they

Delivered at the Cathedral-Basilica of St. James in Brooklyn on May 26, 1985.

apparently didn't think the kind of Catholic education available was worth the higher price. Scholarship aid for needy students was less than the funds allocated for that purpose.

Now that the U.S. bishops, including myself, have made some tentative but highly controversial pronouncements on the U.S. economy, I have become acutely concerned with the meaning these moral principles should have for the Church itself. At prayer, I have anxiously recalled what Jesus said to the scribes and Pharisees after they had harassed him with allegations that he was breaking Jewish law despite his good intention of putting persons ahead of merely human regulations: "Then addressing the people and his disciples Jesus said, 'The scribes and the Pharisees occupy the chair of Moses. You must therefore do what they tell you and listen to what they say; but do not be guided by what they do, since they do not practice what they preach. They tie up heavy burdens and lay them on men's shoulders, but will they lift a finger to move them? Not they!'" (Matt. 23:1-4).

In a recent speech at the University of Notre Dame, the Most Rev. Archbishop Rembert G. Weakland, O.S.B., of Milwaukee, Wisconsin, and chairman of the committee charged with drafting the American bishops' pastoral letter on the economy, remarked that nearly half the voluminous mail he has received raised the question of whether or not the Church would itself live up to the ideals and moral standards it is urging upon the U.S. business community and the federal government. This challenge has been added to pointed assertions that the bishops lack both the competence and the authority to lay out moral guidelines for the management of our nation's affluent economy.

In this relatively brief treatment of a vast topic, I limit myself to three points: (1) the Church's position on justice within its own house, (2) the gap between this official teaching and actual practice, and (3) some ways of closing or narrowing that gap.

None of the great papal encyclicals on economic justice explicitly call upon the Church to make practical applications to itself of the moral principles prescribed for management, labor, and government. Leo XIII's *Rerum Novarum* (1891), Pius XI's *Quadragesimo Anno* (1931), John XXIII's *Mater et Magistra* (1961), Paul VI's *Populorum Progressio* (1967), and John Paul II's *Laborem Exercens* (1981) are classic statements of Catholic social teaching, but one must read between the lines to see their relevance for the Church itself. Neither Vatican II's great *Pastoral Constitution on the Church in the Modern World*, nor the Council's *Declaration on Christian Education*, which extols Catholic school teachers, has anything explicit to say about justice for Church employees.

In November 1971, the second synod of bishops did what Vatican II had envisioned synods doing. It added a new specificity to the Council's decrees and, in effect, updated them. Pope Paul VI approved publication of the decrees of this synod on *Justice in the World* that, among other things, contained a landmark declaration on justice in the Church.

The synod said:

> While the Church is bound to give witness to justice she recognizes that anyone who ventures to speak to people about justice must first be just in their own eyes. Hence we must undertake an examination of the modes of acting and of the possessions and life-style found within the Church itself.
>
> Within the Church, rights must be preserved. No one should be deprived of ordinary rights because of association with the Church in one way or another. Those who serve their Church by their labor, including priests and religious, should receive a sufficient livelihood and enjoy that social security that is customary in their region. Lay people should be given fair wages and a system for promotion. We reiterate our recommendations that lay people should exercise more important functions with regard to Church property and should share in its administration.

With remarkable clarity the synod declared itself on women's rights in the Church, on the right of everyone to be heard in dialogue, on the need for judicial procedures in settling disputes, and on the importance of having a "mixed commission of men and women, religious and lay people, of differing situations and competence," to study all ramifications of the Church's own duty to practice justice. The synod said the Church has an obligation "to live and to administer its own goods in such a way that the Gospel is proclaimed to the poor. . . . In the case of needy peoples it must be asked whether belonging to the Church places people on a rich island in an ambiance of poverty."

Evidently the synod's decrees, though not in the same influential category as Vatican II documents or papal encyclicals, influenced the Commission on Canon Law that took almost fifteen years to recodify the Church's laws in light of Vatican II. (That revised code is now official.) Unlike the synod's heartwarming decrees, however, the canons on justice in the Church are coldly legalistic.

Canon 1274 requires each diocese to have a "special institute" or some other establishment to collect funds for sufficient support of the clergy serving the diocese, and to arrange similar support for all other employees. Richer dioceses, the canon says, should help poorer dioceses, and for this purpose bishops should set up a cooperative enterprise. Social security is to be provided for all employees.

Canon 231, after acknowledging the Church's need for lay ministers, declares: "They have a right to decent remuneration suited to their condition; by such remuneration they should be able to provide decently for their own needs and for those of their family with due regard for the prescriptions of the civil law; they likewise have a right that their pension, social security and health benefits be duly provided."

The revised code also mandates that every diocese must have a finance council of at least three lay members who are "truly skilled in financial affairs as well as in civil law, of outstanding integrity and appointed by the bishop. The bishop must hear the finance council ... on the more important acts of administration in light of the economic situation of the diocese." Parishes also are required to have similar finance councils.

In 1982, the Vatican's Sacred Congregation for Catholic Education minced no words in its statement on *Lay Catholics in Schools: Witness to Faith*. This document is especially significant for the U.S. Church because of our vast commitment to Catholic schools. The sentences I quote here are as forceful as anything I could have composed myself from my long experience in American Catholic education.

> If the directors of the school and the lay people who work in the school are to live according to the same ideals, two things are essential. First, lay people must receive an adequate salary, guaranteed by a well-defined contract, for the work they

do in the school; a salary that will permit them to live in dignity, without excessive work or a need for additional employment that will interfere with the duties of an educator. This may not be immediately possible without putting an enormous financial burden on the families, or making the school so expensive that it becomes a school for a small elite group; but so long as a truly adequate salary is not being paid, the laity should see in the school directors a genuine preoccupation to find the resources necessary to achieve this end. Second, laity should participate authentically in the responsibility for the school; this assumes that they have the ability that is needed in all areas and are sincerely committed to the educational objectives that characterize a Catholic school....
It must never be forgotten that the school itself is always in the process of being created.

So far as unions are concerned, it should be noted that the papal encyclicals never have suggested that the Church need not respect its employees' right to engage in collective bargaining with the Church through unions of their own choice. The encyclicals have upheld this employees' prerogative as a "basic human right." In summary, the universal Church has taught principles of justice applicable to economics with a degree of specificity sufficient to set just management policies for a local Church.

What have the U.S. bishops taught?

In my library I have a collection of the documents issued by the U.S. bishops from 1792 until 1985. In these statements the bishops have condemned all sorts of social evils including secularism, materialism, atheism, racial injustice, evils in government, and immoral weapons of war. They have also recommended solutions to social problems based on the Gospel principles of justice and charity. Without sounding harsh I must say—and having been a bishop for seventeen years I know whereof I speak—that the episcopal pronouncements are often Olympian, particularly in their condemnation of an evil world way out there somewhere. Their high-minded remedies and corrections for those evils often seem to lack feasibility and credibility. Their tone is more heady than hearty. The fact is, however, that the American bishops have tried to apply the papal encyclicals on social justice to the United States and have expressed a sincere readiness to cooperate with the universal Church on matters of social reform.

Rarely, however, have the U.S. bishops as a group spotlighted their own performances as the chief administrators of a 40-million member organization with thousands of institutions and programs to manage. One reason for this is that until Vatican II the bishops' conference was forbidden to function as anything more than a friendly assembly for the exchange of ideas. The conference's first rule was to respect completely the autonomy of each bishop. This rule prohibited collective self-examination, and outlawed even the inference that here and there something might be a little amiss in Church administration.

Occasionally the U.S. bishops' statements might drop a hint about taking a hard look at the Church itself, but like the papal encyclicals, these documents had to be read between the lines to see their practical applicability to the Church. In 1967, however, the American bishops did say in a major document, *The Church in Our Day*:

> The Church has addressed herself to social justice, world peace, the political order, the undeveloped nations. By all this, many were moved to put their hopes in her. If Catholic performance does not match Catholic promise, then truly we shall have failed. We were once warned: It is not your encyclicals that we despise; what we despise is the neglect with which you yourselves treat them. This was said in indictment of the people of God of another nation and another generation, but there is no point in pretending that it cannot be applied with equal force and fury against us in America in our decade.

Nothing like that had been said before to suggest the Church had better practice what it preaches.

Since 1968, the National Conference of Catholic Bishops has come a long way in making its activities compatible with its principles. Salaries, working conditions, and economic security at the headquarters have been improved. Representatives of the bishops have helped Cesar Chavez organize farm workers into a union of their choice. Corporations guilty of antiunion tactics have been openly condemned for that injustice. Staff representatives and some bishops themselves have testified for or against proposed legislation in terms of moral principles. Two formal statements have acknowledged the right of Catholic school teachers and Catholic hospital employees to join unions seeking contracts and improved salaries and working conditions.

By far the most explicit declaration by the Church to the Church is found in the first draft of the pastoral on *Catholic Social Teaching and the U.S. Economy*. In language that would have been startling twenty years ago this document says (and I will quote only the high points):

> The church employs large numbers of people in its parishes, schools, hospitals and social agencies. . . . All the moral principles that govern the just operation of any economic endeavor apply to the Church and its many agencies and institutions. . . .
>
> Increased resources are also needed for the support of elderly members of religious communities. These dedicated women and men have given their lives to ministering, to teaching, nursing and many other forms of care which have greatly benefited Catholics and non-Catholics alike. . . . It would be a great injustice to them if they should be forced to face retirement without adequate resources.
>
> The effective implementation of these objectives will strain the Church's resources. This is the plight we as bishops share with many others who hold the responsibilities we do as administrators. We pledge that we will seek in every way possible to reduce other expenses in order to improve our ability to provide adequate wages and benefits. . . .
>
> We also call on all members of our Church to recognize their responsibilities to contribute to the support of those who carry out the public mission of the Church. . . .
>
> All Church institutions must also fully recognize the rights of employees to organize and to bargain collectively with the institution through whatever association or organization they freely choose, without undue pressures from their employers or from already existing labor organizations. The Church would be justly accused of hypocrisy and scandal were any of its agencies to try to prevent the organization of unions by intimidation or coercion.

When Church-related institutions are shareholders in a corporation, they must, the pastoral says, "make efforts to ensure that the invested funds are used responsibly.... As part owners, they can help shape the policies of these companies...."

The Church has a special call to be a servant of the poor. It should, therefore, the bishops say, keep its inner-city schools open for the education of the poor, open up its doors to the poor neglected by the government or other agencies and insist in season and out of season on a "preferential option for the poor."

All this teaching is what you and I would expect from a Church committed to continuing Jesus Christ's ministry of justice and love in our own day. There is, however, a glaring gap between this official teaching and the Church's record and practices. Often this gap has been due not to malice, or to lack of good intentions, or to fault in the Church's teaching. It has been due largely to neglect and to a dearth of creativity and courage in the management of the business side of the Church. The bishops' pastoral on the economy insists that in making business decisions, management should always ask a pivotal question: "What will this decision do *for* people and *to* people?" My own paraphrase of this is: "People before buildings."

During most of this century, bishops and pastors were caught up in a building craze, and the laity readily joined in the fun. In setting budgets for new buildings, particularly for elaborate churches, the sky was the limit; but diocesan and Church employees, particularly the unskilled, were as poor as church mice and trapped into low-paying jobs with no possibility for advancement and no promise of an adequate pension. To this day, professional fundraisers and "counselors," as they call themselves, insist that a good case, or "pitch," can always be made for a building—a new church or a gymnasium—but that among clergy and laity there is little interest in appeals for funds to pay higher salaries to Church employees.

The U.S. bishops advocate a "preferential option" for the poor, but I have seen little preference shown to the Church's lowest paid and most insecure employees: janitors, domestics, rectory secretaries, and organists. One pastor who moved from parish to parish, often at the request of the bishops and to the delight of the parishioners he left behind, boasted that he always took his housekeeper along. He meant well, of course; he wanted to be sure she had a job. But her explanation was a little different. "I trail along," she said, "only as a slave." All these underpaid persons survive at the whim of their employer. There's no pay scale for them, no passage to a better job, no pension that, even coupled with Social Security's retirement benefits, would be adequate in their old age. Instead of being preferred, the poor employed by the Church are trampled upon. A Christmas turkey and a little bonus are no remedy for a gross injustice.

Allowing for commendable exceptions, I would say that most dioceses and parishes do not assign top priority to salary increases and to improved fringe benefits when they are preparing budgets for the Church's programs. Discussion at budget meetings swirls around questions of the going rate, not around questions of what employees need or deserve. We ask what we can get by with in terms of the employment market, not what these human beings ought to have for a living wage. In Catholic Church management, rugged individualism is more esteemed than cooperation for the general welfare. In some dioceses, each parish is a separate corporate unit. The rich parishes with money in the bank thrive on their income from high-interest certificates of deposit, while poor parishes, often near neighbors, struggle to pay off bank loans at high interest. Interdiocesan patterns and practices, however, are much better. Through the American Board of Missions and other private arrangements, many wealthier dioceses are helping those less affluent.

On the positive side, many Church institutions, after prayerful study of the Church's social teaching, are now putting it into practice. The Archdiocese of Chicago, for example, has a program of universal sharing that encourages every parish, from the richest to the poorest, to take the initiative in helping another parish. By this means, millions flow from affluent parishes to poorer parishes. Though the U.S. Supreme Court has ruled that the National Labor Relations Board does not have jurisdiction over Church institutions' management practices, many schools, notably Catholic high schools, have developed excellent contracts with teacher unions.

The emergence of diocesan finance councils and parish finance councils is, in many cases, helping Church administrators set their sights on greatly increased income as a prelude to improved salaries and benefits. There is, however, a danger that some finance committees, whose members are indeed skilled and experienced in financial matters but are ill-informed or even biased about the Church, may sacrifice a reasonable ecclesiology on the altar of business efficiency. With horror I recall a banker on a finance committee who insisted repeatedly that improved high-school varsity athletics should have a priority over the diocese's liturgical office. In my opinion, all members of diocesan and parish finance councils should be required to participate in a series of seminars on contemporary ecclesiology. Then many of them might realize that, knowing little about the Church, they ought to stick to their expertise on finances and leave pastoral decisions to the bishop and pastor in consultation with diocesan and parish pastoral councils.

My third point has to do with ways of closing that gap between teaching and practice, and I shall deal with it briefly in terms of three C's: conviction, courage, and constancy.

Faith, Jesus Christ said, can move mountains, and it will take faith, graced by God's help, for Church administrators to become convinced that, no matter what the obstacles, they must be just to all Church employees. This faith can overcome the most obvious obstacle, a glaring need for additional income. The generosity of America is great and far superior to that of most other nations. Nevertheless, the full potential of U.S. Catholics' contributions usually is underestimated and, consequently, donations are less than they could be. Studies at the National Opinion Research Center in Chicago prove conclusively that since the Great Depression, Catholics, as a group, have been climbing up the economic ladder at a much faster pace than the general population. Millions of Catholics have moved from middle income to upper-middle income, and millions more have moved from lower income to middle income. In a recent book, *American Catholics Since the Council*, Father Andrew Greeley, citing the results of sociological research, says that "in the 1980's, American Catholics made more money than Protestants excepting Presbyterians and Episcopalians." He further notes, however, that "Catholics under forty, those who were most likely to benefit from the surge in economic and occupational achievement in the last twenty years . . . have become the most affluent religious group in America." But the rate of giving to the Church has not matched the donors' rise up the ladder. Apart from families with children in Catholic schools, I venture to say that few Catholics have ever had the experience of giving until it hurts. Most support of the Church is painless, but low-salaried employees endure plenty of pain.

Bishops and priests will have to deepen and reinforce their conviction that they must raise much more money even though the effort will entail pastoral pain—the nagging irritation of being forced to beg for funds that ought to be given spontaneously. Reluctance to ask for more money is, however, no excuse for paying substandard wages. Ultimately, justice will be achieved when the laity become sufficiently convinced about it to make sacrifices, if necessary, to finance the Church's needs.

Courage calls for the Church to be a model of what it teaches about the moral dimensions of business and economics. This courage will require going to extremes to show people that the Church is living up to its own ideals. Courage will demand a realignment of priorities, with more attention to those lower ones without which there can be no high ones. Courage may necessitate the closing or curtailment of programs that are unquestionably beyond the finances of the Church as a whole. Heaven help the Church, however, if it becomes so narrowly parochial that individual parishes, hard pressed for money, are forced to close schools, while affluent neighbors buy new bells for a Gothic bell tower.

I am distressed (and will cry loudly about it whenever I'm around bishops) that the second draft of the bishops' pastoral on the economy has backed away from the first draft's unequivocal commitment to Church support of Catholic inner-city schools and has retreated into the following ultra-safe declaration: "Our Catholic schools have a well-merited reputation of providing excellent education of the poor. As bishops, we will do our best with the means provided us to continue this tradition of fostering the best education possible for all our students and not neglect those of modest or meager means." That's about as courageous as declaring "we bishops do declare that toothpaste does clean teeth, even the teeth of the poor." The previous (first) draft put it on the line: "We bishops *pledge* [italics mine] to support the effort to provide the best possible education for the poor."

The last "C" stands for constancy. This simply means that every diocese and every parish must have a long-range plan for its finances, instead of periodically launching frenzied drives that inflate income but rarely stabilize it over the long haul. Excessive reliance on bingo will not assure constant income. My hope is that diocesan and parish finance councils will become specialists in the long-range planning that, if convincingly explained to the Church's contributors, will encourage generous and steady donations. That will make it possible to close the gap between our social teaching and our practice.

8

The National Conference of Bishops:
A New Vision of Leadership
and Authority

J. FRANCIS STAFFORD
Bishop of Memphis

We ask a person to speak because we want him or her to redefine the space we live in and to enrich our lives. To speak on a *new vision* of leadership and authority in reference to the National Conference of Catholic Bishops (NCCB) is not necessarily to present the "unheard of" but rather to reaffirm foundations and to bring into focus our home, that is, the Body of Christ.

"May the message of Christ, in all its richness, find its home in you." The image of "home" will be a recurring metaphor in the first part of this presentation. I hope the reason will become obvious.

But first, some background is in order. The publication of the pastoral letter of the NCCB, *The Challenge of Peace: God's Gift and Our Response*, has been the occasion for greater reflection on the teaching authority of episcopal conferences in relation to the universal college of bishops; the limitation and purpose of such letters are also now under discussion. Besides, concern has been expressed about the propriety of religious authorities addressing issues of public life. Many wish to place the religious dimension on the margin of public and political life.

Delivered at the Cathedral-Basilica of St. James in Brooklyn on May 27, 1984.

A statement by Joseph Cardinal Ratzinger, recorded in a *Synthesis* of the "informed consultation" (words quoted from the *Synthesis*) in Rome concerning a 1983 draft of the NCCB's proposed pastoral, is the immediate cause.[1] Recent articles on the question of the teaching authority mentions the following statement by Cardinal Ratzinger: "A bishops' conference as such does not have a *mandatum docendi*." Some authors have dismissed the statement; others, who dismiss the pastoral, have sewn it on a flag.

By far, however, the greatest challenge to the authority of faith and of bishops (both individually in his own diocese and collectively in an episcopal conference) is the attempt of society, of some governments, and even of some Christians to marginalize that faith and its teachers. To marginalize means to remove from the realm of public affairs. The reality of authority is not denied; it is banished from the public realm. This is accomplished in controlled societies by assigning public religious authority to the criminal sector and in open societies by rendering the authority absurd, that is, unworthy of a hearing. Lenin's essay *Socialism and Religion* (1905) is an example of the one extreme; he says: "Religion should be a private matter as far as the state is concerned; however, we can by no means view it as a private matter in regard to our own party." It is so private that the Decree of the Council of People's Commissars, January 23, 1918, states that "no church or religious community has a right to possessions or property. They do not possess the rights of legal persons." And of course religious instructions are forbidden.

The other extreme is William F. Buckley's summary judgment on the 1983 draft of the bishops' pastoral letter on war and peace. "No other declaration has brought home so clearly the dimensions of the philosophical assault on right thought as the draft of the pastoral letter prepared for final consideration by the American Catholic Bishops at their conference in May."[2]

The marginalization of the public authority of faith is not due solely to social theorists (no matter what their ideological leanings); it is also the result of technology whose ascendancy has rendered human interaction, and even the human being, superfluous. This "universalized technology as the dominant form of activity, as the overwhelming pattern of existence, even as a language" imposes itself on our life "without the question of its meaning being asked" (Pope Paul VI, *Octogesima Adveniens*, no. 29). Neutralization of the mind, heart, and soul of human beings means that "man is experiencing a new loneliness; it is not in the face of a hostile nature which it has taken him centuries to subdue, but in an anonymous crowd which surrounds him and in which he feels himself a stranger" (ibid., no. 10).

Public Life and Religious Authority

Nothing could be further removed from the message of the New Testament and the Word incarnate, who is its source, than that humans become strangers to one another or to the foundations of their existence. The fundamental ethic of St. Paul is succinctly stated in Thessalonians 5:11: "Therefore encourage one another and build one another up." The latter expression in Greek could be rendered as "build a home for one another." This fundamental ethic is consistent with the revelation that God has not remained a stranger; the Word was made flesh and dwelt among us. We need to strip evil of its mask, its objective horrors, and see the real terror of its subtle attempts to render human beings superfluous. This attitude can be discerned even in noble persons who dismiss the bishops' peace pastoral with cavalier indifference, or by those who defend abortion as an inconsequential action, or by the vengeful who cry out for more executions.

Faith and its authority are put on the margin by the political executive who cannot face up to an alternative voice, by the technologist who judges his calculations and analyses as morally neutral, and by the otherwise decent man or woman who has a banal appreciation of the first amendment. They claim: "Priests should quit talking about politics and keep Christ in church. Priests should not be meddling parsons." This attitude is the result of people who have allowed themselves to fall victim to the religious alienation that pervades all levels of modern society. The final result is that faith is reduced to the level of sentimentality. Sentiment can have many positive features, but one thing it does not have is authority.

The crucial question in regard to the leadership and authority of faith, and more pointedly to the leadership role of the NCCB, concerns the citizenship of Jesus Christ and his place in human history. In his first encyclical *Redemptor Hominis*, Pope John

Paul II states in section 10: "In reality, the name for that deep amazement at man's worth and dignity is the Gospel, that is to say: the Good News. It is also called Christianity. This amazement determines the Church's mission in the world and perhaps even more so, in the modern world. . . . It also fixes Christ's place —so to speak, His particular right of citizenship—in the history of man and mankind." Being people of faith, we believe in the incarnation and lordship of the Word of God, Jesus Christ. We believe that his authority was communicated to the apostles by him.

The difference between the authority from Jesus Christ and the "eternal ideas" of Plato, or the "predictable conclusion of the dialectic of nature" of the Marxists, or even the "progress" of the technologist, is that Jesus Christ has a right to citizenship; philosophers always consider their *source* to be outside the affairs of men.

What our Church's leaders are trying to accomplish in their teachings on social justice, peace, and human rights is to provide a foundation upon which public life can once again become a possibility for human beings as it once was.

What is meant by the word "authority" and the experience that gives rise to it? The ancient Greeks had no word for "authority." Public affairs had two models. Relationships between citizens were patterned after domestic affairs—persuasion (*peithein*), and foreign affairs were handled by force and violence (*bia*). It is disappointing to note that the Greek word for violence is so closely related to the word for life (*bios*). Plato sought to introduce in human relationships a reality that could give stability and durability to human beings—our mortality declares we are fragile and our institutions no less unstable. As a note of intellectual interest, it was Plato who coined the word *theology*, and it first appears in the discussion on the founding of a city (*Republic* 379A).

Our word "authority" comes from the Latin *auctoritas*. The Greeks had the theory, but the Romans had the experience and the word for it. The experience was that of foundation, "*dum conderet urbem*," as Virgil would put it. *Auctoritas* is derived from *augere*, to augment and strengthen. The work of authority is to reaffirm and to keep in contact with the foundation, grounding all things that are to come. The public experience of being vitally tied to the past (*re-ligare*, whence the word "religion") protected the public realm from the tyrant who would try to rule at whim and from the powerful who would use force as a way of life.

Jesus Christ incarnates a new experience of authority. He announces that he has the authority (*exousia*) to forgive sins, and people marvel at him because, unlike the scribes and Pharisees, he speaks with authority (*exousia*). The Greek word *exousia* is often translated as "authority," sometimes as "full power." It is literally a capacity and a right to act or teach that originates out of one's being. The witness of the Gospel is that this authority on earth does not disappear with the ascension, but is continued through the apostles. *Lumen Gentium* states that bishops are ". . . teachers endowed with the authority of Christ [*auctoritate Christi praediti*], who preach to the people committed to them the faith they must believe and put into practice" (no. 25). The experience of Christ's authority is more than a new foundation that takes the place of Moses. Authority goes beyond vital contact with a divine event in the past; it includes participation in the Body of Christ now and anticipates it in the future. A new vision of leadership and authority incorporates eschatology in our thinking and teaching. It brings into focus the true destiny of the human person and opens up the ministry to hope. Hope puts us into the heart of the public realm, and in the words of David Tracy: "Hope is responsible and public."[3] The Church as the Body of Christ is more than a moral institution, and its teaching and teachers are in touch with the resources "for making possible a future in which it will still be worthwhile to be a person."[4]

These reflections are intended to show that the ministry to the Word of God cannot strike its tent and move to the periphery of life. This ministry must address even those issues and persons which may pretend that they are immune to conscience and the dignity of the person. It is ironic that those who decry the public voice of the Church accuse it of the very problems they precipitate. The radical secularist in denouncing religion as the opiate of the masses is throwing up a smoke screen against the fact that it has been the ideologies of the twentieth century that have been most effective in numbing the mind and conscience of whole nations against the realities of genocide and mass murder. Those who try to discredit Church people as naive and unrealistic are actually seducing whole populations to avoid facing reality by means of selective forgetfulness. The words of Archbishop Weakland are relevant: "The purpose of Catholic social teaching is . . . to stimulate thinking on the ethical and moral implications of decisions which affect the whole of society and to bring to the debate insights which could be forgotten."[5] The thrust of the social doctrine is to make human beings once again capable of experience—experience of themselves as persons with a dignity from the Son of God in a world reconciled to the Father. Because of the need for reconciliation the Church has not only the right but obligation to challenge the world and its citizens in regard to the truth about human beings and the world, and the proper stewardship of both. In the words of Cardinal Ratzinger, "The Church would betray not only her own message, but the destiny of humanity if she were to renounce being the guardian of being and its moral message."[6]

The Authority of Episcopal Conferences

The *munus docendi* (the teaching office) of the National Conference of Catholic Bishops is an alive issue in the Church today. More specifically, in a report by Father Jan Siliotte, secretary of the Pontifical Justice and Peace Commission, Cardinal Joseph Ratzinger, prefect of the Congregation for the Doctrine of the Faith, is quoted as indicating that "a bishops' conference does not have a *mandatum docendi* [a mandate to teach]. This belongs only to individual bishops or the College of Bishops with the Pope." It is true that the new canons on episcopal conferences fall short of the traditional doctrine concerning synods. Even though the law may fall short in its attention to conferences, it is my judgment that there is some kind of teaching "energy" (*Christus Dominus*, no. 37) in an actually existing *communio* of bishops.

It is necessary to put the issue in proper context. The rest of the paragraph of the above-mentioned report reads:

> This belongs only to the individual bishops or to the College of Bishops with the Pope. When a bishop exercises his teaching authority for his diocese, his statements are binding in conscience. Taking into account that the stated purpose of the U.S. pastoral letter is to form individual consciences and

to offer moral guidance in pubic policy debate, how can it be
made clear when, in a statement of a bishops' conference, the
bishops are speaking as bishops who intend thereby to exercise their teaching authority?

The question is not solely one of the authority or the right to
teach, but rather the relationship between authority and public
debate. Later in the *Synthesis* it is stated (and no particular participant is named): "It is wrong to propose the teaching of the bishops merely as a basis for debate; the teaching ministry of the bishops means that they lead the people of God and therefore their
teaching should not be obscured or reduced to one element among
several in a free debate." The bishops' peace pastoral, or any pastoral letter for that matter, does not propose itself as another voice
in a debate. Nor does it hand down a tersely formulated doctrine.
Rather, when issues and situations develop that affect the relationship of one person with another, or when the destinies of whole
societies are being formulated, the various factions cannot be allowed to forget that there are evangelical truths that must be part
of their deliberation. Hierarchical authority, willed by the
Church's divine founder, brings into focus and into the public
forum the voice of the Good Shepherd. It preserves a heritage of
faith in an unbelieving world.

Canon 753 of the new Code of Canon Law states:

> Although they do not enjoy infallible teaching authority, the
> bishops in communion with the head and members of the col-
> lege, whether as individuals or *gathered in conference of
> bishops* or in particular councils, are authentic teachers and
> instructors of the faith for the faithful entrusted to their care;
> the faithful must adhere to the authentic teaching of their
> own bishops with a sense of religious respect.

This canon can be seen as an expansion of the Second Vatican
Council's *Decree on the Bishop's Pastoral Office in the Church*,
which in paragraphs 36, 37, and 38 encouraged the establishment
of episcopal conferences. The language of this decree is more centered on discipline, programs, and juridical decisions, but the underlying thrust is the spread of the faith and "a holy union of

energies in the service of the common good of the churches" (*Christus Dominus*, no. 37).

We are in an age in which the teachings of episcopal conferences are making significant contributions to the universal Church. This sign of the Spirit in the Church needs more theological and canonical reflection in the years ahead. The Vatican synthesis of the 1983 European/American bishops' consultation itself recognizes the broader teaching relationships of which we are becoming aware.

> There was general agreement that in the face of the threats of the present time to life, to basic human values and to the survival of peoples, the *episcopal conferences have to give attention to the problems contained therein.* It was felt that those which are more directly, though in different ways, involved in the problems of nuclear armament should seek to act in concert in order to be informed about the realities experienced in different countries and to examine these realities in the light of their own pastoral mission and in fidelity to the tradition of the Church and the teaching of Pope John Paul II.

Transmitters of the Word

This final part of my paper will develop the idea of what episcopal teaching means, and then I will bring in the idea of *communio*, the community of bishops witnessing to the truth and also searching together for a deeper understanding of the truth within their culture and always in communion with the bishop of Rome.

The issue of the teaching office and mandate of the episcopal conference cannot be handled from a purely legal point of view. It is fundamentally a theological issue. The questions to be addressed are the following:

How is the Word of God alive in a group of bishops?

How can the Word of God be collectively proclaimed by them?

A fruitful source for directing our attention to the word of God is the prologue and first chapter of the *Constitution on Divine Revelation*. The Word of God must be handed on "so that by hearing the message of salvation the whole world may believe; by believing, it may hope; and by hoping, it may love" (*Dei Verbum*, no. 1). Through Christ "God is with us to free us from the darkness of sin and death, and to raise us up to eternal life." We need to entrust our entire self by the obedience of faith to God and His Word and thereby know the joy and ease flowing from the inner unity of God's words and deeds in the history of salvation. Such is the nature of divine revelation.

The bishop transmits this Word through his preaching. He becomes a trustee of this revelation through his sacramental ordination. During the ordination ceremony, the principal consecrator places the open book of the Gospels upon the head of the bishop-elect, and it is held there throughout the prayer of consecration by two deacons. He is later commissioned to preach the word: "Receive the Gospel and preach the Word of God with unfailing patience and sound teaching."

The bishop transmits the Word not merely or chiefly by way of conceptual information; he also witnesses to the sacrament of the Word to the faithful and to the world at large. As the bishop teaches the Word by preaching, the Spirit moves the hearers internally. "If this faith is to be shown, the grace of God and the interior help of the Holy Spirit must precede and assist, moving the heart and turning it to God, opening the eyes of the mind, and giving joy and ease to everyone in assenting to the truth and believing it (*Dei Verbum*, no. 5). When someone makes an act of faith, one accepts both the Word and the Spirit.

While all can proclaim the Word, the Spirit assists the episcopal college in preserving the evangelical message in its purity. There is a specific role for the episcopate in the history of our salvation. Jesus has given divine authority to his Church, to Peter, to the twelve, and to those whom they subsequently delegated. Jesus also declares his solidarity with their authority: "As the Father sends me, so I send you" (John 20:21); "He who hears you, hears me; he who rejects you, rejects me, and he who rejects me, rejects him who sent me" (Luke 10:16).

The bishop has the authority that God gave to Jesus' apostles (consecratory prayer). He is qualified witness "to divine and Catholic truth" (*Lumen Gentium*, no. 25). His testimony is part of an event in the history of the world, bringing the message of God to the human family committed to Him with all its cultural richness.

Bishops are qualified witnesses of the Word through which God reveals Himself and keeps revealing Himself to the world. The memory of God's mighty deeds is preserved by the episcopate. The presence of God to His people is witnessed by the episcopate. This does not mean that others could not do so. But there is a gentle assistance of the Spirit, protecting the memory of the Church in the person of the bishops. This is especially evident in the bishops' overseeing role in the great memory of the Church, the eucharistic *anamnesis*.

Because Jesus Christ is the absolute, irreversible, and invincible climax of salvation history, the authorities of the Church founded by him, namely, the whole episcopate with Peter and his successors at its head, have been endowed by God with formal authority of a fundamental kind. The universal episcopate, that is, the college of bishops, together with the bishop of Rome and under his authorization alone, is competent to give a final judgment in matters of doctrine to be believed by the universal Church.

At times a group of bishops can give stronger witness than an individual one. During the one hundred years after the founding of the first see in 1789, the Church in the United States was governed by the pastoral legislation of the Provincial and Plenary Councils of Baltimore. Some have said that for those years the Church in America was a church of councils.

The successor to these historic councils is the National Conference of Catholic Bishops. It has regularly issued statements having a broadly doctrinal character. In an important address on the mission of the conference, the then Archbishop Joseph L. Bernardin, as president, stated on May 4, 1976: "We have made a number of significant doctrinal statements which have had an impact on our teaching efforts. Consider, for example, the pastoral letters or statements on *The Church in Our Day* (1967), *Human Life in Our Day* (1969), *Basic Teachings for Catholic Religious Education* (1972), and *Behold Your Mother* (1974)."

In 1976 the conference issued a pastoral reflection on the moral life, *To Live in Christ Jesus*, and approved in 1977 a thoroughly doctrinal piece of work, *The National Catechetical Directory*.

The bishops' conference has established a committee on doctrine that periodically appraises the doctrinal soundness of theological works, notably the controversial report on human sexuality published in 1977. Such activity would seem to imply that the conference itself has doctrinal responsibilities. The same committee has also reviewed and continues to review various bilateral ecumenical statements from a theological perspective.

Other national and regional episcopal conferences have made doctrinal pronouncements. For example, the Latin American Bishops' Conference, in its meetings at Medellin (1968) and Puebla (1979), sought to give doctrinal teaching as well as pastoral guidelines on the various questions they addressed. Recently, the German Bishops' Conference has been active in assessing the orthodoxy of such theologians as Hans Küng.

Historically, the Church has shown a great respect for many particular councils, although some others of them deviated from tradition. Many particular councils pioneered doctrinal insights which later were accepted as normative for the whole Church. A few examples are listed:

—The Second Council of Orange held in A.D. 529 rejected semi-Pelagianism. Its canons on grace were later approved by Pope Boniface II in A.D. 531.

—The Provincial Council of Carthage held in A.D. 418 issued the first decrees on the subject of original sin. Its canon 2 was later adopted by the fifth session of the Ecumenical Council of Trent.

—The Third Council of Carthage in A.D. 397 addressed itself to the canon of Sacred Scripture.

—The Profession of Faith of the Eleventh Council of Toledo held in A.D. 675.

—The Council of Braga in Portugal held in A.D. 561 condemned the Priscillianists, a Manichaean gnostic sect, and asserted the fundamental goodness of matter and the human body.

The doctrinal teachings of these local Church councils later became normative for the universal Church.

Since the Word of God is alive today and our understanding of it calls for continuous reflection, bishops speaking and acting as a group ("in conference") can contribute greatly to the process of development within a regional or national culture.

One of the more important theological events of the past generation is the emergence of liberation theology in Latin American Catholicism. The reflections of the Latin American episcopal conference at Medellin in 1968 led to the acceptance of many insights of liberation theology. Pope Paul VI participated actively in that meeting; his addresses to the bishops and his presence showed the importance he attached to that episcopal conference and its deliberations. Pope John Paul II in 1979 indicated the doctrinal and pastoral concern he had for the deliberations of the Latin American bishops at Puebla by his presence and addresses. The official documents of both conferences have been influential world-wide in their pastoral and doctrinal teachings.

Even though canon law makes little reference to the teaching role of the episcopal conferences, my experience is that when bishops share and exchange insights of prudence and experience, there has emerged "a holy union of energies in the service of the common good of the Churches" (*Christus Dominus*, no. 37). The reason is that the bishops do form a *communio* among themselves, even in regional or national groups, and the bond of *communio* enhances their capacity to witness and to proclaim the truth to the people committed to their pastoral care.

In my judgment the present canon law remains deficient in giving scope to episcopal collegiality. I do not mean this in the sense that it goes against such collegiality, but in the sense of not giving a sufficient, legal framework for the operation of a theological gift that is undoubtedly there. The whole of chapter 3 of the *Dogmatic Constitution on the Church*, entitled "The Hierarchical Structure of the Church, with Special Reference to the Episcopate," is a rich resource for meditation on the teaching role of the bishop. The constitution mentions the following ancient practices to attest the collegial nature and meaning of the episcopal order: conciliar assemblies "which made common judgments about more profound matters in decisions reflecting the view of many" and the practice "of summoning several bishops to take part in the elevation of someone newly elected to the ministry of high priesthood" (*Lumen Gentium*, no. 22).

The foregoing is understood in the context of the universal call addressed to every believer to proclaim the good news and in the context of papal and episcopal authority and prerogatives. Yet it remains that there is a potential in the episcopate which has not yet been used sufficiently for the benefit of the Church.

Basically I am saying that the Church, both universal and diocesan, is a community of memory and understanding which requires an authority in doctrinal and moral teaching. The application of this teaching must be done by an authority that can interpret the Good News in the language and culture of the People of God to whom it is being addressed. This is the framework into which I have fitted the *munus docendi*. In local episcopates, assisted by the Spirit and always in union with the Holy Father, the bishop of Rome, the apostolic memory of the Church can come alive for the people of a particular culture; the Good News will not be lost to them.

NOTES

1. Complete text in *Origins* 12, no. 43 (April 7, 1983), 691–96.
2. *National Review*, April 1, 1983. p. 352.
3. *Daedalus* 112, no. 4 (Fall 1983), 250.
4. *Origins* 13, no. 40 (March 15, 1984), 659.
5. *Origins* 13, no. 46 (April 26, 1984), 756.
6. *Origins* 13, no. 40 (March 15, 1984), 664.

Part II

The Pilgrim People of God: The Church in the Modern World

9

Religion and Politics:
The Role of the Church
in Shaping Public Policy

JOHN R. ROACH
Archbishop of Saint Paul and Minneapolis

The topic I am to address, "Religion and Politics: The Role of the Church in Shaping Public Policy," is one I've dealt with on some other occasions, and the bulk of what I'm going to say will be what I originally said in my presidential address to the National Conference of Catholic Bishops in November of 1981.

I've been a priest for thirty-eight years, and in those years I can't remember a time when the Church has received as much attention from the media and the public as is true today. I hasten to add that that is not necessarily a comfortable position for the Church, but because of the nature of the major public issues facing our society today, churches are playing a much more visible role in public debate than has been true at any time in my memory.

In the religion section of a recent issue of *Time* magazine, contributing writers expressed near disbelief at the impact the Church is having in the debate on major issues of our day. Obviously, this has caused a lot of people to be nervous—both in and out of the Church. It has also raised with a new sharpness the question of separation of church and state. As you know, our history has accorded that principle almost the status of a secular commandment.

Delivered at the Cathedral-Basilica of St. James in Brooklyn on April 18, 1982.

We need to be very clear about those issues and those instances when the Church has a responsibility to speak out on public issues and when it does not. At the outset, I want to say that I agree fully with the principle of separation of church and state, but I do not agree that the absence of dialogue about and between religion and politics serves either the church or the state.

It is essential that we initiate explicit public, systematic dialogue about the relationship of religious communities and the political process in the United States. Whether we like it or not, a whole range of policy changes is permeated by moral and religious themes today—from the debate on abortion to the decisions on nuclear armament, from the care of the terminally ill to the fairness of budget cuts. The direction our society takes must include an assessment of how moral and religious convictions relate to the technical dimensions of public policy.

It seems to me that our own faith community must be able to articulate an understanding of how the social vision of faith increasingly caused the Church to develop a public theology and public witness on political questions.

There is another reason for that articulation. Recently, the Connecticut Mutual Life Insurance Company sponsored a survey on American values of the 1980's. The report on that survey concludes: "Our findings suggest that the increasing impact of religion on our social and political institutions may be only the beginning of a trend that could change the face of America." They base that conviction on data showing that people with strong religious convictions influence the political process out of proportion to their numerical strength.

Now there have been times when history has taught vividly that the expression of religious conviction through the political process was not necessarily a blessing to society. The key question is how religious belief is related to political practice. And that is the question which requires that a systematic discussion of religion and politics take place in our religious organizations in the public arena, where people of all faiths, and no religious faith, are called to set the direction of our society.

Let me use a historical kind of example which, I think, validates that theme. It is very clear and very embarrassing to look back historically at the silence of the Catholic Church vis-à-vis the phenomenon of slavery. It would be difficult not to regard slavery as essentially a moral issue, and for all of those years, for the most part, our Church was silent.

There's a short, but I think very good, little book called *The Church and Slavery, 1807 to 1867* written by an historian who teaches at Carleton College in Minnesota. It's an embarrassing book to read. We were very quiet in the face of a great moral evil, and I think we would have to admit that, had the Church articulated a moral position, had the Church raised the Gospel value, slavery could not have lasted as long in this country as it did. That is a comfortable example, because it is in the past. I would argue that that same principle must obtain as we address the major moral issues of our day.

There are two questions that shape the Church's role in society: the theological question and the constitutional question.

The theological question is the way the Church is articulated, the content of its social message. When the United States Catholic Conference addresses the question of El Salvador, or the impact of budget cuts on the poor, when bishops speak, or anyone else speaks on the arms race, when Catholics individually or collectively oppose abortion or capital punishment in defending the sanctity of life, then it must be very clear that these actions are rooted in, directed by, and in fulfillment of a theologically grounded conception of the Church's ministry. That ministry in the social or political order is shaped by two things: The first is a religious conviction about the dignity of the human person, and the second is a spectrum of obligations and rights by which human dignity is preserved and promoted in the political process. These concepts have been key ideas in the Catholic tradition from Leo XIII's first social encyclical, *Rerum Novarum* (on the condition of labor), to John Paul II's *Laborem Exercens* (on human worth). In the intervening years of the twentieth century, each of the social encyclicals has defended the dignity of the person in the face of diverse and changing threats to human dignity.

The moral vision of social ministry was qualitatively strengthened by a second theme: the ecclesiology of Vatican II, particularly the *Pastoral Constitution on the Church in the Modern World*. The decisive contribution of that document is the way it defines the protection of human dignity and the promotion of human rights as properly ecclesial tasks—an integral part of the Church's ministry. This marriage of the moral vision and the ecclesial vision provides the basis of social ministry. In the language of the Council: "The task of the Church in the political order is to stand as the sign and the safeguard of the dignity of the person."

To fulfill this role in a political context (and that is where it must be fulfilled) requires that the Church not only keep the moral truths about the person but must also join the public debate where policies are shaped, programs developed, and decisions made which directly touch the rights of the person—locally, nationally, and internationally. That is precisely what Pope John Paul II was talking about in speaking to American Catholics in his homily at Yankee Stadium. He said: "Within the framework of your institutions, and in cooperation with your fellow citizens, you will also want to seek out the structural reasons which foster or cause the different forms of poverty in the world and in your own country, so that you can apply the proper remedy."

When the Church responds to this theological imperative, then obviously the constitutional question arises. How should it fulfill its social role in the context of the American political tradition? Specifically, can the Church play an active role in the public order without violating separation of church and state? In answering that question, it is essential to recognize the distinction between state and society. The Western constitutional tradition embodies the judgment that the state is a part of society, and not to be identified with all of society. Beyond the state is the realm of free political activity for individuals and groups to give content to the fabric of social life.

On the basis of this distinction between state and society, it seems to me that a twofold affirmation can be made about the Church's role in society. On the one hand, Catholic theology can and should support and defend the separation of church and state. Religious organizations should expect neither favoritism nor discrimination because they are religious. On the other hand, we should not accept or allow the separation of church and state to be used to separate church from society. To accept this would be to reduce the Church or any religious organization to a purely private role. This in turn would prevent the Church from fulfilling an essential dimension of its ministry, that is, preaching the Gospel truth about every dimension of existence—personal and social, public and private—on individual and institutional questions.

At the constitutional level, there is no conflict between the the-ological vision that calls the Church to active engagement in the social arena and the American political tradition that provides religious organizations with the opportunity to participate in shaping society as volunteer associations imbued with the needed moral religious vision.

The concept of religious divisiveness that is thrown at us so often is not only ill-founded in relation to our constitutional traditions, it is noxious when it is used to inhibit our participation in the public process. The theological/constitutional questions keep our understanding of the Church's role in society clear, and they set the foundation for engaging the issues that are at the heart of the social ministry.

Before examining a few of the more obvious specific issues that are very much in the public order today, I would like to touch on a current highly visible instance of these general principles as I try to outline them.

A focal point in this debate over the relationship of religion and politics is the role played by the Moral Majority. In my judgment, two points are to be made. First, some have argued that the Moral Majority's role is an example of why religion and politics should be kept absolutely separate, and religious organizations are to be quiet on political questions. I would reject that contention while defending the right (in terms that I tried to define above) of the Moral Majority or any religious organization to address the public issues of the day.

The right of religious organizations of varying views to speak must be defended by all who understand the meaning of religious liberty and the social role of religion. But religious organizations, including the Moral Majority and the Catholic Church, must be subjected to the same standards—rational, vigorous presentation of their views—as any other participant in the public debate. Moreover, religious organizations that address the moral dimensions of public issues are to be judged by the standards of competent moral analysis. Particularly relevant, it seems to me, are the issues of how one defines a moral issue and then, above all, the consistency with which moral principles are defended across a range of moral issues.

Here is where I have my problems with the Moral Majority. I find it very difficult to find consistency in a political and moral position that is very strongly pro-life, but indifferent to the question of nuclear warfare. I find those two issues as part of the spectrum of life issues, and I find it inconsistent to defend the one and ignore the other.

Now those same standards of discourse should be tested. Neither the vigor of reasonable argument nor the controversy that surrounds the role of religion and politics should make us timid about stating and defending public positions in key issues. On the other hand, once we enter the public debate we will be challenged, and should be challenged, and we must be able to defend our position as coherently as those with whom we differ.

Let me outline three issues against the backdrop of principles I have tried to establish up to this point.

The Arms Race

On a global scale, I believe more each day that the most dangerous moral issue in the public order is the nuclear-arms race. The Church in the United States has a special responsibility to address this question. Our country is one of the major superpowers of the world, and that responsibility was underscored by Pope John Paul II in his remarks at the White House in 1979.

The United States Catholic Conference has addressed this issue often, most notably in Cardinal Krol's testimony in the Salt II debate a few years ago. It is an unhappy fact that strategic arms-control discussions are stalemated, even as the technological and strategic dynamics of the arms race proceed. And it is perhaps a convergence of these two themes that has moved a number of American bishops to address the arms race recently in terms that are both prophetic and profoundly important. There is a ground swell of concern about that issue in the United States.

People are being forced to see the nuclear-arms race as a classically religious, moral question. We may not remain silent in the face of the moral gravity of such a build-up of arms. We have a responsibility to speak to the question, and it is my belief that we are being heard at very high levels. But heard or not, we must continue to speak to the issue; for it is above all a moral issue, a religious issue that is the work and the responsibility of the Church.

Certainly, that sense of moral urgency about the arms race is what stands behind the establishment of the Bishops' Committee on War and Peace chaired by then Archbishop Joseph Bernardin of Cincinnati.

It is useful to say clearly what we already know from Catholic teachings. The Church needs to say "no" clearly and decisively to the use of nuclear weapons. This is surely the direction of Vatican teachings on the arms race and its condemnation of attacks on civilian centers, and the "no" we utter should shape our policy advice and our pastoral guidance of Catholics. It is not useful to blur the line of moral arguments about the use of nuclear arms at a time when a secular debate is openly discussing the use of nuclear weapons and the viability of nuclear war.

The Abortion Issue

The horrors of nuclear war, though certainly not fantasies, are at the moment possibilities, but the horror of legalized abortion is tragically real. The destruction of unborn life now as it appears in this nation is, as you know, at the staggering rate of one and one-half million abortions annually. Nine years after the Supreme Court decision initiated this carnage, who can doubt that today is time to say "enough"? Human dignity, human rights are mocked by the scandal of abortion. The concept of just law is mocked by the invasions used to create and continue this slaughter of the innocents. There is, thank God, some reason for hope at this moment. Our elective representatives increasingly recognize the need to correct this situation. The Conference of Bishops gave support to a realistic constitutional remedy that holds out hope for undoing some of the damage done by the abortion decision. That amendment, as you know, is out of committee and will be acted upon by our legislative body.

Law, of course, is not the total solution to the evil of abortion. We remain committed to the proclamation of the Gospel message concerning the sanctity of human life and to the steps required to eradicate the conditions that cause some to turn to abortion as a solution to personal and social problems, but we also recognize the need for a remedy in law in order to undo the harm done under the guise of law. Without this, the sanctity of human life can only be a hollow phrase. At this moment, the abortion issue is difficult.

There is an enormous split in the ranks of pro-life groups, and my prayer every day of my life is for unity among those who believe in life. It would be a tragedy if, because of division about means, we were somehow to lose the golden moment that I believe we have to effect a change—to save lives.

The Poor among Us

Papal statements on the arms race have consistently condemned the build-up of armaments, considering it a misallocation of scarce resources. These statements have typically referred to the global dimension of the issue, but at a time of scarce resources here at home, they take on meaning in a domestic debate on public policy. The proposed expenditure of $1.5 trillion for defense over the next five years stands in stark contrast to budget cuts that threaten food, the health care, and the education of the poor.

In the past, it was presumed that we in the United States could spend whatever we wanted for defense and still be a compassionate society. That assumption today is denied in fact. What we spend for guns directly reduces what is available for the quality of care and life for the least among us. In the past few years we have often heard from the Church in Latin America the pastoral principle of the "option for the poor." Now, implementing that principle in our more complex economy poses different challenges, but the principle has meaning for us. It means simply that while we are concerned about the larger questions of the economy, we will give specific weight to any overall solution that touches the poor.

We are called to this role of advocacy for the poor not only by our social teachings, but also by the kind of experience we have had in the Campaign for Human Development in our Catholic Charities. This ministry with and for the poor confirms the moral vision of our teachings. The Old Testament prophets were right. The quality of our faith is tested by the character of justice among us.

You and I know from experience the impossible choices the poor face in our society, not, as is normally said, between guns and butter but between bread and rent, between money for heating oil and health care for children. We also know that private agencies of the nation cannot close the gap created by recent cuts. We have the will, please God, to help, and even as we exhaust our resources we will do our part, but our own social teachings call upon the state to do its part as well.

Religion and politics always come back to the person, to the way society respects or fails to respect a person. The Church must raise its voice clearly about justice, because choices now before us as a nation can erode the conditions that support the human person's dignity. Today those of us who represent a religious tradition must be very clear about our task. We must carry forward the debate about religion and its role in the political order, because both have a central contribution to make—preserving all that is valuable to the life of each person and the lives of all the people who constitute this society.

To serve the person is to honor the Creator, and you and I are called to reverence both. This is an exciting time. I believe that from the depths of my heart. It is a time the Lord has offered to us to make a very special contribution to this society and this world we love. It will require prayer, patience, wisdom, and strong doses of the spirit of God speaking to us, but it is worth it. We have a contribution to make, and thank God, we have become alive to the fact.

10

Institutionalized Racism

JOSEPH A. FRANCIS, S.V.D.
Auxiliary Bishop of Newark

There's a story of an elderly black man who spoke to God in prayer every day at two o'clock in the afternoon. On one occasion, God was just about three minutes late and He apologized to the man: "John, I'm sorry I'm late, but we'll carry on as usual."

John said: "Today, Lord, I have a lot of questions. I hope that you don't become disturbed. I hope that you don't think I'm disrespectful, but I have to ask you these questions, because they've been bothering me. You won't be bothered if I ask you a few questions, will you, Lord?" And the Lord said: "No, John. We're old friends. We've talked things over for many, many years." John then asked: "Lord, why is it that my skin is black and that people think I'm different and treat me differently and discriminate against me?" And the Lord answered: "Well, John, in Africa the sun is very hot, and if you had fair skin like people in Scandinavia and Germany and Ireland and places like that, you would be burned to a crisp. Your dark skin absorbs the harmful rays of the sun." John said: "You mean ultraviolet rays?" God replied: "That's right, John. The ultraviolet rays."

John continued: "Well, Lord, that's very good. I realize now why you are all wise; why you are all knowledgeable; and why you created the world." So God settled back very happy that He had answered the question successfully. But John then said: "Lord, why is my hair so curly and short and the rest of these people

Delivered at the Cathedral-Basilica of St. James in Brooklyn on April 25, 1980.

have long, flowing hair?" "Oh!" God replied, "In Africa you do a
lot of hunting; sometimes you chase the wild boar and sometimes
the wild boar chases you, and if your hair would be long and flowing, you might get caught in the underbrush and the wild boar
might gore you to death." John said: "Lord, great is your wisdom
and your providence. But I still have two more questions to ask
you. If you answer these successfully, I will never ever question
you again. Why, Lord, is my nose so wide and dilated? The rest of
these people have long, aquiline noses." "That's an easy one," God
said. "You see, in Africa the air is laden with moisture and in order
to breathe and get the oxygen out of that moisture, you have to
breathe deeply. Whereas people living in Scandinavia and in Northern Europe where the air is frozen, if they breathed that deeply,
their lungs would freeze and they would die." So John prayed:
"Lord, that's good enough for me. One more question though. If
all those things that you said about me are true, what in the hell
am I doing in Pittsburgh?"

I'm not going to answer all of those questions, but the questions
I am going to try to raise are perhaps much more serious than the
ones mentioned in the story. The topic about which I write has
finally come out of the closets of our churches and Church-run institutions. It is now being discussed openly and, hopefully, seriously. Back in the early thirties, I never heard terms like prejudiced, bigoted, hateful, spiteful used in characterizing the perceptions of blacks about whites. We never analyzed these perceptions nor did we go beneath the surface to discover and articulate
why white people were prejudiced, bigoted, hateful, and spiteful.

We did not use the word "racist" or "racism." Perhaps the reason was that blacks could not or would not think negatively about
white people. Whites would not or could not think that negatively
about themselves. Whites and blacks in the North looked upon
whites in the South as bigoted segregationists. Whites and blacks
in the South looked upon whites in the North as hypocritical.

There was general consternation in this country when we began
to hear that the whole society in America was racist. "Racist" was
a term reserved for whites in Rhodesia and South Africa. I can remember angry outcries in April of 1968 when a group of black
priests, brothers, and seminarians, meeting in Detroit, Michigan,

after a hot and prolonged debate, issued a statement that proclaimed the Catholic Church in the U.S.A. was a white racist institution.

I spent days, weeks, and even months discussing the statement, defending the statement. And, at the same time, wondering whether I, along with my black brothers, was being too harsh, too judgmental, and too dramatic. But the more I reflected upon this statement, the more I reflected upon my experiences in the Church—North, East, West, and South—because I have lived in all of those places, I knew that the statement was dramatic, judgmental, but not harsh. Realistic, yes. And, like Dr. Martin Luther King, Jr., we were calling our Church to look at itself as we saw it and experienced it then, and sadly, as we still experience it in many places today.

Remember that our Catholic bishops at the Council of Baltimore elected not to condemn the most severe form of racism, namely, the slavery of blacks in America. Not that all American black Catholics were and are as Christian in their response to racism as was Dr. Martin Luther King, Jr., but racism was and is a fact whose time has come.

In the pastoral on racism entitled *Brothers and Sisters to Us*, the Catholic bishops of the United States declare: "Racism is a sin. A sin that divides the human family, blots out the image of God among specific members of that family, and violates the fundamental human dignity of those called to be children of the same Father."

Racism is a sin that says some human beings are inherently superior and others essentially inferior because of race. It is the sin that makes racial characteristics the determining factor for the exercise of human rights. It mocks the words of Jesus: "Treat others the way you would have them treat you."

Indeed, racism is more than a disregard for the words of Jesus. It is a denial of the truth of the dignity of each human being revealed by the mystery of the incarnation.

Racism, like hatred, like envy, like greed, like covetousness, like anger, and like lust is both individual and institutional. The two are interdependent. They feed on each other, and normally, they reinforce each other. Individual racism is that form of racism which finds, at least in this country, individual whites thinking, acting, and teaching against individual groups of blacks and now

Hispanics. Institutional racism finds a total community or nearly all corporate segments of the community thinking, acting, and teaching against all blacks and other people of color.

Individual racism is easily recognized and documented; but corporate, institutionalized racism is often subtle, subversive, sinister, and, in many instances, enjoys the protection of laws specifically enacted to protect, further, and justify this kind of racism.

Institutional racism often assumes a posture of condemning obvious individual racism, while at the same time it denies its own racism and enters litigation to prove otherwise. I would like to dwell primarily, at this point, on institutional racism and on some of the effects it has produced and continues to produce today.

Looking at racism from an economic perspective, a book entitled *Institutional Racism in America*, edited by L. Noels and Kenneth Pruitt, asserts:

> The United States has built the strongest, the most productive economy known to man. The abundance is spread among not only the entrepreneurial class, but also the laborers. It is safe to say that no people has ever enjoyed a standard of living as high as that found in white America. Yet black America remains bound in a poverty resembling that found in underdeveloped nations. The discrepancy between unprecedented white affluence and black poverty is the result of the almost total exclusion of black Americans from entrepreneurial activity and the market. The vast majority of blacks function only as menial workers and exploited consumers. The present division of the economy along racial lines is a result of both intentional and unintentional institutional racism.

Certainly, there are those who will point out how much progress blacks have made over the past 150 years. This is more fictional than real. We cannot judge how far blacks have come since slavery in isolation from how far whites have come in the same period of time. We have to recognize also that the same forces which held blacks in slavery over 200 years ago are still operative today. It is inconceivable that a Constitution written during slavery would include slaves within its consideration.

Racist legislation after the Civil War continued to be enacted, and the highest courts in the land upheld most of that legislation.

It was only when blacks themselves began to challenge those laws that we began to see how firmly entrenched racism was and still is in this country. Is it any wonder that cities all over the country are still opposing integration in their school systems and in housing? Is it any wonder that Catholic institutions in many parts of the country are still under the gun for noncompliance in racial matters? And as recently as April 1980, in one of our Southern cities, two Catholic hospitals were threatened with withholding of funds because they had not complied with the guidelines that the federal government had set for a racial balance both in acceptance of patients and in the staffing of those hospitals.

That pastoral on racism stated very clearly: "We do not deny that changes have been made, that laws have been passed, that policies have been implemented; but neither can it be denied that too often what has happened has only been a covering over, not a fundamental change. Today the sense of urgency has yielded to an apparent acceptance of the status quo."

One of the factors that indicates the power of racism over the life and development of blacks and Hispanics today is the exclusion of black people from effective, fair, and meaningful participation in the free-enterprise system. The exploitation of the black worker is partially evidenced by his or her relationship to unions in most parts of this country. Granted the national posture of our major labor unions is antiracist in word, the local unions are, in fact, racist. They reflect the current posture of racism as it exists in other areas of their lives—education, housing, church membership, you name it.

Another factor is the exploitation of the black consumer. No group of persons has been more exploited than blacks, and now Hispanics and other minorities are experiencing the same thing. They are living in the urban areas of the North, the East, the West, and the rural and urban areas of the South. Friendly loan companies, furniture stores, auto dealers, etc., have made millions by overcharging, by interest gouging, and swift foreclosures. Landlords have gotten more for less and given less for more. Real-estate companies and individuals have done their best to buy cheaply and sell beyond the ability of blacks and other nonwhites to pay for and retain their property.

Among a whole litany of abuses that could be cited, there are several other areas that must be mentioned—areas where racism rules supreme, namely, in the education of black children and the miseducation of white children. Blacks are undereducated or, in many instances, not educated at all. Whites are not educated about blacks or, what is even more devastating, are given erroneous and often false notions about blacks.

I remember that, a few years ago, a friend of mine, Walter O'Keefe, had a radio program called "Okay O'Keefe." Walter became a very close friend during the civil-rights days when we went to a lot of meetings together and gave a lot of speeches out in California. Well, he tells the story about one occasion when he was a master of ceremonies for a very prestigious gathering of scholars. He was sitting next to a young Oriental gentleman, and Walter, who is something of a comedian, said to the gentleman while they were eating their salad: "Likee salad?" And the gentleman turned to him and obligingly said: "Likee salad." Then, when the steak finally came around, he said to his Oriental dinner companion: "Likee steakee?" And the gentleman replied: "Likee steakee." When the meal was over, the president of the group that had invited Walter to be master of ceremonies for the evening got up to introduce the guest speaker. He proceeded to give a biography of a man who was a Shakespearean expert both in England and in America, who had written many books, and who had been a drama critic for some large newspapers both in the United States and in the Orient. The Chinese gentleman who had been Walter's dinner partner got up and gave a brilliant speech in flawless English. When he sat down, he turned to Walter and said: "Likee speechee?"

This is an example of what I have been talking about—miseducation, stereotyping, and the whole manifestation which can still be found in the media today of the image of black people and other minorities.

Racism is also responsible in large part for the disproportionate political power held by whites in this nation. Racism has filled our prisons disproportionately with blacks—especially young black men. All of the evils I have ascribed to racism may seem like an exaggeration. But taken together as manifestations of institutional racism, they are interdependently linked, and each reinforces the other and contributes to the growth and cancerous effects of racism in our society.

Racism plays a part not only in politics, education, finance, housing, labor, but most remarkably in the delivery of health care. While I am aware that progress has been made in this area, blacks and other nonwhite minorities are still less healthy than whites. There are many factors contributing to this. Housing and environment are two significant factors, and again, these are also racially conditioned. Where sick, diseased, and elderly blacks are concerned, racist policies and persons often determine how, how much, and when health care is available to them. Educational institutions, beginning at the primary level and leading all the way up to the universities, often make it difficult and even impossible for talented and gifted blacks to enter health fields where they could make the difference. Even those who make it often find themselves effectively prevented from becoming members of health-care facilities.

There are so many good people in this world who maintain that they are not racist, and because they are not racist, they feel racism does not exist. Yet, these are the very people who give stature and respectability to institutional racism. Such good persons can deal with the avowed racism of the Klan and the Neo-Nazis, but they are unwilling to deal with a program of institutional racism in both the public and private sector.

Institutional racism hangs over our cities like an unhealthy, ugly-smelling smog. And like environmental pollution, it affects all of us. The new form of urban racism is marginalization and containment of blacks and other nonwhites. Many persons in white society see no good reason for blacks to live in their midst. Hence, its institutions marginalize them in every manner possible, and what marginalization does not cover is taken over by containment.

That containment is as evident in the inner chambers of corporate institutions as it is in the basement tenements of a blighted urban ghetto. White America, unlike South Africa, feels it does not need blacks. Blacks, like the unborn, the elderly, the handicapped, are looked upon as burdens: the white man's, the white woman's burden. In their pastoral letter on racism, the bishops of this country tell us:

> Rude and blatant expressions of racist sentiment, though
> they occasionally exist, are today considered bad form. Yet

racism itself persists in covert ways under the guise of other motives. It is manifest in the tendency to stereotype and marginalize whole segments of the population whose presence is perceived as a threat.

It is manifest also in the indifference that replaces open hatred. The minority poor are seen as the dross of post-industrial society without skills, without motivation, without incentive. They are expendable. Many times a new face of racism is a computer printout, the graph of profits and losses, the pink slip, the nameless statistic.

Today's racism flourishes in the triumph of private concern over public responsibility, individual success over social commitment and personal fulfillment over authentic compassion. Then, too, we recognize that racism also exists in the attitudes and behavior of some who are themselves members of minority groups. Christian ideals of justice must be brought to bear in both the private and the public sector, in order that covert racism be eliminated wherever it exists.

The new forms of racism must be brought face to face with the figure of Christ. It is Christ's word that is the judgment of this world. It is Christ's face that is the composite of all persons, but in a most significant way of today's marginal people, today's minorities.

I believe at this point that many, if not all of you, are wondering if I shall allude to racism within the Catholic Church. Will this bishop condemn the Catholic Church for its racism? I cannot condemn the Catholic Church. I cannot condemn anyone. I am not God. I love the Catholic Church. I love the Church because the Church is God's gift to me, and I in turn have given myself to God through that Church. What I have always done, not always very well, and what I will continue to do (and I hope better), is to call my brothers and sisters in the Church to accountability, while struggling, at the same time, to be accountable to them.

I fight against racism, not because I'm one of its victims, but because we are all its victims. Yes, there is still institutional racism in the Catholic Church in the United States of America. It is alive and well, and very few institutions in our country have done less to combat racism than the Church, given its mission to witness the presence of Christ among us.

Men and women who exercise leadership in a multitudinous variety of institutions have been, and continue to be, the products of exclusively white institutions. These institutions are dioceses, religious orders, Church-related organizations, societies, and universities. Because individual members of many of these institutions have condemned racism, many of them have marched with Dr. Martin Luther King, Jr. and Cesar Chavez and have identified with minority struggles, we and they tend to ignore the fact that many have marched with the oppressed but have not marched against the oppressor in their own religious institutions.

I really become sad when many of my women friends condemn me for saying that the ordination of women is not one of my priorities. The baptism of blacks is one of my priorities; the acceptance of blacks into religious communities of men and women is one of my priorities; the acceptance and welcoming of blacks into communities of faith that we know as parishes is one of my priorities. I cannot give priority to an effort which, if it happens at all, will still be a lily-white affair complete with all of the same scandal that has kept seminaries, monasteries, and convents lily white even to this day. I would like to see just one community of religious, just one seminary, just one Catholic organization, just one Catholic hospital take an ad in a newspaper committing itself to eradicating racism within its own institution and then demonstrating this through policy and action.

What is your response to racism? Whether you are black or white, that's the answer you will have to give for yourself. But the response of a Church speaking to its people, speaking to all of us as brothers and sisters in the pastoral on racism is the following:

> Racism is not merely one sin among many. It is a radical evil that divides the human family and denies the new creation of a redeemed world. To struggle against it demands an equally radical transformation in our own minds and hearts, as well as in the structure of our society.

I am not naive. I am a realist. I offer no simple solutions. I offer a challenge. I invite you to look upon the reality of racism and the havoc it brings about. I ask you to know that racism has destroyed more lives than wars. Racism is so much a part of us that in order to eradicate it we must die, not a little, but a lot. In doing so, however, we give life to others and to ourselves.

My heart is heavy as I realize that after sixty-one years of carrying the burdens placed upon me and my contemporaries, I shall bear that burden to the end of my life. Is it less a burden, I ask myself, than the burden borne by a child without arms or feet or eyes? Has the burden harmed me? Yes. But it has also taught me how to forgive and how to love. It has taught me that perhaps, just perhaps, I can teach my Church that it is possible to be good, to be holy, to be dignified, and to be great without being racist.

11

Capital Punishment and the Sacredness of Life

RENE H. GRACIDA
Bishop of Corpus Christi

If anyone had suggested to me a few years ago that I would be addressing the subject of "Capital Punishment and the Sacredness of Life," I would have considered the whole idea absurd. While I have always had a keen interest in the subject, I am not an expert on the question. In fact, prior to a radical reversal in our national policy and practice with regard to the death penalty, I would have refused to deal with this subject had I been asked to do so. But then everything changed for me on May 18, 1979. On that day, Robert Graham, Governor of the State of Florida, signed two death warrants. The death warrants for John Spenkelink and Willie Darden were the first ever to be signed by Robert Graham. Willie Darden's execution was subsequently stayed, but on May 25 of that same year, John Spenkelink was executed at Raiford State Prison in Stark, Florida. The fact that Governor Graham signed the death warrants in Tallahassee and announced the signing in Tallahassee, combined with the fact that John Spenkelink's execution was the first execution in Florida and in the United States in over twelve years, focused the attention of many people in the United States and certainly everyone in Florida on Tallahassee and on Raiford. If interest throughout the country was great, you can well appreciate that the interest of those of us living in north Florida was even greater.

Delivered at the Cathedral-Basilica of St. James in Brooklyn on April 18, 1980.

108

The title of this series, *Shepherds Speak: American Bishops Confront the Social and Moral Issues That Challenge Christians Today*, in its own way indicates precisely the situation in which I found myself as bishop of the Diocese of Pensacola-Tallahassee following the signing of the death warrants and subsequent execution one week later of John Spenkelink. The local newspaper, *The Tallahassee Democrat*, conducted a survey between the time the governor signed the death warrant and the time of John Spenkelink's execution. The survey indicated that eighty-seven percent of those who responded to the survey were in favor of capital punishment in the Tallahassee area. *The Tallahassee Democrat* itself is opposed to capital punishment. It seemed to me at the time that I had an obligation to speak out on the matter, not only of John Spenkelink's execution, but also on the more fundamental question of the fitness of capital punishment as an instrument of public policy in our times. Yet, because I am a religious leader and because my first obligation was to my own people, it seemed even more appropriate that my first public utterance on the subject of capital punishment should be in the form of a pastoral letter addressed to the Catholics of Northwest Florida, written to help them form their own consciences on the policy of their state to employ the death penalty.

I immediately set to work on a pastoral letter that was to be entitled "Capital Punishment and the Christian Conscience." Within three days I had completed the first draft, and on May 28 I sent copies of it to some of my consultors and advisors in the diocese asking for their critiques. After several revisions of the letter, it was published in the secular papers of Northwest Florida on Saturday, June 17, 1979.

It should be obvious to everyone that a pastoral letter whose first draft was written in just three days, and even with subsequent revisions over a period of three weeks, could not possibly pretend to be a definitive teaching on the subject of capital punishment. Nor could it pretend to be the result of exhaustive research and a presentation of data assembled from a wide variety of sources. The letter was simply an intuitive response of my own conscience to a situation in our society that was troubling not only my conscience but those of many others and which demanded some statement on my part as a shepherd which would help them to put the various issues in the capital punishment controversy into clearer perspective.

Since the publication of the pastoral letter, I have necessarily become very involved in the ongoing controversy over capital punishment. I still do not claim to be an expert on the subject. I must admit, however, that events forced me to focus my attention on the subject to such a degree that I can say without boasting that I am better informed on it today than when I began. If my experience can be of any benefit to others who are also struggling to understand the complexities of this issue in the light of scripture and the call to be God's people, then I am happy to share with you what I know and what I believe on this subject.

It would be helpful to begin with an historical presentation in order that we might have a common understanding of how we have arrived at this point in history with regard to capital punishment.

The earliest historical record of capital punishment is to be found in the legal codes of ancient Near Eastern kingdoms. The codes of those kingdoms usually prescribed capital punishment for homicide and for some religious or sexual offenses. For example, among the Babylonians the code of Hammurabi distinguished between manslaughter and willful homicide and also proclaimed the *lex talionis*, which we know popularly as "an eye for an eye and a tooth for a tooth." Death and mutilation were frequent penalties.

The law of ancient Israel is of more particular concern to us because we are, after all, heirs of the Judeo-Christian tradition. The law of ancient Israel mandated or authorized the death penalty for a wide variety of crimes. Crimes punishable by death included sacrificing to or worshipping an alien god, specifically offering offspring to Moloch, and leading others to worship alien gods; being an unauthorized or false prophet, sorceress, medium, or fortune teller, or a client of a medium or fortune teller; committing blasphemy and profaning the Sabbath. Murder was punishable by death. Premeditated murder was distinguished from other homicide. Striking a slave with a rod was punishable, whether by death or otherwise is not clear; only if the slave died within a day was it clear that the penalty was death. A blow to a pregnant woman that caused a miscarriage and subsequent death was punishable by death. An owner of an ox that habitually gored people could be punished by death if the owner had been warned and if the ox again gored someone other than a slave resulting in the injured person's death; however, the death penalty was not mandatory in this case. It was considered murder to beat a burglar to death during daylight but not considered murder to beat a burglar to death at night. A person bearing false witness in a capital case was to be punished with death and so were persons who disobeyed judicial decisions in certain types of cases. Also subject to the death penalty was the kidnapping of an Israelite in order to enslave him. Other crimes punishable by death were beastiality, male homosexuality, various incestuous relationships, and adultery involving a married woman. Both parties to these crimes, including the animal in cases of beastiality, were subject to the death penalty. A man who raped a betrothed girl could be punished by death, and so could the victim of such a rape if it occurred in the city and she was not heard to cry out for help (Deut. 22:23–27). A bride accused by her husband of not being a virgin who could not provide evidence that she was a virgin might be punished by death (Deut. 22:20–21). Both parties to intercourse during a woman's menstrual period were to be "outlawed" or "cut off from their people." The death penalty also was prescribed for striking a parent (Exod. 21:15) or cursing a parent. A stubborn and rebellious son, if incorrigible, could be denounced by his mother and father to the elders of the city and punished by being stoned to death by the people of the town (Deut. 21:18–21).

I am indebted to Professor Germaine Grisez of the Catholic University of America for much of this research into the penal code of ancient Israel. Professor Grisez points out that the law of ancient Israel had sterner legislation regarding deliberate homicide than did other ancient Near Eastern codes. It is not clear that the death penalty was mandatory in other cases in which it was authorized, except for those offenses having a specifically religious character and the bearing of false witness in a capital case, which obviously is tantamount to murder. When death was prescribed the sentence was more often carried out by stoning, although hanging, beheading, strangulation, and burning were also used.

Roman law also knew the death penalty. In fact the term capital punishment derives from *caput*, a word used by the Romans variously to mean the head, the life, or the civil rights of an individual. In addition to death, Roman law looked on perpetual hard labor and banishment, which usually consisted of the denial of fire, water, and shelter, as lesser capital punishments. Banishment meant in effect a grave loss of one's civil rights or status and, frequently, ultimately one's life. During the Republic, death was imposed mainly for crimes among the military. But under the emperors, it became increasingly common as the penalty for a much wider range of offenses. Rome early embraced the *lex talionis* in its Law of the Twelve Tables (450 B.C.). Ancient Greece and Rome generally looked on homicide, treason, and sacrilege as capital offenses. Later Roman law put other crimes, such as arson and false coinage, in the same category. The Greeks imposed death in several ways, for example, sometimes a free man would be permitted to take poison, but a slave would be beaten to death. Roman usages included strangulation, exposure to wild beasts, crucifixion, and the *culeus* which consisted of drowning a condemned man tied up in a sack with a rooster, a viper, and a dog.

Two patterns of grave punishment emerged in Europe before the Middle Ages. The law of Germanic peoples generally, and of a few countries such as Ireland, tended to see homicide and attacks on person or property chiefly as wrongs done to individuals, not wrongs done to the state. The proper penalty in such cases came to be a fine paid to the injured party or to the heirs of the injured party. However, capital punishment was employed elsewhere. From the Middle Ages on, Britain, France, and the Latin peoples decreed death for a variety of crimes. Moreover, the methods of execution took on added refinements of brutality and degradation, as in death by pressing, burning at the stake, or hanging and quartering.

When the United States gained its independence, the death penalty was called for by all the criminal codes of European nations and their colonies. English law under King George III made hundreds of crimes punishable by death. These were not only major crimes such as treason and murder but included also such offenses as picking pockets and poaching deer, pheasants, or rabbits from a landlord's property.

Beginning in the eighteenth century the history of capital punishment in the West begins to take on a two-fold nature. It is not only a history of the practice of capital punishment but also a history of the birth and development of the movement to abolish capital punishment. Prior to the eighteenth century the only voice questioning the use of capital punishment was the magisterium of the Catholic Church. Even so, the Church has never taken a formal position with regard to the question of the rightness of capital punishment per se. Nowhere does the magisterium directly treat the subject. There is an indirect acceptance of it in the decrees of two councils: the Council of Toledo in 675 and the Fourth Lateran Council in 1215. These two councils in their decrees recognized the existence of capital punishment by forbidding clerics to take part in a process or a sentence involving capital punishment. But when the *licitness* of the death penalty was attacked by the Waldensians, along with a broad attack on all society, the Church did not hesitate to condemn them for their opinion. Therefore, we can say the Church has never directly addressed the question of the state's right to exercise the death penalty; the Church has never condemned the use of the death penalty by the state, although the Church did condemn the denial of the state's right to use the death penalty. Recent popes have stressed the rights of the person and the medicinal role of punishment instead of focusing upon capital punishment. I will have more to say about the Church's teachings on this subject later in this paper.

It was a young Italian, Cesare Beccaria, who opened the modern debate on capital punishment with his essay entitled *Of Crimes and Punishment* published in 1764. On the basis of his own theory of society, he rejected the state's right to take a citizen's life. Far more influential, however, was his critique of the death penalty as cruel, unreasonable, and ineffective. Within two years his essay had appeared in French translation and had become known all over Europe. Beccaria merits the title "father of modern penal reform." He is the originator of the now famous dictum: "It is not the severity of punishment which deters crime but rather the certainty of punishment."

By the year 1776 a movement to limit or abolish the death penalty already was underway. This movement had been accelerated by Christians and humanists following the publication of Beccaria's essay.

The law of the American colonies never used the death penalty as extensively as did the law of England. William Penn's "Great Act" of 1682 restricted the penalty of death in his colony to murder and treason. In the eighteenth century, however, partly because of pressure from the English crown, Pennsylvania and the American colonies generally punished with death such crimes as treason, murder, piracy, arson, rape, robbery, burglary, and sodomy.

After independence, Pennsylvania was one of the first states in which a significant movement against the death penalty developed. In 1794 Pennsylvania ended the death penalty except for first degree murder. In this law the familiar American distinction between degrees of murder was made for the first time.

The movement for abolition or restriction of the death penalty has continued throughout the world and in the United States to the present day. Many times in various jurisdictions the death penalty has been reinstated after having been abolished or extended after having been restricted. Such reversals of policy have resulted from various factors: for example, changes in regime, the existence of a state of war or its aftermath, and the reactions of public opinion to particularly horrible crimes. Still, the long-term trend has been toward abolition or restriction. Often the death penalty has been abolished a second time after having been first abolished and then reinstated.

By 1962, about twenty nations, mostly in Europe and Latin America, had abolished the death penalty while other nations never used it or narrowly restricted its use. For all practical purposes, the United Kingdom eliminated the death penalty in 1965, and Canada has suspended the use of the death penalty by statute since 1968. By 1968 nine states of the United States had completely abolished the death penalty. In 1972 the California State Supreme Court declared the death penalty incompatible with the cruel or unusual punishment clause of that state's constitution, thus making California the tenth state to abolish the death penalty. Five states had severely limited use of the death penalty by 1971. These states allowed the death penalty in unusual cases such as those in which a prisoner, or one already convicted of murder, committed another murder. In practice, however, these five states seemed to have abolished the death penalty; Rhode Island and North Dakota, for example, have not executed anyone since 1930, and as of 1971 none of these five states had anyone under sentence of death.

Since 1930, a total of 3,861 persons have been executed in the United States—that is, in the states using the death penalty, in the District of Columbia and under federal civilian, but not military, jurisdiction. Of the 3,861 executed, 1,753 were white and 2,066 were black. Executions for murder numbered 3,334; of these 1,664 were white and 1,630 were black. Executions for rape, mostly in Southern states, numbered 455; of these only 48 were white, 405 were black. There were only 70 executions for other crimes. Of the 3,861 persons, only 32 persons executed out of the entire sum were female.

The executions were not spread evenly over the period under consideration. In the 1930's executions averaged 167 per year; in the 1940's, 128 per year; in the 1950's, 72 per year. In the 1960's executions tapered off annually as follows: 56, 42, 47, 21, 15, 7, 1, and 2. So, from an annual average of 167 in the 1930's it tapered off gradually to zero in the 1960's. The tapering off of executions during the 1960's can be accounted for in part by the fact that the United States Supreme Court was then expanding procedural protections in criminal process under the Bill of Rights, for example, the famous Miranda decision.

In 1972, the United States Supreme Court addressed the challenges which were being made on the constitutionality of capital punishment. The Court addressed the issue in the case known as *Furman* v. *Georgia*. The Court reversed and remanded the Furman case but it did *not* declare the death penalty unconstitutional, as many people believe. There was no majority opinion. The five justices of the majority each wrote their own separate opinion. Justices Marshall and Brennan dissented. They believed that the death penalty was unconstitutional per se. Justices Douglas, White, and Stewart, especially the latter two, did not view capital punishment, per se, as unconstitutional. They focused on the discretion given to the jury and the judge under existing statutes and concluded that the manner in which capital punishment was imposed was so arbitrary that it constituted cruel and unusual punishment which would make its use clearly against the Eighth and Fourteenth Amendments to the Constitution.

The lack of a single majority opinion in the Furman case created much confusion in the United States. The decision left unanswered many questions regarding what procedural features were necessary for a state statute to comply with the decision of the Supreme Court. Thirty-five states and the federal government promptly enacted new death penalty statutes. Attention was focused on the manner in which capital punishment was to be imposed, with the expectation that if the process were not arbitrary Justices White and Stewart would support the imposition of capital punishment.

It was believed that the first post-Furman procedural issue the Court would address would be the mandatory imposition of the death penalty for murder, as it was under review in the case *Fowler* v. *North Carolina*. Instead, in July 1976 the Court chose to respond to five cases from Georgia, Louisiana, Florida, North Carolina, and Texas. The cases from Georgia, Florida, and Texas were affirmed while those from Louisiana and North Carolina were reversed and remanded. The net effect of affirming the cases meant that the Court upheld the imposition of the death penalty under the new laws of the states of Georgia, Florida, and Texas. From these cases, it appears that there must be certain conditions and procedures existent for a capital-punishment statute not to constitute cruel and unusual punishment and therefore to be constitutional. And repeatedly since 1976, the Supreme Court has upheld the statutes of these states that have been brought before it.

In 1977, the United States Supreme Court considered two other types of capital punishment cases other than murder, namely, nonhomicidal rape and a mandatory death sentence in the killing of a police officer. In the case of *Coker* v. *Georgia* the Court declared that a statute imposing a sentence of death in the case of a nonhomicidal rape of an adult female was not constitutional. The Court also concluded in the 1977 case of *Roberts* v. *Louisiana* that a statute which imposed a mandatory death sentence in the killing of a police officer was not constitutional. The Court felt that it was incorrect to assume even in such cases that there were *no mitigating circumstances* which could be considered. It's significant that although hundreds of men have been executed for rape in Florida, no white man has ever been executed there for raping a black woman. But practically every black man that was ever accused of raping a white woman was executed or at least found guilty and given a capital sentence, which may have later been commuted in some cases to life imprisonment.

The present situation, then, with respect to capital punishment in the United States is this: Thirty-five states have death-penalty statutes that presumably meet the test of constitutionality as proposed by the United States Supreme Court. Fifteen states do not have death-penalty statutes. On the international scene, capital punishment is, for all practical purposes, nonexistent in the following countries: Argentina, Australia, Austria, Belgium, Brazil, Colombia, the Federal Republic of West Germany, Great Britain, Israel, the Netherlands, Sweden, Denmark, Norway, Switzerland, Venezuela, and Canada. At the beginning of April 1980 the wire services reported that the Law Committee of the Council of Europe had recommended that at the next meeting of the Parliament of Europe (it represents for all practical purposes the European states that are members of the European Common Market) a bill be adopted which would in effect abolish the death penalty in those few European countries which still have it. Also the bill would make it impossible for those countries that have already abolished the death penalty to reinstate it in the future.

This historical survey would not be complete if I did not mention that paralleling the efforts of many to achieve the abolition of capital punishment are the efforts of others to make capital punishment more palatable by constantly seeking less repulsive ways of executing people. The more brutal methods of the past have given way to methods which supposedly are more humane. We should recall that Dr. Guillotine proposed his invention as the most humane way to execute a person. We today would be horrified if our government were to adopt the guillotine as the standard method of executing people. We are currently witnessing the introduction of legislation in more and more states calling for execution by lethal injection. I think four or five states at the present time do use lethal injection as the means of execution. The whole question of lethal injection becomes complicated, especially when one considers the question of euthanasia and the necessary involvment of physicians in the execution of people.

I should now like to focus on the question of capital punishment in its relationship to the sanctity of human life. The historical survey was important in order to make clear that over the millennia, not just over the centuries, there has been such a wide disparity in the use of capital punishment by different peoples, different cultures, different civilizations, different generations, as to make the whole picture of capital punishment in human history one of caprice and arbitrariness. All of which defies any effort to systematize a logical development in the use of capital punishment as a means of achieving justice in society.

I am again indebted for much of the following theological development to Professor Germaine Grisez of the Catholic University of America. The first point to notice in a theological consideration of the justifiability of the use of the death penalty is that "Thou shall not kill" was not understood originally to rule out the use of the death penalty. The law of ancient Israel mandated or authorized the death penalty for a variety of crimes that I have listed. Should we consider the prescription of the death penalty for such crimes in the law of ancient Israel to express a divine teaching that use of the death penalty is morally right and proper? That's the question for us Christians today. Many legal codes have imposed the death penalty much more freely than did the ancient law of Israel. Crimes involving property, for example, were not punished by death in Israel; the death penalty for pickpockets is a relatively modern development. Still, Christians could hardly approve a death penalty for many of the crimes thus punished in accord with the law of Israel, anymore than we can approve of what is evidently the current practice in Iran of executing people for adultery—but only the woman, not the man—as well as for prostitution and drinking alcoholic beverages.

In particular, Christians always have taken the position that ecclesiastical authority should not use the death penalty; clerics or even potential clerics directly involved in the imposition or execution of a secular death penalty, regarded as legitimate in itself by the Church, perhaps, are nevertheless considered unfit to receive or to exercise Holy Orders. That's a significant aspect of the way the Church has viewed capital punishment throughout the centuries. The Church has traditionally said that participation in the imposition or carrying out of a sentence of death on the part of a priest or deacon or subdeacon or a seminarian rendered that person unfit to receive Holy Orders or to exercise Holy Orders if they had already received them.

The Second Vatican Council, in its teachings on religious liberty, clearly precludes the use of secular penalties to enforce religious conformity. It follows that from a Christian perspective there can be no general moral justification for the use of the death penalty by secular society in specifically religious offenses.

Clearly, the Christian's moral judgment on the rightness of using the death penalty cannot be based directly and simply on Sacred Scripture. The law of ancient Israel has had to be modified by Christians in very many respects, not to conform to humanistic philosophy and modern secular practices, but rather to harmonize with specifically Christian beliefs and traditional Christian practices.

Moreover, in working against the legalization of abortion, Catholics and other religious believers cooperating in the struggle on behalf of innocent life have been forced to meditate upon and to base their actions on the value and sanctity of human life. They have done so not on a scriptural basis, since in debating with nonbelievers they could not appeal to the teaching of faith that the killing of the innocent infringes upon the dominion of God, the Lord of life. In this struggle, also, some who have participated by articulating jurisprudential arguments have been compelled to reconsider the proper role of law in respect to all human life; they have tended to conclude that public authority has an unqualified duty to protect human life but has no right to destroy it.

Our Holy Father, Pope John Paul II, in his homily delivered at the Washington Mall in Washington, D.C. said:

> A distinguished American, Thomas Jefferson, once stated: "The care of human life and happiness and not their destruction is the just and only legitimate object of good government" (March 31, 1809). I wish therefore to praise all the members of the Catholic Church and other Christian Churches, all men and women of the Judeo-Christian heritage, as well as all people of good will who unite in common dedication for the defense of life in its fullness and for the promotion of all human rights.

In thinking about and working to defend innocent life against legalized injustice, many of us have come to a more intense appreciation of the value of the human life of every person, whether innocent or guilty, and have also focused attention upon the requirements of justice and the criminal law.

The result is that in recent years certain Catholic thinkers who have shown their fidelity to the Church's teaching office and their dedication to the values of human life and just law have argued that the use of the death penalty is itself a morally unjustifiable attack upon human life. That is my own position. I deny to political society any special dominion over life, and I maintain that the good end of just punishment cannot justify the bad means of killing a person.

As George Bernard Shaw is reported to have asked: "When will we stop trying to convince people to stop killing people by killing people?" The testimony of Catholics who hold this position is significant. It cannot be dismissed as the reflection of secular opinion; these are persons accustomed to thinking with the Church and of acting in accord with their own faith. They have taken a position against the legalization of abortion—a position often unpopular among their acquaintances and associates—and have acted upon this position with an energy born of Christian commitment. Their reflective articulation of the fruit of this experience must be considered with respect.

The fact that the ancient law of Israel on the use of the death penalty had to be modified considerably to harmonize with Christian beliefs and practices, together with the fact that contemporary reflection, rooted in specifically Christian belief and action, has begun calling the *received position* from the Old Testament on the justifiability of the death penalty into question, lends some initial plausibility to the proposal that the *received position* might be mistaken. *Might be mistaken.* Perhaps the more ancient books of Sacred Scripture show that the use of the death penalty was authorized by God only in the sense that other practices common in those days but now believed to be immoral by Christians were also authorized by God. In other words, perhaps God merely permitted the use of the death penalty as He merely permitted the practice of polygamy and merely permitted the practice of slavery until the deepening of faith and a growing sense of human personal dignity nurtured by faith would lead to replacement of these practices by alternatives consonant with the natural law and with the new law of Christ. The law of Christ does not replace natural law, but fulfills and elevates it by assuming it into union with the grace of the Holy Spirit, who teaches and guides Christians from within.

If God only permitted use of the death penalty, then it must be said that the belief that its use is morally justified is not strictly speaking part of Catholic tradition. Statements in the New Testament and in traditional teaching that can be taken to exclude the justifiability of the death penalty would have to be interpreted without the limitations and qualifications hitherto commonly introduced to permit justification of it, while elements of the New Testament and definitive Christian teaching that seem to justify use of the death penalty would have to be interpreted as only tolerating it, not approving it. The question is: Is such a reinterpretation possible without infringing upon anything essential to Catholic faith?

This question cannot be answered without a very careful, intensive and extensive study of all the teaching of the Church relevant to the morality of using the death penalty.

Unfortunately, no such study has yet been made. Most of the ancient doctors of the Church and Catholic theologians of the past who have written on the subject seem to have defended the morality of using the death penalty. The teaching office of the Church itself, however, seems to have had little to say directly bearing upon the issue. Statements of popes often have touched on the use of the death penalty; they have assumed it to be morally justified, accepting the *received position* from the past without expressly considering whether that position is essential to Catholic teaching and life or not.

One thing is certain. A matter of this kind cannot be settled solely by an examination of Sacred Scripture. Whether or not the Catholic Church is irrevocably committed to the position that the use of the death penalty is morally justifiable—and to other positions included in her received moral teaching from the past—can be determined only if the teaching of the Church through the ages is taken fully into account. Moreover, the judgment of the kind of assent due to any teaching received in the Church is not the function of individual conscience or private opinion based upon theological scholarship. The teaching of the Church binds the consciences of Catholics and is the criterion against which theological opinions must be measured. The judgment of the kind of assent due to any received teaching must be made by the teaching office of the Church.

The development—assuming it is possible—of Catholic teaching to exclude the death penalty would occur partly in virtue of a more intense appreciation of the value of human life as such, a clearer recognition of the indivisible unity of human bodily life and human personal dignity, and a more refined grasp of the manner in which fundamental personal values render morally unacceptable anything that would directly attack them. Such a development would by no means indicate that other received Catholic teachings with respect to the value of human life might also be reversed.

So a development with respect to the moral justifiability of the use of the death penalty would not imply that the teachers in the Church failed in times past in their mission of leading the faithful along Christ's way of salvation. The situation would be similar to the development of Christian moral teaching with respect to slavery. The fact that such a development has occurred (and we have come a long way in the Church over the centuries with regard to the Church's view of slavery) does not imply that modern Christians are morally superior to our ancestors in the faith. The Spirit gives different gifts to Christians of every age, so that they might use the special opportunities of each age to redeem it.

In summary, I claim that the *theoretical possibility* exists that the use of the death penalty is *in principle* morally unjustifiable, and that Catholic teaching might eventually develop in such a way as to make clear that this is the case. Further, I claim that the *use* of the death penalty is morally unjustifiable. If the use of the death penalty cannot be shown to be absolutely necessary to protect society and to deter potential criminals, and I do not believe that it can be shown to be absolutely necessary for such purposes, then the use of this penalty in the United States today is morally unjustified. Finally, on the basis of all the evidence concerning the inability of our penal system and our judicial system to mete out punishment fairly and equitably, it seems to me that if the death penalty cannot be imposed and executed fairly, then it should be abolished.

I began this paper on a personal note, and I should like to conclude it on a personal note, but first I wish to refer not to my own person but rather to a man living in England today, one Albert Pierrepoint.

Albert Pierrepoint was the last "Number One," as Britain's official executioner used to be called. He was the chief hangman of England for twenty-five years. Now, at age 74, he lives quietly and as anonymously as possibly in the quiet northern seaside town of Southport in England. As he commented in his very discreet memoirs entitled *Executioner Pierrepoint*, published in 1974 and reprinted in 1977: "I accept that even educated men are fallible, I accept the possibility that an innocent man has been hanged in error by my hands, and it is not a pleasant thought. But I know that there was never anything that could be done about it by me." Normally a talkative, humorous man, Pierrepoint always in the past refused to discuss his work as a hangman. Another kind of man would have exploded without some such outlet or been unable to sleep at night, but Pierrepoint perhaps was saved by his sense of vocation. Recalling his early days, he once said: "I was later to find—from the number of assistant executioners who shot off the list of names with monotonous repetition after two or three experiences—that it was the memories, dreams and fears that broke the men up. But at that time having every confidence in my own balance of mind, my youthful priority was to get the technique right and the speed unsurpassable."

His father was also chief executioner in England. It was said that his father could complete an execution—from the taking of the prisoner from his cell to the moment of death—in the time it took the prison clock to strike eight. "Our Albert," as his family called him, set out to do even better. Greater speed meant less torture for the prisoner. Asked by the Royal Commission on Capital Punishment exactly how many executions he carried out, he reluctantly added them up but then had the public report changed to read merely "several hundreds." Although he insisted that a prisoner's guilt was not his business, that he was merely doing his job as well as possible, a much stronger reaction can surely be read into his claim that it was his vocation to be a hangman, that he believed he was "chosen by a higher power for the task which I took up, that I was put on earth especially to do it." Certainly we know that after twenty-five years as an executioner Pierrepoint was left with a disquieting sense of the failure of capital punishment. He wrote: "Executions solve nothing and are only an antiquated relic of a primitive desire for revenge which takes the easy way and hands over the responsibility for revenge to other people."

He added:

> It is said to be a deterrent; I cannot agree. There have been murders since the beginning of time and we shall go on looking for deterrents until the end of time. If death were a deterrent, I might be expected to know. It is I who have faced them last, young lads and girls, working men, grandmothers. I have been amazed to see the courage with which they take that walk into the unknown. It did not deter them then, and it did not deter them when they committed what they were convicted for. All the men and women whom I have faced at the final moment convinced me that in what I have done I have not prevented a single murder.

When Albert Pierrepoint retired prematurely in 1956 as the last "Number One," he refused to explain his reasons. He said, "The authorities have asked me to keep the reasons for my resignation confidential," and that's all that he would say. But after reading his memoirs, published years later, one can only assume he resigned because he had lost all belief in what he was doing. There is a limit to even a craftsman's self-effacement.

It took Albert Pierrepoint twenty-five years to reach his conclusion about the true nature of capital punishment. It has taken me somewhat longer.

I fought in the Second World War and was acutely aware not only of the Nazi Holocaust but also of the frightful cost in human lives that the Allied victory required. I have lived through the decades of the terrible experience of Vietnam, the autogenocide of the Pol Pot regime in Cambodia, and the violence of the Middle East. It seems to me that in the face of the continuing spiral of violence in the world, there is no other solution than for us to take seriously what Our Lord Jesus Christ himself taught us about the sacredness of human life. He came to give us life and to give life to the fullest. Life not only in the world to come but in the present world as well. I suggest that if we have learned anything we must surely have learned by now that all human life is sacred and worthy of defense, even the life of a convicted criminal. To execute criminals is to brutalize society and to render more easy the taking of human life in other circumstances.

May the risen Christ in whose life we are privileged to share inspire us, help us, encourage us to weigh seriously the challenge posed to us by the use of capital punishment as an instrument of public policy in these United States. May we join together to achieve its abolition.

12

Poverty in America:
The Social Sin of Our Time

JOSEPH CARDINAL BERNARDIN
Archbishop of Chicago

In the autumn of 1957, the World Union of Catholic Women's Organizations convened in Rome at the headquarters of the Food and Agricultural Organization of the United Nations to discuss world hunger. As a prelude to the congress, presentations were made on three hungers of the human family: the hunger for food, the hunger for truth, and the hunger for God. In the more than twenty-five years since that eventful congress, the human family has passed through as turbulent a period of history as perhaps we have ever witnessed. Brilliant, mind-staggering technological developments have put us on the moon and made it possible for us to explore the outer limits of space. The same technology has given us new life-styles with more ease, more comfort, more affluence than our parents ever dreamed of. But that same technology has also given us sophisticated and lethal weapons systems that threaten this world with a nuclear holocaust. In these twenty-five years the human family has looked beyond itself and tried to make real its deepest aspirations for peace and human freedom, but too often has had to face the ugly reality of wars and revolutions, civil and religious fratricide, tyranny and terrorism. For all our achievements and gains in this quarter century, we still suffer the deep pangs of our hungers—for food, for truth, for God.

Delivered at the Cathedral-Basilica of St. James in Brooklyn on May 2, 1982.

It is true that men and women do not live by bread alone, but they must have bread if they are to live and to seek truth and come to know God. In our present-day world the hunger for bread is bound up with a poverty that here and abroad cries to heaven for alleviation and confronts us, our institutions, and our governments with ever increasing direful consequences. This poverty is not unique to any one nation. It is a common enemy to the entire family. For wherever people are forced to live without the basic necessities required for a decent life, the result is the same— human dignity is threatened and impaired. The existence of poverty, whether in the Third World or in our own nation, diminishes the dignity not only of the poor, but of the entire human community. Poverty makes us all less human. Here I will discuss one aspect of this global problem: poverty in America, the social sin of our time.

Most Americans who are under middle age have never really seen the face of poverty. The national experience that we know as the Great Depression has been our only mass exposure to what it means to be without the means of sustenance and to have no way to remedy the situation. To be sure, we have had several "recessions" which have caused us to think, even in personal terms, of depriving ourselves of some of our customary amenities; but these have been for the most part temporary and for most of us more annoying than really troublesome.

In the last few years we have even been told that there is in fact no poverty to speak of in the United States, that the so-called "War on Poverty" has at last been won. The United States Chamber of Commerce asked a few years ago, "Have we licked poverty without knowing it?"[1] One economic observer has argued that "the day of income poverty as a major public issue would appear to be past."[2]

The poverty picture surely has changed in the last two decades and, despite the critics, government programs have been important in bringing the change about. The final report of the National Advisory Council on Economic Opportunity (NACEO) tells us that "in 1959 a little over 22 percent of the American population was poor; by 1969 only 12 percent was poor."[3] Since then there has been little change, although poverty rose during the recession of 1975 and again during the recession of 1979.

An interesting aspect of this picture is the geographical distribution of poverty over this period. From 1959 to 1979, 14 million Americans ceased being poor, and 9 million of these were in the southern part of the United States. During the 1969–1979 decade, however, the number of poor people in the North and West rose by 1.5 million.

Another significant detail reveals that the rate of poverty for black Americans in the North has changed only marginally in twenty years. The Economic Opportunity report tells us that "there are one million more black poor in the Northern and Western states today than in 1959."[4] The general picture is very much the same for Americans of Hispanic origin. Big-city poverty has been especially troublesome: New York City's poverty rate increased by about 25 percent in the 1960's and late 1970's, Philadelphia's increased by 38 percent, Chicago's by 47 percent.

Let me close these references to poverty statistics by recording that 29.3 million Americans who in 1980 lived below the poverty level represent a 3.2 million increase over the previous year. This means that we are talking about a current, staggering human reality in deprivation.

If the cold statistical data are insufficient to convince us of the growing severity of poverty in our midst, we need only look to human examples all around us. In particular, I would point to the hundreds of Church-sponsored programs that provide emergency assistance to the poor. We have seen in recent months a dramatic increase in the number of the homeless and hungry, the destitute and the desperate, who show up on the doorsteps of Church agencies, emergency shelters, and parish rectories.

Several months ago, for example, the doors of Holy Ghost Church in Denver were opened at night because it was anticipated that thirty or forty people needed emergency shelter. Within a month the numbers swelled to hundreds of homeless men, women, and children sleeping in the pews of the church.

In Detroit, at an emergency food center run by the Capuchin Fathers, the demand for assistance has doubled in the past year. Close to a thousand people are being served there every day.

There are some misconceptions about the poor that circulate widely and should be responded to directly. The most ugly of the misconceptions is that the poor do not want to work. This is a polite way of saying that they are lazy and shiftless and expect others to support them. The fact is that 17 percent of the poor work full time, and 13 percent work at some time during the year. What about the rest of them? Actually, over 70 percent of the poor simply cannot work—they are either too old to work, are severely disabled, are mothers with small children, or are themselves under sixteen years of age. This means that 90 percent of America's poor either work full time or are persons who, because of age or disability, simply cannot work.

Associated with this myth about the poor being lazy is the notion that they spend their money more frivolously than anyone else. On the contrary, studies indicate that the poor spend most of their money on the necessities of life—88 percent for food, clothing, medical care, and shelter. This is actually a higher percentage than those who have more money.

A second misconception sees the poverty picture in racial terms —the poor are mostly black. The truth is that almost 70 percent of the poor are white Americans. Furthermore, a large percentage of those who are poor live in rural areas, contrary to the popular perception that poverty is confined to the inner city.

Up until now, we have been talking about the "official" poor —those eligible for certain welfare programs. There are, however, millions of Americans who are just above the poverty line, those who manage to get by as long as they can continue to work. Here the specter of unemployment appears with all the harsh realities that follow in its wake. As I write these words in the fourth month of 1982, our own government figures for current unemployment tell us that more than 10 million Americans are out of work. This means that 9 percent of the labor force in the United States is without a job—the highest percentage since the Depression. Here is where the social sin of poverty breeds its most noxious byproducts.

Unemployment has an immediate psychological impact on the human person, assaulting self-respect and indeed personal human dignity. Pope John Paul II reminded us in his encyclical on work:

> Work is a good thing for man—a good thing for his humanity —because through work man not only transforms nature, adapting it to his own needs, but he also achieves fulfillment

as a human being and indeed in a sense becomes "more a human being."[5]

Significant changes in self-esteem occur when unemployment is extended over any lengthy period, and studies indicate that its effects are most pronounced in workers in low-level employment. Thus those least able to cope with it are the ones most often afflicted with joblessness. Not merely emotional malaise, but serious mental health disorders can take their origin in loss of employment. One study found that a one-percent increase in the jobless rate could be expected to increase psychiatric admissions by 3.4 percent. Other studies make it unmistakably clear that loss of employment is linked to increased suicide, so much so that some researchers have claimed that the suicide rate is one of the more reliable indicators of a change in the economy.

These destructive effects on the human person emphasize the moral dimensions of both poverty and unemployment. To regard these as mere economic or social phenomena is to miss their real significance. They are assaults on men and women that crush the human spirit and render the victims ever more vulnerable to almost any of the "shocks that flesh is heir to."

Beyond all this, one must take some measure of what poverty and joblessness do to family life. Pope John Paul II has remarked on this relationship in his recent encyclical:

> Work constitutes a foundation for the formation of family life, which is a natural right and something that man is called to. These two spheres of values—one linked to work and the other consequent on the family nature of human life—must be properly united and must properly permeate each other. In a way, work is a condition for making it possible to found a family, since the family requires the means of subsistence which man normally gains through work.[6]

When a person's need and right to work go unmet and unacknowledged, the consequences are both dire and predictable. Here again the unemployed—or the marginally employed in low income and unstable jobs—are those most easily stricken. Studies verify the increase in marital dissatisfaction and the deterioration of family relations in jobless family situations. This is especially true among younger families and those with preschool children, and it is aggravated as unemployment is extended. Nothing more graphically indicates the rise in family tensions than abusive behavior. Researchers find joblessness a crucial component in the incidence of "battered wives" and abused children. Declines in such indicators as school attendance and scholastic achievement also measure family tensions in the home, and these effects live on in another generation.

If one seeks further evidence to document the effects of the social sin of poverty and its step-sister, unemployment, a glance at studies in criminal justice will suffice. Both crimes against property and crimes of violence are strongly linked to unemployment and underemployment. One study estimated "that one percentage point increase in the unemployment rate increased state prison admissions by about four percent."[7] Similar links have been demonstrated in the area of juvenile delinquency. An increase in the use of narcotics and alcohol has also been observed, a strong factor in relation to both crimes against property and violence.

In the face of the massive evidence, of which we have mentioned only a fraction, can any citizen—can any Christian—be complacent? Is it enough to recite once again the sad statistics of poverty and unemployment and their deadly effects on millions of Americans? Can we leave the task of healing to the political leaders, the social scientists, and the economists alone? I think not. We have a role to play in the rescue of America, the fate of the American worker, and the future of America's poor. Our voice must be heard, not just in pleas for charity for those in want, but in cries of justice for the poor. We must not merely mourn for the jobless, we must see their right to work fulfilled in fact.

But how do we do it? More specifically, what is our role *as Church* in addressing the problem? I would like to focus on that particular question now.

As you well know, the Church has a rich tradition of social teaching. Beginning with Pope Leo XIII's *Rerum Novarum* in 1891, there has been a continual development in this area. This teaching, reflected so clearly in papal, conciliar, and synodal documents, is rooted in the dignity of the human person who is created in God's image and likeness and the rights and obligations that flow from that dignity. Unfortunately, it is not so well known, or at least it does not seem to make as much of an impact, as many other teachings. It is critically important, therefore, that we bring this teaching, together with its far-reaching implications, into the public debate. The Church does not claim any special expertise in the political, economic, or social order; as the Second Vatican Council reminded us, its mission is religious.[8] But its social teaching does provide an indispensable framework within which to make a moral analysis of today's problems. It also can give the direction and motivation needed to work out viable solutions.

One reason why the Church's social teaching needs more exposure at this time is that it clearly spells out what the basic rights of people are, as well as the responsibility of the various elements of society, both private and public, to protect those rights. In recent months an increasing amount of emphasis has been placed on the responsibility of the private sector and, in particular, the churches, to provide for the needs of the poor. For example, in a Cincinnati daily, one of the editorial writers said recently in a signed column: "Fundamental human needs need not be the concern of governments, but of individuals, of families, of communities and of charitable and religious organizations." Earlier this year the Reagan administration said that if each church adopted ten poor families, we could eliminate all government welfare in this country.

I am the first to admit that the churches, as well as all segments of the private sector, need to do more, and I will say more about that in a moment. But I wish to affirm as forcefully as I can that government also has a responsibility from which it cannot escape. Important as voluntarism is, it cannot alone resolve the problem of poverty. In his 1979 address to the United Nations, Pope John Paul II spoke about the need for creative collaboration among nations to overcome the global causes of poverty. That evening, in his homily at the Mass in Yankee Stadium, the pope challenged American Catholics in a very direct way. He first talked about the charitable work of the Church which he commended and encouraged. Then he added:

> But this is not enough. Within the framework of your national institutions and in cooperation with all your compatriots,

you will also want to seek out the structural reasons which foster or cause the different forms of poverty in the world and in your own country, so that you can apply the proper remedies. You will not allow yourselves to be intimidated or discouraged by over-simplified explanations, which are more ideological than scientific, explanations which try to account for a complex evil by some single cause. But neither will you recoil before the reforms—even profound ones—of attitudes and structures that may prove necessary in order to recreate over and over again the conditions needed by the disadvantaged if they are to have a fresh change in the hard struggle of life.[9]

These powerful words, which call not merely for more charity but also justice, are rooted in the thinking of Pope John XXIII who, in *Mater et Magistra*, addressed the issue of the role of government in developing public policy in two crucial sentences:

To safeguard the inviolable rights of the human person and to facilitate the fulfillment of his duties, should be the essential office of every public authority.[10]

One of the fundamental duties of civil authorities is to coordinate social relations in such fashion that the exercise of a person's rights does not threaten others in the exercise of their own rights nor hinder in fulfillment of their duties.[11]

It is clear, then, that there are two sides of the coin. The common good, which civil society is obligated to defend and promote, requires that the individual's rights be respected. But it also requires the public authority to take action as needed and appropriate to defend those rights.

I wish to conclude by making some suggestions which, I believe, flow from what has already been said. It is important that we assume a position of advocacy for the poor, both by insisting on a just economic and social order and by providing for their immediate needs. This is a work of justice and charity. The Latin American bishops at Puebla spoke about a "preferential option" for the poor. "We affirm," they said, "the need for conversion on the part of the whole Church to a preferential option for the poor, an option aimed at their integral liberation."[12] Such a preferential option would seem to call for the following.

1. In all matters of public policy, but especially those affecting the poor, we must insist on the truth. The problems are so complex that it is difficult enough to arrive at a clear analysis of their causes and possible solutions. We must, therefore, demand that the facts not be slanted or manipulated for political, ideological, or personal motives, as so often happens in the political process today. The urgency of the situation demands that everyone rise above the prejudices, divisions, and myths that delay solutions or make them impossible. Insisting on the truth—both in analyzing the facts and presenting the consequences of the proposed solutions— will bring about a clarity that will be immensely helpful. As Pope John Paul II told the Latin American bishops at Puebla, in the light of truth "we see that human beings are not the pawns of economic or political processes, that instead these processes are geared toward human beings and subject to them."[13]

2. As a Church, as I indicated before, we do not have any special expertise in the political, social and economic orders. While all may share a common goal, there may be a number of legitimate ways to achieve it. Moreover, we must acknowledge that there are real problems and limitations that must be taken into account. For example, there is no doubt that the United States presently faces a serious economic crisis which will probably not improve significantly for some time. Our specific contribution to the public debate about priorities and particular programs or legislation, therefore, must be more in the form of principles which should serve as the criteria for evaluating and developing public policy. In 1975, the American bishops outlined seven such principles that should guide our citizens and policy makers as we plan and provide for the human rights and dignity of all our people. Each flows from the Church's social teaching as it has evolved over the past ninety years. All are so essential to the issue we are discussing that I must repeat them at this time.

i. Economic activity should be governed by justice and be carried out within the limits of morality. It must serve people's needs.

ii. The right to have a share of earthly goods sufficient for oneself and one's family belongs to everyone.

iii. Economic prosperity is to be assessed not so much from the sum total of goods and wealth possessed as from the distribution of goods according to norms of justice.

iv. Opportunities to work must be provided for those who are able and willing to work. Every person has the right to useful employment, to just wages, and to adequate assistance in case of real need.

v. Economic development must not be left to the sole judgment of a few persons or groups possessing excessive economic power, or to the political community alone. On the contrary, at every level the largest possible number of people should have an active share in directing that development.

vi. A just and equitable system of taxation requires assessment according to ability to pay.

vii. Government must play a role in the economic activity of its citizens. Indeed, it should promote in a suitable manner the production of a sufficient supply of material goods. Moreover, it should safeguard the rights of all citizens and help them find opportunities for employment.[14]

Another aspect of advocacy for the poor might well be added to the category of principles to be observed in developing public policy. This is the relationship between the cost of the arms race and the plight of the poor, not only in our own country but throughout the world. This topic is intensely debated today. Pope John Paul II, as well as his predecessors, has spoken about it many times. The bishops also address it in their pastoral on war and peace. It is more than just the choice between "butter" and "guns." It is the choice between feeding the children of God and refining the tools of war; it is the choice between life and death. I mention it now only to affirm that it is a serious problem that cannot be ignored.

3. The Church as an institution must find new ways of increasing its own charitable outreach to the poor. There is no doubt that we are already doing a great deal. In every diocese, a sizable portion of the resources are earmarked for the poor and disadvantaged. But the needs are increasing. I met recently with the urban

ministers of the Cincinnati area who are deeply concerned about the rapidly growing number of people who are without work or desperately need assistance. Urban ministries throughout the country are faced with the same situation.

What do we do? I do not have any ready answers in the form of specific programs or strategies. But I do think that the growing crisis requires a special effort on our part. We simply cannot proceed on a business-as-usual basis. We must examine our priorities to see what adjustments might be needed. To succeed in our efforts, much more needs to be done to sensitize our people to their responsibilities. Sometimes, because of publicized abuses of welfare programs (which frequently are attributable to those who deliver the services rather than the recipients), they seem ready to write off all the poor as lazy or shiftless and undeserving of any help. It is also true that even the suburban parishes do not always find it easy to make ends meet today. Still, when one sees how much money they can raise for their own special projects, one must wonder about their priorities. I believe the time has come for those of us who are in leadership positions to challenge our people to be more sensitive and responsive to the needs of the poor.

The Holy Father put it very bluntly in his Yankee Stadium homily to which I referred earlier.

> We cannot stand idly by, enjoying our own riches and freedom, if, in any place, the Lazarus of the twentieth century stands at our doors. In the light of the parable of Christ, riches and freedom mean a special responsibility. Riches and freedom create a special obligation. And so, in the name of the solidarity that binds us all together in a common humanity, I again proclaim the dignity of every human person: the rich man and Lazarus are both human beings, both of them actually created in the image and likeness of God, both of them equally redeemed by Christ, at a great price, the price of "the precious blood of Christ" (1 Pt. 1:19).[15]

4. Finally, in what may be the most difficult yet potentially most useful step of all, I believe the Church should undertake—and encourage others to undertake—a fresh appraisal of poverty: its causes, its effects upon the poor and nonpoor alike, and its solutions.

For example:

Traditionally, we have regarded America as a land of opportunity, and so it has proved to be for many. Yet for others this is
not the case. Indeed, some seem locked in an inter-generational
prison of poverty. What are the systems, the structures, the attitudes, and practices which cause this state of affairs, and how can
they be changed?

Are schools and other agents of socialization breaking down
class barriers in our society—or is it possible that, without intend-
ing it, they are helping to create a new elite class, while at the same
time perpetuating and reinforcing the existence of an under-class
mired in poverty and despair?

What is being done to prepare the poor and the near-poor and
their children for advancement in the emerging American service
economy which places a declining premium on physical labor and
a rising value on relatively sophisticated skills? How adequate are
schools and other educational institutions, as well as public and
private antipoverty efforts, in this regard?

How should the Church carry out its duty to make a preferential option for the poor, in light of the fact that its efforts tend to
become counterproductive to the extent they are perceived as
merely "political" in nature? How, in other words, can we speak
to real issues—employment, housing, education, and federal
budget, and the rest—without being ignored or resisted by precisely those whom we need to reach and persuade?

These are complex, difficult questions, but I believe the Church
should lead the way in raising them and encouraging the search
for answers. Our preferential option for the poor must be as informed as it is wholehearted, as realistic as it is sincere, as oriented
to the eradication of poverty as to its relief, and rooted at all times
in a vision of the integral dignity of the human person. For this
purpose let us make our own the conviction of Pope John Paul II,
that "such a task is not an impossible one" and also that "this difficult road of the indispensable transformation of the structures of
economic life is one on which it will not be easy to go forward without the intervention of a true conversion of mind, will and
heart."[16]

NOTES

1. National Advisory Council on Economic Opportunity (NACEO), Final Report, September 1981, p. 34.
2. Ibid.
3. Ibid., p. 36.
4. Ibid., p. 37.
5. Pope John Paul II, *Laborem Exercens*, no. 9.
6. Ibid., no. 10.
7. NACEO Final Report, p. 78.
8. CF. *Gaudium et Spes*, no. 42.
9. Pope John Paul II, Homily at Mass in Yankee Stadium, in *The Message of Justice, Peace and Love* (Boston: St. Paul Editions, 1979), p. 81.
10. Pope John XXIII, *Pacem in Terris*, no. 60.
11. Ibid., nos. 62, 63.
12. Third General Conference of Latin American Bishops, *Puebla* (Washington, D.C., NCCB Edition, 1979), p. 178.
13. Ibid., p. 8.
14. The Catholic Bishops of the United States, "The Economy: Human Dimensions" (Washington, D.C.: USCC Publications Office, 1975). In this statement, each of these principles is referenced to the particular conciliar or papal document from which it was drawn.
15. Pope John Paul II, Homily at Mass in Yankee Stadium, *The Message of Justice, Peace and Love*, p. 86.
16. Pope John Paull I, *Redemptor Hominis*, no. 16.

13

Woman as Person
in the Church and Society

P. FRANCIS MURPHY
Auxiliary Bishop of Baltimore

As Christians, we all share or should share a common concern about women as persons in the Church and society. As I prepared this paper, I thought often of the sign and symbol of bishop as a shepherd of the people. I have prayed often over the thirty-fourth chapter of the book of the prophet Ezechiel. Ezechiel tells us that the Lord God speaks thus: "Behold I, even I, will both search after my sheep and seek them out. . . . I will deliver them out of all places where they have been scattered in the cloudy and dark day. I will seek that which was lost, and bring again that which was driven away, and bind up that which was broken, and strengthen that which was sick. . . ."

I have spent most of my priesthood in a ministry to my brother priests. I consider this a great blessing. I have recently concluded a nine-month study and report of a twenty-priest task force on questions of the morale and support of priests. It was a very enriching and rewarding experience for me to listen to the faith of and to see the commitment to service of my fellow priests.

As my ministry has evolved as a priest and now as a bishop, I have experienced a rewarding dimension of working closely with women as persons and friends, including administrators, educators, medical and health professionals, lawyers, housewives, and

Delivered at the Cathedral-Basilica of St. James in Brooklyn on May 9, 1980.

pastoral ministers. I count all of them as a great blessing, and I thank them for all they have shared with me in my growth as a person and a minister.

I want to say at the outset that, here and elsewhere in my paper, if my comments sound critical, they are not intended to be judgmental. As human beings, we are blessed with only a limited vision of the truth. My point here is to emphasize that the Church has systematically, and not without purpose, promoted separateness in the formation and apostolic experiences of men and women. As a result, there is something of a mood of discovery now among women and men seeing, as if for the first time, one another's contributions and gifts. A sense of humor is indispensable.

My experience convinces me that there is an urgent need to continue to identify and clarify women's participation in ministry and in society. May I state here that the main focus of my paper is not the question of women's ordination. I am addressing a much broader question: "Woman as Person in the Church and Society."

This is the outline I intend to follow:

I. Is the position of women in society and ministry a moral and social issue for a Christian Church?

II. What do we learn from the lives of Jesus and Mary about "personhood?"

III. What does the Church, as a representative of Christ, say in her teaching about woman as person, both in the Church and in society?

IV. What do we find in the practice of the Church at various levels of her life in response to this teaching? Does it draw all possible conclusions from its noble teaching?

V. In conclusion, I will emphasize one specific action that I believe is essential for the journey of the pilgrim Church.

What Is the Issue and Why?

It is a widely accepted insight into human development that we human beings discover and develop our sense of self, our personhood, in and through interaction with others. That is to say, we become persons in community. The quality of the communities to which we belong and the structure of the societies that encompass those communities, then, assist or impede each individual's realization of the God-given dignity of personhood that is hers or his.

The Church, as a social reality and community, must continually be concerned with the quality of her own life and with the witness she gives to the world about the human person. This concern ought to be so intense that the Church would welcome all true progress achieved by other institutions and groups and would undergo the same self-scrutiny. "The Church knows from experience that her ministry of fostering human rights in the world requires continued scrutiny and purification of her own life, laws, institutions, and policies" (Pope Paul VI to the Synod of Bishops in 1974).

Today, we of the Catholic Church in America are being seriously challenged to just such self-scrutiny as a result of the struggle of women to achieve full personhood in American society, a struggle that has extended its criticisms of unjust laws and structures beyond our political institutions to the Roman Catholic Church herself. In many ways, it is the very ideal of American democracy that has brought women to this pass, for many of the assumptions of our society about women have been at odds with founding principles of individual freedom and individual responsibility for human persons.

Most damaging to the self-respect and the self-image of women has been the assumption that women are by nature inferior to men and consequently subordinate. This view of women is called "sexism," and the discrimination that is its outward expression is just as detrimental to the development of human persons as the prejudices that we have recognized longer and combatted more vigorously, such as racism and nationalism.

The first issue implied in my topic, then, is the effect of sexist attitudes and discriminatory practices on the development of women as persons. It is my belief that a sexist view of women—one which sees them as secondary, inferior, subordinate, or derivative with respect to their human nature—when institutionalized in laws and customs, deprives women of their God-given rights as human persons and thus constitutes a moral problem calling for a response from the magisterium of the Church.

The second issue implied in my topic is the demoralizing effect that discrimination based on sex has on the Church and civil society. It has long been a teaching of the Church that no society can be united and strong unless the rights of all, especially of the weak and the underprivileged, are respected. History shows that no society can endure unless its laws and customs truly reflect the ideals to which it has committed itself. Discrimination against any citizen is contrary to the ideals of the American people, however long it may take us to recognize the particular forms in which such discrimination appears.

As the larger society makes progress in identifying the ways in which it has institutionalized sexism, so must the Church. Our faith in the reality of our communion with one another in the Mystical Body makes it imperative that we do so, for we believe that when one part of the body is wounded, the whole body suffers. To be true to the vocation entrusted to her, the Church must strive to eradicate every kind of division among us; we must become ever more a community based on faith in God and not on any of the distinctions due to "flesh and blood." This applies to distinctions based on sex as well as to those based on economic status, national origin, or racial grouping.

I speak, then, as one concerned about what effect our failure to facilitate the full personhood of women is having on women, the Church, and our world. I speak as one who has great hopes for what it will mean to women, to the Church, and to the world for us as a people, in word and in deed, to recognize women as persons created in the image of God, called to the imitation of Christ, and destined for the fullness of life. I speak as one who hopes that in time discrepancies of ideals and practices will be fully recognized. I speak as one who loves and hopes in the Church, which has grown in so many other areas under the guidance of the Holy Spirit. I believe she can grow in this respect as well and be a light to all the nations. I believe the decade of the 1970's has raised the Church's consciousness.

Now let me address in a more concrete way five reasons for thinking that the matter of women as persons is so important for the Church today:

1. The women's movement has raised important questions about the Church's interpretations of revelation about women. Some have charged that the Judeo-Christian tradition is inherently sexist and therefore constitutes one of the main blocks to the development of women as full persons. I am increasingly aware that some scholars, like Rosemary Reuther, and many persons regard the Church's exclusive delegation of authority to men as the closest

contemporary example of ancient patriarchal society founded on male privilege. As a shepherd of the Church, I feel that it is time we undergo a profound examination of our theological anthropology.

2. My concern for other moral and social issues cannot be isolated from my concern for women. I do not believe that the Church can be a credible voice speaking to the urgent questions of family, the nation, and the international community without first requesting and including the perspectives of women on these questions. Eli Ginsburg has stated that women in the work force in our country have had the most dramatic impact on our society of any other single event in the twentieth century.

3. The tensions building in the Church about the role of women, the disaffection expressed by some women and men, and the defensive attitudes of others, all challenge the credibility of the Church as sacrament of unity. We all know that if tensions are suppressed, they become potentially destructive to the effectiveness of our mission as Church. On the other hand, the existence of tensions can give rise to an opportunity for constructive action.

4. Another serious reason for addressing the topic is the very mission of the Church. The reality of the decline in the number of traditional ministers and the overall increase of Church membership has challenged the Church to be more innovative and creative in establishing new ministries in order to fulfill the Church's mission and to meet the pastoral needs of the people. In a word, today there is a need for women in ministry. Women have demonstrated their willingness to serve, and yet women are still being denied the official confirmation in such ministries as reader and acolyte, which are open to laymen.

5. As a bishop of the Catholic Church in America, I believe our recent experiences of consciousness-raising can enable us to make a great contribution to the development of doctrine and of discipline in the ministries of the universal Church. But this will be possible only if our commitment to the Kingdom of God is sincere and if we—women and men alike—are willing to seek the truth together, even when it may be a two-edged sword separating us from customary male and female privileges. Yet what we must seek together is the development of the full potential of all persons that is not incompatible with the paschal mystery at the heart of our Christian faith.

Jesus and Mary

I have commented on the meaning and significance of my topic on woman as person in the Church and society. I will now place the issue of sexism in the light of Jesus and Mary, and then take a look at the recent teaching and pronouncements of the universal magisterium of the Church as it attempts to interpret for a pilgrim people, in a living culture and history, the teaching of Christ.

A brief glimpse at the Gospel story of Jesus shows that Jesus both related well and delighted in the company of women. He was a celibate, but he had close women friends. He dined at the home of Martha and Mary. He challenged the stereotyping of women by telling Martha, the cook, that he preferred to have her sister Mary remain and listen to his teaching, for she had chosen the better part. We, in our modern-day culture, forget that women were not welcome to study the Torah with the rabbi in the time of Christ. Jesus overthrew the traditional place of women as upheld by Martha. He associated with a woman recognized as a prostitute. Women were with him at his death. Though women were not allowed to be *witnesses* by Jewish law, Jesus appeared to the women as well as to his male disciples, thereby making them witnesses to his resurrection.

Jesus taught in parables. He told the story of the prodigal son and imaged God as a Father. But he associated "feminine" concepts with Father, Son, and Spirit in Scripture. To offer a few examples:

In Luke we hear: "What *woman* who has ten silver pieces and loses one, does not light a lamp and sweep the house in a diligent search until she retrieves what she has lost?" Jesus then relates this to the joy in heaven when one sinner repents.

In Matthew: "O Jerusalem, how often I have longed to gather your children as a hen gathers her brood under her wings...." This was at a critical moment of disappointment for Jesus as he describes himself as a mother hen.

Among those women who entered into a relationship with Jesus, in and through which they develped as full human persons, none equals the example of Mary of Nazareth. Sacred Scripture preserves for us the memory of the earliest community regarding her, the memory of a woman fearless enough to question the angel at the time of the annunciation, great-souled enough to endure the correction of her son and learn to go beyond the claims of family ties, heroic enough to stand beneath the cross and share the agony of Jesus' death. Generations of the faithful, meditating on this memory and praying to this lady, came to understand that she, too, is sinless, that she, too, has gone before us to the presence of God, being body and soul in heaven. This belief about Mary has been incorporated into the official teachings of the Church in the doctrines of the Immaculate Conception and the Assumption.

Is it any wonder, then, that Pope Paul VI referred to Mary as

> the perfect model of the disciple of the Lord; the disciple who builds up the earthly and temporal city while being a diligent pilgrim toward the heavenly and eternal city; the disciple who works for that justice which sets free the oppressed and for that charity which assists the needy; but above all, the disciple who is active witness of that love which builds up Christ in people's hearts. . . . Mary of Nazareth, while completely devoted to the will of God, was far from being a timidly submissive woman . . . on the contrary, she was a woman who did not hesitate to proclaim that God vindicates the humble and the oppressed and removes the powerful people of this world from their privileged positions (*Marialis Cultus*).

If it is true that human beings develop their personality in interaction with others, we can only conclude that Jesus grew in wisdom, age, and grace through his relationship with Mary as well as that with God the Father.

Woman as Absolutely Equal and Complementary to Man

To understand Church teaching and the developing consciousness of the discrimination against women in society and in the Church, let me quote from a pivotal document on Catholic social teaching and the unique dignity of the person. I refer to Pope John XXIII's *Peace on Earth* of April 11, 1963.

> Since women are becoming ever more conscious of their human dignity, they will not tolerate being treated as inanimate objects or mere instruments, but claim, both in domestic

and public life, the rights and duties that befit a human person.

Two other key texts to be considered in this document include one in which John XXIII sets forth the basic argument about human dignity and human society:

> Any human society, if it is to be well-ordered and productive, must lay down as a foundation this principle; namely, that every human being is a person; that is, his nature is endowed with intelligence and free will. Indeed, precisely because he is a person, he has rights and obligations flowing from his very nature. And as these rights are universal and inviolable, so they cannot in any way be surrendered.

There is a second key text in which the person is placed in a social context, for the person cannot come to full human potential outside a social context:

> Since men are social by nature, they are meant to live with others and to work for one another's welfare. A well-ordered human society requires that men recognize and observe their mutual rights and duties. It also demands that each contribute generously to the establishment of a civic order in which rights and duties are ever more sincerely and effectively acknowledged and fulfilled.

Two other documents that are very significant in developing the Church's teaching on women in society are the *Declaration on Religious Freedom* and *Gaudium et Spes*. Both clearly enumerate forms of discrimination against basic human rights which must be eliminated as being contrary to God's plan, and first place is given to discrimination based upon sex.

In the 1971 synod document on *Justice in the World*, we see the first acknowledgment of the need for the Church to relate its social teaching to its own life, structures, and practices:

> While the Church is bound to give witness to justice, she recognizes that anyone who ventures to speak to people about justice must first be just in their own eyes. Hence we must

undertake an examination of the modes of acting and of the possessions and life-style found within the Church herself. We also urge that women should have their own share of responsibility and participation in the community life of society and likewise of the Church. We propose that this matter be subjected to a serious study employing adequate means; for instance, a mixed commission of women and men.

In a 1974 address to Italian jurists, Pope Paul VI, while speaking on one hand of "the recognition of the civil rights of women as the full equals of men" and the need for "laws that will make it really possible for women to fill the same professional, social, and political roles as men," also speaks of the "protection of the special prerogatives of women in marriage, family, education, and society" and of "the maintenance and defense of the dignity of women as persons, unmarried women, wives, and widows; and the help they need, especially when the husband cannot fulfill his function in the family." Some would criticize this text as reminiscent of the adage: man's world and woman's place.

In January of 1977, the Vatican *Declaration on the Admission of Women to Ministerial Priesthood* made a clear distinction between civil and social equality and the question of women's human rights and the ministerial priesthood. The Sacred Congregation for the Doctrine of the Faith acknowledged that discrimination against women has existed and does exist in the Church and in society. The declaration emphasized the need for new ministries and positions to be found and opened for women. It clearly stated that the Church, in fidelity to the mind of Christ, does not see herself authorized to change an unbroken tradition and admit women to the ministerial priesthood. The Church's official teaching states that the maleness of the bishop or priest is constitutive of divine revelation about the economy of salvation as based on Jesus' intention and decision to choose only men as his apostles.

The declaration is careful to point out that the matter of ordination does not constitute a human right and concludes by speaking of the concept of complementarity—men and women are equal but not called to the same roles.

The declaration was mandated by Pope Paul VI. On numerous occasions, including his recent visit to the United States, Pope

John Paul II has reiterated the traditional decision of the Church.

This brief summary indicates the variety and complexity of official Church teaching relative to women and their place in the Church and in society.

How Does the Church Practice Its Teaching?

Having examined the high points of the Church's theory, I now wish to ask the following question: What do we find in the practice of the Church, and do we draw all possible conclusions from her noble teachings on person?

Presently, a national women and ministry study, a project of the Leadership Conference of Women Religious, is being conducted. While the study is not complete, some details that are available might be of interest here. A total of 950 women in ministry have been interviewed. Of the 950 respondents, the overwhelming number are laywomen and only 52 are women religious. Eighty percent of these women are married and living with spouses. In reporting on the types of ministries in which they are engaged, nine types of activities, both traditional and innovative ones, were reported by the women. Within liturgical ministry, 120 women are active in groups such as altar societies, 71 women are serving as lectors, and 101 are eucharistic ministers. Similarly, while many ministries involve supportive secretarial, fundraising, and church-maintenance functions, a sizeable group of women serves on parish councils or as parish officers. New types of ministry can be observed particularly in the social activist and in the spiritual category (e.g., preaching retreats).

It is clear to me that the consciousness of many people has been raised in the Church about the need to be sensitive to the role of women, and there are numerous examples where we can point to increased types of ministries and the practice of women in ministries. The National Association of Catholic Chaplains, for which I serve as episcopal liaison, is a professional organization of Catholic chaplains, primarily health-care chaplains. It has grown from no women members in 1972 to fifteen hundred presently involved in pastoral ministry.

Regarding the question of drawing all possible conclusions from the teaching on women as persons, I believe that we, at every level of Church life, have failed to be creative enough in implementing the possibilities these documents seem to indicate.

I wish to address two areas that are problematic, namely, attitude and Church system.

The Church at one time in her history of religious formation taught men and women to avoid interaction and to fear its possible consequences. Now, the Church is encouraging dialogue, shared ministry, and acceptance of women in new ministries and positions of influence in the Church. I believe it is natural that we men may feel threatened and fearful of the consequences to our own role of authority and service by interacting with and by inviting women to assume ministries. As an example of this insecurity in us, I recall the extreme sensitivity and caution which surrounded the appointment of a qualified person, who happened to be a woman, to the position of dean in a large Northeastern Catholic seminary.

In addition to such personal fears or anxieties, I believe the Church experiences systemic short-sightedness regarding women. In my evaluation of the systemic changes possible in the Church, there are, I feel, many more acceptable options than we have honored. Considering that the number of women who are preparing themselves for theological degrees has risen dramatically in recent years (there are 48,000 persons in seminaries of all Christian denominations; just three years ago, there were 3,000 women among these, and now there are 10,000), we need to ask the question: Where will we include these women in our local dioceses? In our parish system? They have no access to canonical office. Considering the number of Catholic women fully qualified at the top levels of the academic scene in this country, I do not believe we have often turned to them, formally, for consultation and expertise. Is there fairness in the fact that officially young girls cannot serve at the altar table? Is it fair that women who read the Word and plan the liturgy cannot be recognized by the Church in an official way?

While there are many women working in diocesan centers who have administrative responsibilities, few have access to active participation in the decision-making process at the highest levels. The same can be said at the national level and at the international level of Church decision-making.

Canonically, the vestiges of subservience remain: a woman's

domicile is her husband's; the constitution of religious communities of women must be approved by the Sacred Congregation of Religious, an all-male group; when people of different rites within Catholicism marry, the woman must change her rite to accommodate the man; only males can be diocesan vicars for religious because jurisdiction is tied to ordination.

These are only a few examples. It seems to me that, even excluding the possibility of ordination, there are many, many possibilities yet untapped for women to fulfill their call to serve and to promote the Church's mission.

I began this presentation by mentioning my firsthand exposure to the struggle of women within the Church. That same experience has made me aware that the ideas that I am stating are not universally accepted. There are men and women of good will within this Church who would take exception, and in fact have done so, to my own interpretation of the current experience. Perhaps no single event more dramatically and graphically illustrates this point than the reaction to Sister Theresa Kane's introduction of the Holy Father, Pope John Paul II, to the representatives of women religious gathered at the National Shrine of the Immaculate Conception. Sister Theresa became an instant symbol—for proponents of women's rights, she was a heroine; for antagonists, she was the symbol of all that is wrong with ecclesial feminism. Sister Theresa obviously did not cause the present disunity on this issue; she simply revealed the depth of feeling that exists on both sides of this sensitive question.

As a pastor, I feel a profound responsibility to engage in the search for a symbol of unity, a point toward which good-willed persons of different persuasions might come together. The pastoral task before us is to reflect, pray, speak, and listen until we come to that symbol or sign, to that sacramental reality, where we can stand together in unity.

Let me begin the dialogue by suggesting a symbol—a traditional image from Scripture—in the hope that it will encourage others to continue the search for the appropriate sign. In doing this, I also admit the limits of the suggested symbol.

The symbol I suggest is that of the "Body of Christ." I immediately want to state that I am not suggesting a literal interpretation of this image. A literal interpretation of the physical body of Christ

can lead only to the divisions flowing from the Vatican document
on the ordination of women. Viewed literally and physically, the
body of Christ becomes the grounds for a distinction and separation of men and women within Church society.

I am speaking here of the image of the Body of Christ as used by
St. Paul, especially in his first letter to the Corinthians, and to a
lesser extent in his letter to the Ephesians. In Corinthians, the body
becomes an analogue for the communal interaction of the members, the Church. The Body of Christ becomes, then, the focal
point of unity of disparate but interrelated parts. What the parts
are to the body, we are to Christ. This passage is Paul's attempt to
affirm the two values of unity and diversity.

I think it is important to note that the pastoral use of this image
does not assert that all members are the same, but it does asert that
all members, though different, are bound together in mutual interdependence.

In the twelfth chapter of Corinthians, where he is speaking of
the variety of the spiritual gifts of the community, Paul uses the
analogy of the human body to describe this relationship of those
gifts. He makes three applications of that analogy that might well be
seen as a framework for pastoral approaches to the issue of women
in the Church.

The first application is the necessity of differences within the
body. "If all the parts were the same," Paul states, "how could it
be a body?" "Nor is the body to be identified with one of its many
parts." Paul's statements constitute not just a recognition that differences exist, but he affirms the necessity of differences. This
point suggests to me that the current structure of the Church ought
to reflect a healthy acceptance of differences. Especially in decision-making bodies on the parish, diocesan, institutional, and
international levels, a balanced representation of men and women
would more fully express the reality that is the whole body. In
practice today, I believe that the local parish community is leading the way by the balanced inclusion of women on parish collegial bodies and in public ministerial roles. Diocesan structures are
beginning to feel the impact of women's voices as women share in
such key roles as vicar for religious, personnel directors, and in at
least three dioceses as chancellor. The international level of Church
structure has been strong in the area of articulation of women's

rights. The development of a practice, however, generally seems heavily influenced by the sometimes contradictory multiplicity of cultural norms that affect any international body.

The second application of Paul's body analogy is the statement of mutual need. "The eye cannot say to the hand: 'I do not need you'; nor can the head say to the feet: 'I do not need you.'" The more universal integration of women into the Church is not an act of tolerance; it is an act of necessity. There is something missing when the voice or the presence of women is not impacting on the whole Church. We have long recognized that women have unique and indispensable gifts to share in the Church's mission. In this country, the Catholic school system, the health-care system, and, to a lesser extent, the social-service system were created and controlled by women. We need now to rethink our ministry-call system. Longstanding assumptions about what is a man's work and what is a woman's work may not be valid. Our starting point must be—here is a real pastoral need. The next question is: Who is the gifted person who can respond to that need and is willing to do so? We then need to find creative ways of structuring, supporting, and publicly calling gifted persons to the fulfillment of that ministry. If pastoral need is our starting point and recognized giftedness is the test, the limits placed upon men and women in Church service will be natural ones and not socially discriminatory ones.

The third application in Corinthians is the mutual vulnerability of all members. "If one part is hurt, all parts are hurt with it. If one part is given special honor, all parts enjoy it." As a pastoral concern, I ask the question: Who are the groups who are especially vulnerable on this issue of the place of women in the Church? The two that come to mind immediately are: first, women who are actively trying to raise our consciousness and transform the Church system; and secondly, the current male leadership of the Church, especially the ordained clergy. May I say just a few words about the latter?

Many men were prepared for a priesthood that consolidated all the functions of ministry in themselves as priests. With the advent of the Second Vatican Council, there emerged the whole concept of the place and role of all the baptized in the mission and ministry of the Church. Many priests were not prepared for this development either theologically or practically. Many did not have the necessary skills to order logically the new ministries that were developing and the capacity to work with them. Nor were our laypersons well prepared to assume the new roles implied by this changed understanding nor sometimes to receive such services from their peers.

Many priests regard as a diminishment of their priesthood the sharing with the laity of the functions that had always been associated with the priesthood. I am deeply troubled by this perception of diminishment. Is something being withdrawn from the priesthood on behalf of the developing new ministries, or are priests being liberated for a new and deeper understanding of their ministry of preaching the Word and servant leadership?

It is clear that no bishop could fulfill his ministry without an effective relationship with his priests as his principal collaborators. In my view, thousands of our priests in this country have responded with outstanding faith, good will, and generosity to the tremendous expectations and new demands made upon them as we have tried to renew ourselves as a Church and as a presbyterate. I have deep concern for the feelings of displacement and the fatigue factor in the lives of many priests. As we continue to call forth ministries of women, it is my hope that we can also enhance and strengthen the essential role of the ordained priesthood.

Conclusion

Pope John Paul II, prior to becoming pope, contributed his own understanding of the person in a philosophical book entitled *The Acting Person*. His insight in this book is that *acting*, taken in the widest sense, both reveals and completes the meaning of being a person. Action, you might say, is the *signature* of the person because it manifests the interior potential that lays hidden in the depths of personal life. In reading his first and programmatic encyclical, *Redemptor Hominis*, and his address at the United Nations, we see the theme of human dignity as central to his philosophical and theological perspective. The person is central to the theological vision, but the human person can only be understood in light of a christological vision; and both the person and Christ shape one view of the ministry of the Church.

There are many actions we can take as together we create a

Church and a society through the influence of the Church as a leaven, a light, and the salt that truly is perceived as and is just and equal in its teaching and practice toward men and women as persons. Most important, I believe, is the patient, painful dialogue that needs to be carried out in love at every level. The words of John Paul II in the homily given at Grant Park speak eloquently of the necessity of unity:

> Love is the power that gives rise to dialogue, in which we listen to each other and learn from each other. Love gives rise, above all, to the dialogue of prayer in which we listen to God's word, which is alive in the Holy Bible and alive in the life of the Church.
> Let love then build the bridges across our differences and at times our contrasting positions. Let love for each other and love for the truth be the answer to polarization, when factions are formed because of differing views in matters that relate to faith or to the priorities for action.

Presently, the National Conference of Catholic Bishops and representatives of the Women's Ordination Conference are in dialogue on the theme "To discover, understand, and promote the full potential of woman as person in the life of the Church." This has been an important step in developing both a level of trust and a new understanding of the issues surrounding women in the Church and in society.

I urge each of you to have hope in your own selves as you contribute your gifts to this movement toward Church unity.

May I close with a simple story in which a fifth-grade girl wrote a letter to God. She wrote: "Dear God, are boys really better than girls? I know you are one, but please try to be fair." And God answers: "Male and female I made them in my image." And St. Paul speaks for Christ: "There does not exist among you slave or free man, male or female. . . ."

14

The Continuing Arms Race: Waging War against the Third World

ROGER M. MAHONY
Archbishop of Los Angeles

In my own pastoral letter of December 1981 dealing with the issues of war and peace in the nuclear age, I emphasized that the continuing nuclear and conventional arms race was not only a folly, but that it was also a serious attack upon the economic life and development of most Third World countries.

I quoted the Holy See's testimony at the 1976 United Nations Conference on Disarmament:

> The arms race is to be condemned unreservedly. By virtue of the nature of modern weapons and the situation prevailing on our planet, even when motivated by a concern for legitimate defense, the armaments race is in fact a danger, an injustice, a mistake, a sin and a folly.
>
> The obvious contradiction between the waste involved in the overproduction of military devices and the extent of the unsatisfied vital needs is in itself an act of aggression against those who are its victims (both in developing countries and in the marginal and poor elements in rich societies). It is an act of aggression which amounts to a crime, for even when they are not used, by their cost alone armaments kill the poor by causing them to starve. (May 7, 1976)

Delivered at the Cathedral-Basilica of St. James in Brooklyn on April 29, 1984.

In the U.S. Catholic bishops' pastoral letter on the same topic, *The Challenge of Peace: God's Promise and Our Response,* we raised the same theme and pointed to the same contradictions:

> We see with increasing clarity the political folly of a system which threatens mutual suicide, the psychological damage this does to ordinary people, especially the young, the economic distortion of priorities—billions readily spent for destructive instruments while pitched battles are waged daily in our legislature over much smaller amounts for the homeless, the hungry, and the helpless here and abroad. (par. 134)

We quoted the Second Vatican Council's *Pastoral Constitution on the Church in the Modern World* when we stated:

> The arms race is one of the greatest curses on the human race and the harm it inflicts upon the poor is more than can be endured. (par. 13)

In section three of the bishops' pastoral letter, we call attention to the sinful relationship between massive arms expenditures on the one hand, and the frightful neglect of millions of people's basic needs on the other:

> If the arms race in all its dimensions is not reversed, resources will not be available for the human needs so evident in many parts of the globe and in our own country as well. (see paragraphs 269–73)

This paper affords me the opportunity to expand upon these themes and to outline some of the many dimensions of the worldwide arms production and trade, as well as how the economies of both developing and developed countries are adversely affected by the spiraling arms race.

In section one of my paper, I will survey how military expenditures are a major factor of underdevelopment in the Third World or Southern Hemisphere nations.

In section two, I will outline the impact and implications of military spending upon the developed countries.

And finally, section three will touch upon our collective call as "artisans of peace" to work toward full disarmament so that genuine resource development—both human and material—will propel us as a world community into a new era of peace, justice, health, prosperity, and broad development.

Introduction

The arms race, for a long time restricted to developed countries only, has become a world-wide phenomenon. For a number of years, new arms have been devised that threaten mankind with mortal and unprecedented danger.

The available nuclear arsenal is presently 1 million times more deadly than the Hiroshima bomb. Nations live with the dangerous illusion that they can protect themselves through increased armaments that, on the contrary, result in decreased efforts at combatting poverty. Since the last World War more than 130 armed conflicts have threatened the peace of the world, while at the same time massive hunger is still plaguing mankind.

The threats to security are not limited to armaments only. They are part of the total economic crisis in developed countries, the increase in unemployment and unjust conditions of life, underdevelopment and the ravaging of the environment. "Economy" has become an instrument for domination. The economic war kills tens of millions of children each year through hunger and malnutrition.

Meanwhile, military spending reached $850 billion in 1983, according to the estimate of the general secretary of the United Nations.

The sum of $850 billion seems to be an amount of military expenditures acknowledged by the majority of the international community. The financial output in defense spending by governments increased five times over during the period between 1948 and 1984. It is interesting to note that while the NATO and Warsaw Pact countries accounted for more than 85 percent of world military spending in 1960, they represented only 65 percent of total military expenditures in 1984.

In contrast, the developing countries increased their share of military spending between 10 percent and 16 percent of the total expenditures. A group of experts from the United Nations studying the economic and social consequences of the arms race published additional figures that are very significant, as follows:

• Military budgets represent 6 percent of total world production, and they amount to over 25 percent of the regular investments in a world that is in such economic and social crisis.

• The military-industrial production amounts to $180 billion and is concentrated principally in the developed countries of the United States, the Soviet Union, France, and Britain.

• The budget for military research and development represents one quarter of the money spent in world research and development as a whole. One must also point out that it is not always easy to determine whether the nature of research is nonmilitary or military. It would seem that the published figures concern only the research and development that is exclusively military, which clearly underestimates the actual financial effort in military research and development.

Although the total amount of military spending in world production has decreased (it was 9 percent in 1950), this evolution is not as favorable for peace as it would appear, for at least two reasons.

First, the expenses devoted to armed forces, especially in the nuclear area, are more and more effective for each dollar spent. In other words, the effectiveness in potential deaths through armaments increases without a comparable increase in cost. Consequently, the nuclear weapons that are so frightening to us all represent less than 20 percent of the world military expenditures.

Secondly, since 1978 the superpowers have definitely increased their military spending, thus being responsible for the frightening acceleration of funds destined for military purposes.

The problem that confronts us is to determine what could be done alternatively with $850 billion now being spent in the military sector. Allow me to share a few informative examples with you:

• According to the Food and Agriculture Organization of the United Nations, roughly 1 percent to 2 percent of world military expenditures would be enough to transfer 2 percent of the world's cereal production to those who need it most to eliminate malnutrition.

• The price of one aircraft carrier ($500 million) would suffice to finance a campaign to eradicate debilitating and crippling diseases such as malaria, trachoma, leprosy, and intense suffering in the developing countries.

• The price of two strategic nuclear bombers ($200 million) would enable UNESCO to wipe out illiteracy from the face of the world within ten years.

• World military expenditures are twenty times larger than the amount of aid being given to all the developing countries in the world.

The importance of the world military effort cannot be measured only in terms of the funds assigned to it. Actually, military expenditures are unproductive expenditures, and because of this, their influence over the world economy becomes negative at a global level. They exert negative effects on the growth and development of the underdeveloped as well as the developed countries.

1. Military Expenditures: A Factor in Underdevelopment

The analysis of the impact of military spending on economic development in the more underprivileged countries is generally focused upon four main aspects: (1) the link between military expenses and economic growth; (2) the massive arms trade; (3) the industrialization caused by setting up an armament industry in the poorer countries; and finally, (4) the sociological, political, and economic effects of the militarization of national economies.

Military Expenses and Economic Growth

The effect of military expenses over economic growth in the countries from the Southern Hemisphere was the subject of a passionate debate following the publication of Emile Benoit's study that stressed the lack of a permanent link between military expenses and the gross national product of forty-four developing countries.

A few analysts had too hastily concluded from this that military spending had no negative effect over the economic growth of developing countries. Several empirical studies were subsequently conducted and they underlined the weaknesses in the methodology and theory of Emile Benoit's analysis. Several general conclusions could be derived from this empirical research.

First, an increase in military spending is conducive to increased budget deficits and often results in a flaring up of inflationary tensions. This situation discourages saving and investment. Besides, an increase in military spending is detrimental to overall investment because the consumption of developing countries is almost impossible to reduce. Consequently, useful resources are sidetracked toward military spending.

Secondly, there is often a direct or indirect relationship between military spending and economic growth in underdeveloped countries. It is generally a negative relationship but there are a few exceptions. The Southern Hemisphere countries that benefit from an increase in military spending have special characteristics. On the one hand, they receive important amounts of aid from abroad during periods of international tensions, and they are constantly manufacturing arms, even exporting them.

On the other hand, they are very dependent upon the superpowers. These characteristics underline the very precarious character of this growth caused by an increase of military spending. The political support of both aid and the sale of arms can be withdrawn at any time, which would then lead such countries into a frightful recession.

And thirdly, even though, in the short term, an increase in military budgets can be favorable to economic growth, it exerts in the long run a negative effect over the country's entire economic development, which is a more extensive phenomenon than the mere increase of the national product. It is not enough to increase production year after year. This must be a cumulative process, which evidently is not the case in a development policy based on the spending and the exportation of military supplies.

Military expenditures have a negative effect over the economies of developing countries. The arms trade widens the gap between Northern and Southern Hemisphere countries.

The Arms Trade

Most developing countries buy their military equipment from already overarmed developed countries, and about one-third of all arms imports are delivered to the Third World. These arms sales and imports have different goals.

First, for the supplying countries, this kind of exportation helps reduce the cost of arms that are mass produced in their own countries, and it provides an opportunity to receive a sizeable amount of foreign currency. Consequently, these supplying countries exert strong pressure on the Third World countries to buy military equipment that improves the former countries' balance of payments and increases the dependency of the poorer countries.

Secondly, some areas in the Third World are still politically unstable. Decolonization has created new ambitions that the purchase of sophisticated armaments satisfies or escalates.

Thirdly, the national armies of the poor countries play a role that is part of the international division of labor. They support the national elites who are themselves often subservient to the ideologies of the larger world. Close to half of the governments in underdeveloped countries are led by military regimes of one kind or another.

Fourthly, recently independent countries are convinced of the necessity to create an army that would assert their national sovereignty. This attitude is always perilous.

The consequences of these arms purchases by poor countries are very serious, and for these reasons:

First, the cost of military equipment abroad is relatively low compared to the political and economical gains to be made by such arms purchases. The buying nations are, in addition, very vulnerable to the cultural values transmitted through the technology of the armaments vendors. This can result in a cultural domination that is not favorable to local development.

Secondly, from an exclusively economic point of view, the developing countries use up their national resources or their currency reserves in order to buy materials that will not further their much needed growth. Not only are military expenditures substituted for investments, but such expenditures squander the scant currency reserves that are needed to import goods essential to the growth of the local national economies.

And thirdly, in order to maintain their security through military means the developing countries are usually still underarmed. Even if they spent their entire national wealth on armaments the situation would not be altered appreciably.

The developing countries must act on the international scene in order to force the larger powers to begin a genuine disarmament process.

If the international arms business is so harmful to the economic growth of developing countries, must they then manufacture their own armaments?

Arms Production

The negative impact of military spending over investments in the developing countries is not always realized by the governments that supply the armaments. Some of the Third World countries have partly founded their developmental strategy on the armament industry. They stress the advantages of the home manufacturing of arms that reduces the political and military dependency on the supplying countries, limits the importation of arms, saves currency, improves the balance of payments, definitely improves the competency of the national labor force, and results in a more satisfactory mastering of modern technologies.

India and Argentina, for example, have practiced this policy of import substitution that aims at increasing the national manufacturing of imported products. These two countries believe that arms production is "industrializing," that is, favorable to industrialization, an essential factor of development. This concept omits the negative factors in this approach, as we shall note:

First, the arms systems are very costly if they do not benefit from important savings on a large scale (that is, a reduction of cost per unit through mass production). A fighter plane is sold in the United States in units of 1,000 to 5,000 planes. The Third World countries often only need ten of them, which results in elevated costs for developing countries unless they resort to mass exportation. This is quite a risky gamble economically, given the competition from the big armaments companies in developed countries. This approach, obviously, cannot be extended to all countries.

Secondly, military investments are very costly in terms of capital expenditures, and they require a highly qualified labor force. In addition, the armament sector is characterized by a rapid pace in innovation, and the Third World countries can hardly keep up, owing to the limited size of their research and development sector.

Thirdly, arms production often requires importing more goods. Most of the time it is restricted to the assembling of foreign parts or manufacturing them under the control of the developed countries. Among forty-five types of airplanes manufactured in 1982 by the Third World countries, twenty-three (or almost half) were under foreign patent. This ratio rises to more than two-thirds in the home manufacture of missiles.

And fourthly, military and civilian technologies do not have the same goals or the same limitations. The former focuses on technical performance, whereas the latter is primarily concerned with the marketability of the project. The armaments industry tends to use costly investments with mediocre profit potential, which the civilian industry could not sustain for long since it is concerned with profit or added value.

This analysis leads me, consequently, to the view that arms production in developing countries does not further economic growth since the economic dependency that it imposes remains very significant. The overall effects on a nation's industries appears extremely negative. Countries with mediocre military power become very dependent on the international markets and on the vendors themselves.

The Military Sector: An Instrument for Possible Domination

The threat of using armaments, or their actual use, have traditionally been decisive factors in the dissemination or transplantation of the dominant economic system. In the nineteenth century, colonization took place through war, through force, through hard labor and slavery, or through the expulsion of the country people from their lands. Through armed coercion colonized countries very often underwent a process of the destructuring of their societies.

Decolonization has not resolved the problems created by military domination. The national armies of weak and needy countries have a role within the international distribution of work, and they often ally themselves with the social groups that are subservient to a foreign power as a foreign political system. It is not correct to say, however, that all the armed forces in the Third World countries have a negative role. Sometimes they are instrumental in increasing the rate of exploitation of available resources, in transferring the agricultural surpluses into industrial uses, and in managing the surplus released through collective discipline in order to implement social and economic growth.

Sometimes military leaders seem to be on the side of progress since they train recruits, they develop the national infrastructure, they nationalize some sectors that are of vital interest to the country, and they introduce new techniques to their countries. Examples are abundant in our contemporary world, however, of military powers that are incompetent, dictatorial, dependent on a foreign political and/or cultural model, and unable to overcome the economic crisis. It is difficult to generalize, but it would seem that at a global level, the military governments have not yet arrived at adequate formulas to solve the problems of their countries.

On the other hand, the developed countries, because of their military power, derive profit from their huge commercial strength. In times of international conflict, the big powers strive to guarantee delivery of their supplies, and in order to achieve this they use every means available (intimidation, military aid, political destabilization, etc.). In times of détente the big powers endeavor to encourage their partners in that type of production that commits the selling country more than the buying country, resulting in the former's increasing subordination. An example of this is Cuba, which has become exclusively dependent upon the Soviet Union for the sale of its sugar.

The developing countries cannot manufacture their own armaments without running the risk of seriously endangering their potential for development. The importation of arms weakens these countries and opens the door to all sorts of economic, political, and technological domination. The arms race condemns them to play the role of the victim, for they lack the means to create a military force able to compete with the larger powers. Military spending does not really preserve the independence of the developing countries nor does it allow them to build their own positive future.

2. Military Spending: A Factor of Impoverishment in Developed Countries

For the last six or seven years the developed countries have been plagued by a grave economic crisis. The growth in world production went from 4.6 percent in 1978 to less than 2 percent in 1983. This widespread decline in growth rates was accompanied by strong inflation and a disturbing rate of unemployment. In this situation the option for military expenditures assumes a considerable significance, for it neither stimulates consumption directly nor does it improve the capability for production.

The burden of military expenditures is measured in "opportunity costs," that is, the civilian goods and services which could have been available with the equivalent of the amounts spent by the military.

A Factor in the Slowdown of Growth

Military expenditures have increased at an approximate real rate of 3 percent a year since 1978, thus increasing the overall economic burden. Historically, expenses were associated with a strong economy. This general rule, however, is not verified any longer since military expenditures have obviously expanded in a period of recession. What are the consequences of such a state of affairs?

First, when the factors of production imply unemployment or underemployment, military expenditures have a momentary stimulant effect upon the economy as a result of the effect of multiplication. Some governments have sometimes used military expenses to combat unemployment and reduce global demand. Some Marxist economists (Baran and Sweezy, for example) even think that the increase of American military spending is necessary to the American economic system in its effort to counteract cyclical long-term declining profits. This theory, however, is at present rejected by many empirical analysts, which clearly underscores the negative role that military expenditures have in the long run on the growth of developed market economies.

Whereas it is possible, in the short term, to use military spending in order to reinvigorate the economy, one must point out that other expenditures in the fields of health and education produce the same effects. The implementation of a policy of increased military spending leads to militarizing the economy, developing military-industrial complexes, and creating conflicting political strategy.

When full employment is secured, the choice between "guns and butter" has to be faced. Military expenditures exert effects that are immediately negative on lowering inflation, budget deficits, and economic growth. This is not to say that the military effort is of necessity useless as far as security is concerned, since the people of a country can accept the risk of an unbalanced economy in order to safeguard their security.

Our own country's policy, in this respect, is a very good example. In an economy whose industrial potential is largely underutilized, it proposes to compete with the alleged military superiority of the

Soviet Union and to relaunch the economy on a more sound basis. It proposes both an increase in military spending compensated in part through a reduction in other public expenditures and a tax reduction.

In fact, this policy has led to formidable federal deficits in spite of a cut in social-service expenditures. By directly preventing a balance of public finances, the military effort leads to high interest rates and the development of inflationary tensions. This has several consequences, as follows:

First, according to the United Nations report on the "Economic and Social Consequences of the Arms Race," $1 billion spent in nonmilitary sectors of the economy generally creates two to four times more jobs than the same amount spent for military purposes. By increasing military spending one does not fight unemployment; one increases it and this, consequently, leads to increased poverty.

Secondly, military expenses are in direct opposition to social-service expenditures, and as a result, the poor bear the costs.

Thirdly, the increasing value of the dollar has resulted from the shrinking supply of capital and has depressed the economies of the allied countries, leading to a new wave of unemployment worldwide.

And fourthly, those who bear the brunt of inflation are those people living on fixed incomes and those working for the lowest salaries. Inflation leads to a redistribution of income that is primarily favorable to people in higher-income brackets. Military spending leads to a soaring of inflationary tendencies.

According to the United Nations report on "Disarmament as a Stimulus to Broader Development," military spending generally affects unfavorably the economic growth of countries, whether they are on a planned economy or a market economy. In both cases, the stepping up of the arms race has cumulative effects harmful to the economy that, as time elapses, are more and more difficult to correct.

Not only do military expenditures not improve poor people's lot, they tend to be detrimental to their total social welfare. In addition, the military monopolize certain occupations that, later on, will not be easily transferred back to the nonmilitary domain. Such is the case, for example, with nuclear energy.

Nuclear Proliferation

In 1955, the international scientific community compiled exchange information about nuclear energy and explored all the potential civilian uses of nuclear energy. Born during the Second World War, nuclear energy was to offer to the world a new era of peace and abundance as the result of increased control of man over nature. By 1981, however, some 300 nuclear-energy plants had been built producing 3 percent of the world's energy, but benefitting only four countries: the United States, the Soviet Union, France, and Japan.

Nuclear energy, however, also means 300 ships and submarines propelled by nuclear reactors and a stockpile of weapons with an incredible destructive power equivalent to 16,000 megatons of conventional explosives.

While nuclear energy is now well entrenched in the world, civilian nuclear achievements have remained far beneath what had been projected, and the reverse has resulted with the military use of nuclear power. Several reasons can help explain this trend.

First, nuclear-energy plants are often confused with nuclear weapons. This confusion is misleading and mistaken, but it is firmly implanted in many people's minds.

And secondly, the military and civilian uses of nuclear power cannot be disassociated. A country that can control the techniques for the production of nuclear energy and the whole cycle of plutonium production is in control of the processes necessary for the production of nuclear weapons. This phenomenon explains the crisis of the nuclear-energy industry. The nuclear powers have tried to set up legal protections acceptable to all governments that would guarantee exclusive civilian use of nuclear-power installations, but regrettably no international accords have proved binding and effective.

The development of nuclear energy also promotes as an inevitable consequence the potential for the destruction of all mankind.

While it is exaggerated to assign nuclear reactors to military spending, experts are persuaded that there is danger in the proliferation of nuclear weapons, for the present reactors provide more than eighty tons of plutonium a year, sufficient to construct 8,000 nuclear weapons as powerful as the Hiroshima bomb.

Nuclear energy is potentially a factor for the progress of mankind in its nonmilitary uses. But because of the arms race, it is unfortunately a factor for destruction. The militarization of this energy source makes its wider development extremely dangerous and thereby prevents its acceptability to resolve the serious energy problems of all countries.

3. Working toward Disarmament for Development

In my opinion, total world economic development is closely linked inevitably to real progress in the area of disarmament. It is unjust to produce weapons of destruction while the fundamental needs of so many peoples remain unmet. Since they are not genuinely productive, military expenditures are squandering vital resources at an extraordinary rate and level.

Disarmament implies setting limits to international competition and the firm refusal to found economies on power struggles. Any disarmament plan that would not reduce relationships based on domination or exploitation would simply perpetuate the inequalities among people in our world community. Disarmament has genuine meaning only when based on respect for the dignity of each person, the guarantee of human rights, the promotion of social justice, and sovereignty and equality among nations.

A study by Nobel prize recipient Wassily Leontieff and Faye Duchin emphasized the significance of disarmament for development. This study includes several armament scenarios and provides economic predictions based on those criteria. The main results of this study are helpful in our present discussion, as follows:

First, a decision for a 1.2 percent reduction per year of military expenditures until the year 2000 would lead to an additional economic growth of:

- 3 percent for Eastern Europe
- 1 percent for Japan
- 1.5 percent for North America and Western Europe
- 3 percent for Latin America
- 13 percent for sub-Sahara Africa

And secondly, this same reduction coupled with development aid from richer countries to poorer countries would create no growth reduction for the developed countries, but it would enable the developing countries to attain a substantial economic growth. Supposing that in the year 1990 15 percent and in the year 2000 20 percent of the reduction in military spending would be allotted to the development of sub-Sahara Africa, we would see this area's per-capita gross national product increase 246 percent; among Asian countries with low incomes, a 40 percent increase would result; among Latin American countries with moderate incomes, a 17 percent increase would result; and among the countries of tropical Africa, a 56 percent increase would result.

This study clearly stresses the advantages of choosing a disarmament policy from a purely economic point of view. Needless to say, a limitation of the arms race—both conventional and nuclear —is our greatest desire for the sake of peace and fraternity among nations. The Institute of Research on Disarmament at the United Nations is at present investigating the creation of an International Disarmament Fund for Development, founded on a simple principle: It would collect part of the proceeds from the reduction in military spending in the more affluent and better-armed countries, and it would redistribute these funds in the form of grants or loans to the poorer and less-protected countries. This idea deserves our support to complement a more general move toward disarmament.

Through their direct and indirect effects, military expenditures affect quite unfavorably economic development, and the more underprivileged social groups in our world community are the main victims.

Governments seek to protect themselves, and to that end, they arm themselves. The constantly escalating arms race becomes frighteningly irrational for the whole of mankind while the dangers of pursuing suicidal privileges threaten to multiply the number of world-wide conflicts.

Our genuine hope for a better and more just world lies precisely in our authentic discipleship of our risen Lord. May each one of us allow that limitless power of Christ Jesus to change our own hearts, to make us artisans of his peace, and to work for that full development of all peoples and nations that is his will!

REFERENCES

Benoit, E., "Growth and Defense in Developing Countries," *Economic Development and Cultural Change*, no. 2, January 26, 1978.

Fontanel, Jacques, Directeur-Adjoint, Centre d'Etudes de Défense et de Sécurité Internationale de Grenoble. Several Articles between 1977 and the present dealing with the question of the arms race and developing countries.

Leontieff, W., and Duchin, F., "Worldwide Implications of Hypothetical Changes in Military Spending," United Nations, New York, 1980.

Mahony, Most Reverend Roger, "Becoming a Church of Peace Advocacy," December 30, 1981, Stockton, California.

National Conference of Catholic Bishops, *The Challenge of Peace: God's Promise and Our Response*, May 3, 1983.

United Nations, New York. "Study of the Relationship between Disarmament and Development," 1981.

———."Reduction of Military Budgets," 1981.

———."Economic and Social Consequences of the Arms Race and Military Expenditures," 1978 and 1983.

———."Relationship of the Reduction in Military Spending," 1982.

15

A Gospel Life-style
in a Consumer Society

REMBERT G. WEAKLAND, O.S.B.
Archbishop of Milwaukee

Some texts of the Bible seem to remain smothered for centuries—
and then pop out to haunt us as if never seen before; the many texts
on the role of women in the Gospel and life of the early Church are
examples of such passages. Other texts seem to be constantly before our eyes, in every moment and for every generation, but sel-
dom do they find a neat resolution. An example of this kind of text
is Matthew 6:24–31; we cannot serve two masters, God and money;
we should not worry about what we are to eat, drink, or use for
clothing; we should look at the birds of the air and the lilies of the
field; we should stop worrying about tomorrow: our heavenly Father knows all of our needs.

These latter texts, in addition to those on renunciation, the story
of the rich young man, the story of Lazarus and the rich man—all
of these continue to prick our consciences and leave us with a sense
of unresolved ambivalence. They bothered the Church of every
age. We argue, for example, for days on the meaning of the beati-
tude "Blessed are the poor" as found in Luke and then in Matthew
as "poor in spirit," and the differences between the two. Often we
come away with a bit of existential *angst*: Are we seeking easy
ways out by preferring Matthew's "Blessed are the poor *in spirit?*"

For me these texts have been the object of much personal medi-

Delivered at the Cathedral-Basilica of St. James in Brooklyn on May 1, 1983.

tation and examination for the past five years, that is, since I was named a bishop. The first years of my life, those that coincided with the Great Depression, were spent in fighting and rising above poverty and the indignities it inflicted. My happy years as a Benedictine monk—some thirty-two—seemed to pose no problems. With a vow of poverty, life was more or less cut out for me. Only now must I make constant decisions for myself: What kind of car should I drive? Where should I live? Where should I buy my suits? Should I be seen in such and such a restaurant? What hotel should I stay at? And a thousand others. I feel guilty with such a fine grand piano; I feel guilty with such a fine stereo; I feel guilty with a thousand fine books. (It is easy to see why I yearn again for the cloister!) But it has all been helpful to me as a person, and I hope the confrontations of life-style and Gospel have not been without their positive effects.

It has been helpful, because more and more doctors, more and more lawyers, more and more professional people have been talking to me in similar ways. Life-style is now important for every Christian. We are being forced to make choices and ask what the biblical texts just cited mean to us personally today.

Perhaps it is the contrast with Third World countries, perhaps it is a new awareness of poverty in our own urban areas that forces us to a personal reexamination of our own values and how we project them in our lives.

What I wish to reflect on are some rudimentary values and attitudes concerning the Kingdom and the "poor" that I have had to make my own and that I want to share with you.

The first I will call the need for personal conversion. It is only proper that the Church today examine the economic system under which it has to function and point out those aspects of the system that produce effects in a society that one could call unjust or un-Christian. The National Conference of Catholic Bishops, having undertaken such a study on communism, is now engaged in a similar study of the American economic system in the light of the values proposed in the papal social encyclicals.

What is more important to remember, however, is that Christian and Gospel values become a part of a social fabric through people. People must be converted and bring their values to the economic fabric they live in. Thus my paper is not about systems, but about people today. One could say that it is beginning from the bottom up and not from the top down.

Although we live in a consumer society and must bring our Gospel values to bear on that society, we must still ask ourselves the question: Are there values and attitudes grounded in the Gospel that should be ours as Christians—regardless of the time, period of history, or economic system we must live under? Vatican II rightly pointed out that the Church has no proper mission in the economic order as such, that is, one cannot find in the Gospel an economic system; nevertheless, the Gospel does expect us to bring to this world those values that are inherent in the Gospel message and that will, thus, affect the whole of the social fabric in which we live, including the decisions made that bear on the economic system. But it is people who use such systems. So often, however, they feel manipulated by the system rather than its controller.

In addition to personal life-style one has to ask a question about a communal life-style for Christians today. These two questions go hand in hand, but it seems to me that the first—the personal life-style—should be our place of beginning. The reason again is that conversion is in the heart of the individual, and there is no substitute for that personal conversion.

When I was abbot of my monastery at Latrobe, I used to say that the poverty of the monastery had to be the sum total of the poverty of each individual. Many times I visited monasteries that lived very frugally—but out of necessity, not out of conviction. One can have little but be constantly distressed and preoccupied to have more. One of the poorest monasteries I had visited as abbot primate of the Benedictine Confederation was Koubri in Upper Volta. The monks were diligent and industrious, but there was no real market for their banana soda. I was indeed edified when they asked to discuss with me—in all their poverty—if their life-style was still too high compared to their neighbors around them. Such sensitivity is uncommon in nations striving for development.

If this paper deals with personal conversion, a follow-up could deal with that conversion and the role of the community.

Next I would like to deal with the concept of renunciation and the things of this world because it is involved in that conversion. There has been so much ink spilled on the word "poverty," especially among us religious, that I almost hesitate to use it. They told me that my vow of poverty was "suspended" when I was made a bishop; and yet, for the first time, it has become a reality of choice to me.

In biblical terms one can talk about "the poor," or detachment, or renunciation, but not really about poverty as a virtue. From the story of Jesus' life we see that he was voluntarily poor, born in poor circumstances, living as son in a poor family. His life-style should have meaning in itself for us. He never refused gifts from those with means—the apostles had a purse, but he did not cater to the rich. Often he was found eating in the homes of the rich if they were generous and sharing. Never did he try to convince all the rich to give up their possessions, as a class, to be like him. On occasion, however, he demanded that kind of renunciation from his own disciples, or from those like the rich young man, who would then follow him like early charismatic nomads; but he did not demand this of all his followers.

On the other hand, he certainly pointed out the dangers inherent in riches. He knew all too well that riches could become the end in themselves, leaving no time for the Kingdom and its pursuit. He also knew that riches could corrupt. It is interesting to note in the story of Lazarus and the rich man—often called Dives—how the rich man, even after death, while in his torment, thought he could command the services of Lazarus. People cease to be considered persons when their services can be bought.

If we return to the concept of renunciation, we find that it is incumbent on all followers of Christ. A certain discipline of self is needed to pick up one's cross daily and follow Christ. This renunciation also goes beyond that need to avoid evil, to avoid sin. It is a positive call for the Kingdom. It is that enthusiasm on finding the pearl of great value and renouncing all else for it.

Most of all, renunciation is freeing. That is the key word. It helps us break through those barriers that keep us from being free to give of self for others in obedience to God's call to build the Kingdom. It should be noted that Jesus demands of the rich young man that he give to the poor those valued possessions of his. Jesus does not ask—as became customary in religious life—that he add his riches to the already stored up riches of the community, namely, to add to the greater security of all. Charity is always associated with renunciation. Generosity comes from the freedom gained and is the source of the hundred fold Jesus speaks of.

Lest we deceive ourselves into taking an easy way out, we must reflect on the preferential option Jesus had for the poor. Jesus does have a special place in his heart for the poor. Rosemary Haughton put it well when she stated that Wisdom will find a home in the poor Christ, the oppressed, denounced, shunned, tortured, and dying Christ; in that place, she remarks, Wisdom will be "wearing an apron rather than a crown." But to discover that kind of Wisdom, she writes,

> poverty is needed. To "lay aside bias," to strip oneself of the protection not only of colonialism and a cassock but of the cultural self-confidence of those with a rich and deservedly loved tradition is the kind of *kenosis* demanded: to go to the poor, and be poor, means to give up all the props of social and emotional security. It is not just a "spiritual" poverty, if by that we mean a kind of poverty which allows us to go on having all things we think we "absolutely have to have." It means just plain poverty.[1]

The poor can be free because they can risk all; they have nothing to lose. We all have met, however, jealous, envious, and selfish poor. Although they should be more open to the Good News of the Kingdom and although the preaching of the Kingdom equally and fully to them (that is, the fact that the Kingdom is not the prerogative of the wealthy) is a sign of its authenticity, there is no guarantee that all the poor hear that Word. Just as there is no guarantee that all the rich reject it.

This idea is well summed up by Hans Küng:

> Jesus then was not a naive enthusiast in economic matters, making a virtue of necessity and adding a touch of religion to poverty. Poverty may teach men to pray, but it also teaches them to curse. Jesus glorifies poverty no more than sickness; he provides no opium. Poverty, suffering, hunger are misery, not bliss. He does not proclaim an enthusiastic spirituality which suppresses all thought of injustice or provides a cheap promise of consolation in the hereafter. On the other hand, he was not a fanatical revolutionary, wanting to abolish poverty by force overnight and thus mostly only creating more poverty. He displayed no animosity toward the rich, brutal as they were in the East at that time. He was not one of those

violent men offering happiness to the people who merely give a further twist to the spiral of violence and counterviolence, instead of breaking through it. Certainly he in no way agreed with social conditions as they existed. But he saw definitive solutions in a different way. To the poor, the suffering and the hungry, in the midst of their misery, he called: "Salvation is yours," "You are blessed, happy."[2]

Or perhaps from a positive point of view it was better expressed by Rosemary Haughton:

First of all it means what it most obviously meant in the life of Jesus himself and has meant through the centuries: that the gospel message gets through very easily and directly to people who have little to lose. Poverty means that people cannot find security in the circumstances of their lives. The certainties are the regularity of the landlord's demands for rent, the contempt of officials of whatever kind, and death. Virtually everything else can and does fail—jobs, crops, health, justice, the Church. Family members may support each other but they cannot create jobs; they may reject, they may be split up, they may die. So the poor have always been the beloved of God in the very simple sense that being poor means being vulnerable, and therefore divine love finds it easier to break through.[3]

From this I assume that being "poor" implies one's willingness to accept one's fragility, one's dependency.

The next question I asked myself was: What is the greatest change today in the seeking of wealth and riches? The economic system has its own laws and inner dynamics that are not dependent on the Gospel; but economics are but one aspect of the whole of the social fabric and, because money signifies power, it is often difficult for the aims of society to be pursued for the benefit of all because of the imbalance created by the use of wealth and the dependency on it.

I do not want to ascribe motives to those who are concerned about the acquisition of wealth. Many times, I am sure, those motives are highly mixed and not without a selfless base. On the other hand, money for the sake of power, in our age, cannot be ignored.

The Church in capitalistic nations tends to be naive vis-à-vis such use of money. Perhaps the forces that have opposed the bishops' efforts to bring a moral dimension into the arms race and the nuclear-arms question, in particular, will leave us less naive about the power of money and the aims of numerous foundations spun off from such money and that serve the interests—not always of society—but of their own corporate concerns.

These examples are cited because there remain today, as always, mixed motives behind the acquisition and use of wealth, and we should not be so naive as to forget the admonitions of the Gospel.

My next question was: How can poverty be the object of a vow? Jesus never advocated poverty for its own sake. One could say that for accepting the Good News of the Kingdom the poor are advantaged, but poverty is never called a virtue. Poverty is an evil. So often it is not freeing; it does not permit the full development of the human person, of the human potential. The Good News of the Kingdom must be a freeing and liberating news, not a pat on the back or a handout. Perhaps this confusion was perpetuated by religious life, which demanded a vow of poverty rather than renunciation. Poverty, to be the object of a vow, has to be a virtue; it is only if it creates freedom by renunciation. Such ambiguity remains in our speech today and continues to cause much confusion.

Edward Schillebeeckx put it this way:

> From Jesus' eschatological message we hear only God's radical "no" to all forms of evil, all forms of poverty and hunger that lead to tears. That is Jesus' message; and it has enormous consequences. That in it God is also refusing to acknowledge the superior strength of evil and so with his own being as God is standing surety for the defeat of evil in all its forms can in no way be turned to reactionary or conservative ends. Jesus gives us on God's behalf only the message that God stands surety for us. And therefore the poor, the suffering and the deprived do indeed have grounds for positive hope.[4]

My last question was this: Within what spiritual and theological context is renunciation for the Kingdom a positive Christian value? Jesus came preaching that the Kingdom of God was at hand; nothing else really matters. Or perhaps one should say that everything else must be seen in the light of that Good News. In that preaching of the Kingdom, however, lies the very tension that is at the basis of our attitude toward the world and ultimately toward poverty and riches.

The Kingdom implies a "nowness." Jesus came preaching that the Kingdom is now with us. We live in the time of that "nowness." At the same time we know that the fullness of time has not come, that we live in the in-between times. This tension between "now" and "not yet" is integral to the Christian message and to Christian living. Because the Kingdom is "now," Jesus has said a "no" to poverty, as to all evil. Because that Kingdom has not been fully realized in our midst, the "not yet" pulls us forward to a more just and equitable world. The important concept in the "not yet" is that the Kingdom is God's, not ours, that he is our hope and our security, that he will realize that Kingdom in and through us. Thus, for the poor he is the assurance of hope. How often he calls us back to that verity!

On the other hand, he does not expect us to sit idly by. He committed his message and also his mission to the Church. For this reason we are, by baptism, involved in that positive mission of the "now/not yet" tension. Instead of denying the values of this earth and society, we must take them up into the dynamics of the Kingdom in a positive way.

Theologically this dynamic has often been called "incarnationalism." I notice that spiritual writers today talk of "inclusion." It could be described as the acceptance of this secular world for its own intrinsic values (a concept that Vatican II affirmed) and at the same time the conferring on this secular world and its values a higher destiny because they are taken up into the dynamics of the Kingdom.

Jesus is the model for such "inclusion." He took on our human nature to draw all things to himself and ultimately to hand them over to his Father. It is within that dynamic that the Christian of today must live. Where there is evil, conversion must take place, so that nothing will be excluded, but all brought to "inclusion"— that is, raised up with Jesus on the cross to be offered to his Father.

For this reason, too, if someone is in need, Christ is in need, because the fullness of his offering remains incomplete; evil continues to exclude itself. If people anywhere in the world are starving—

anywhere in the world, I say—Christ is starving. Our mission as received from him is lacking. On the positive side, our proper use of secular values can only lead to building the Kingdom and completing his offering.

In the light of this perspective I would conclude that perhaps my original guilt came from asking the wrong question. The challenges are not—What kind of car do I drive? In what kind of house do I live?—but, rather: Does my car help me to be a good bishop and aid me in my service of others? Does where I live help me fulfill the function of bishop? Does my computer or word processor help me teach and proclaim the Good News? And so on!

Most of all, in all of this dynamic and tension there must be no anxiety, no real concern about the outcome. The Kingdom belongs to the Lord. On him rest our hope and joy and happiness as we sense how poor we are.

NOTES

1. Rosemary Haughton, *The Passionate God* (New York: Paulist Press, 1981), p. 332.
2. Hans Küng, *On Being a Christian* (Garden City, N.Y.: Doubleday, 1976), p. 269.
3. Haughton, p. 326.
4. Edward Schillebeeckx, *Jesus: An Experiment in Christology* (New York: Crossroad, 1979), p. 178.

16

Sanctuary for Latin American Refugees: Biblical Values and the Politics of Repression

JOHN J. FITZPATRICK
Bishop of Brownsville

My subject is a new phenomenon that is highlighted by front-page contradictions: On the one hand we are to spend millions to refurbish the Statue of Liberty, and on the other we refuse to heed and follow her welcoming words: "Give me your tired, your poor, your huddled masses yearning to breathe free, the wretched refuse of your teeming shores; send these, the homeless, tempest-tossed, to me: I lift my lamp beside the golden door."

My subject is the Sanctuary Movement, the reasons for its recent beginning in this nation, the Christian and American idealism that fosters it, and some of the problems it faces. Many Christians and members of other faiths here are faced with the question of possibly divided and contradictory loyalties. Their loyalties run deep back through the early Christian era to the Israelites in Egypt at the time of Moses, over 3,000 years ago; back also through our own two centuries of American freedom and growth to the days in the early 1600's when our refugee ancestors sought freedom from oppression and famine here on American shores. Ever since then it has been part of our glorious heritage to open our shores to the oppressed and the hungry alike. They have helped to make us a great and honorable nation.

Delivered at the Cathedral-Basilica of St. James in Brooklyn on April 28, 1985.

Until recently! Now we routinely deport thousands of refugees to our shores from neighboring El Salvador, and we persecute Americans who still believe in the First Amendment of the Constitution, which protects our right to practice the dictates of our faith.

We make grandiose political statements about the great heritage of our nation—the home of the free and the land of the brave—and then show clearly we do not have any more room here for people who have lost their own freedom in their own land and who come here to seek what our ancestors—many of them refugees themselves—sought and found on these shores.

Too bad about Salvadorans whose fathers have been killed, whose mothers have been raped, whose baby brothers and sisters have been disemboweled from the bodies of their mothers even before birth, whose brothers and relatives have been kidnapped, tortured in the closest thing to fratricide we Americans have ever seen. If you are from El Salvador, do not seek asylum in the United States that you have admired for so long. We do not want you! We prefer to disregard your civil war, your 50,000 people killed by death squads, your forced expulsion from your own homes and neighborhoods. We have time only to clean up the beautiful Lady in our New York harbor but not enough American idealism anymore to heed its glorious message to the poor and to the oppressed. And not because our Congress has made that decision but because our Immigration and Naturalization Service has so decreed.

The phenomenon started with the civil war in El Salvador with its concomitant genocide—tens of thousands killed, kidnapped, tortured.

Let me say a word about El Salvador, a country about the size of Massachusetts bordering on Guatemala and Honduras. It is one of the most densely populated and poorest of our countries in the Western Hemisphere. Less than 1 percent of the population (around 5 million) owns 40 percent of the land, while over 90 percent of the population owns less than 5 percent of the land. The average wage for a worker in 1979 was $1.95 per day. About 90 percent of the Salvadorans earn less than $100 per year. Sixty percent are illiterate. The country has the lowest per-capita caloric intake of any country in Latin America; about three-quarters of all children under the age of five die from malnutrition. Of every 1,000 babies born, 100 die before they reach the age of one. There are fewer than 3 doctors for every 10,000 people.

El Salvador has been ruled by the world's longest succession of military dictatorships. In 1931, the country's last civilian president was overthrown by army officers following a series of strikes and mass marches by coffee workers demanding unemployment benefits and a minimum wage in the face of deteriorating economic conditions. General Maximiliano Hernandez Martinez assumed the presidency and ordered the massacre of over 30,000 people during a peasant uprising in 1932.

The current president of El Salvador, José Napoleon Duarte, in 1981 told us:

> This is a history of people starving to death, living in misery. For fifty years, the same people had all the power, all the money, all the opportunities. Those who did not have anything tried to take it away from those who had everything. But there were no democratic systems available to them, so they have radicalized themselves, have resorted to violence. And, of course, the second group, the rich, do not want to give up anything, so they are fighting.

In 1979, with the aid of the U.S. State Department, the Pentagon, and the CIA, the ruling president was overthrown. Under the next president human-rights violations spiraled. Among the targets of violence during 1980 was Archbishop Oscar Arnulfo Romero, of San Salvador, who was killed while offering Mass. He had been quite outspoken against the abuses on the part of the government and a champion of the human rights of the people. In 1980 alone more than 10,000 Salvadorans were killed or disappeared. Almost 20,000 disappeared or were killed in 1981.

A report to the then Secretary of State Haig in 1981 said:

> Analysis of all available data suggests that the majority of the reported human-rights violations, including torture, disappearance and deliberate cold-blooded killings, have been carried out by the security forces and have been directed against people not involved in guerrilla activities.

The violence in El Salvador that has taken so many lives outright also has spawned a refugee crisis of overwhelming proportions within El Salvador, in surrounding Central American nations and within the borders of the United States as well.

There are more than 300,000 displaced persons within El Salvador itself with another 350,000 having fled to surrounding countries in Central America.

The United Nations High Commissioner for Refugees recently stated:

> Much of the violence in El Salvador today is politically motivated in order to instill fear and submission into the populace whose political sympathies are suspect. Persons fleeing this kind of violence are bona fide political refugees and not simply war-displaced persons and should under no circumstances be compelled to return.

Well over 300,000 have fled to the United States, seeking a temporary refuge from the violence and terror wracking their country. These refugees tell stories of terror, disappearance, rape, mutilation, and murder at the hands of Salvadoran government forces. Fifty thousand, 1 percent of the population, have been killed in the last five years.

In Texas we began to see almost immediately an increase of illegal Latins crossing our Rio Grande. They had walked 1,500 miles through parts of El Salvador, all of Guatemala, all of Mexico where many of them were robbed and poorly treated, to the only hope they had—the United States of America. They arrived utterly exhausted, poorly clothed, haggard from lack of sleep and food, and they collapsed on our American doorsteps. They found little welcome. The border patrol immediately scooped them up into patrol cars, lodged them in any prison they could find, and even built larger ones to hold them and denied them any hope they ever had for protection in this country, any hope that America would accept them as refugees as it had accepted *our* forefathers fleeing oppression, hunger, and war in days gone by.

This flood of civil-war victims spawned the American response that eventually became the Sanctuary Movement. Hundreds of individual American families and then hundreds of churches, parishes, and congregations opened their doors and hearts to the refugees who knocked on them seeking help. They were motivated by our American tradition and policy toward the oppressed as well as by their religious beliefs, both learned during early childhood.

Most religious people will recall hearing the passage in Leviticus: "When an alien resides in your land, do not molest him. You shall treat the aliens who reside with you no differently than the natives born among us; have the same love for them as for yourselves; for you too were once aliens in the land of Egypt" (19:33–34).

And in Isaiah: "Hide those who have been driven out, do not let the refugee be seen. Let those who have been driven out of Moab stay with you; be their refuge against their destroyer" (16:3–4).

All of us here can recall the flight of the Jews from Egypt, the flight of Jesus, Mary, and Joseph to Egypt, warned by an angel that the child was to be killed, and the flight of religious people from their European oppressors at the beginning of our own history. We also recall that at the last judgment God Himself will judge us precisely because of our acceptance or rejection of the homeless, the stranger, the oppressed. And, of course, our Statue of Liberty for some 100 years has boasted "give me your huddled masses."

Perhaps we do not generally know the American laws that govern or should govern the activities of both private citizens and our American government officials.

Under our Constitution we are bound by treaties that our government enters into. These treaties are to have the force of law. They are to be respected and followed as absolutely as any law that Congress enacts. Treaties are supposed to be part of the supreme law of the land and courts are supposed to follow them. One of these treaties is the Geneva Convention relative to the treatment of civilian persons in time of war. President Eisenhower signed this treaty in 1955. According to article three of the Geneva Convention no government that signed that document can expel or return a refugee, in any manner whatsoever, to the frontiers or territories of a country where his life or freedom will be threatened on account of race, religion, nationality, membership in a political social group, or political opinion. That means that the United States is not allowed under international and U.S. law to return to a state or country anyone whose life is going to be threatened for those reasons. This applies whether the refugee came through one country or fifty countries after he left his own country. That means that Salvadorans, whether or not they come here immediately after having gone through Guatemala and Mexico, are still refugees. Unfortunately, as A. Bates Butler III said recently: "The United States seems to recognize these international laws and agreements only when it is perceived to be convenient to do so or it is perceived that following such agreements is in our own national interest."

Nevertheless our government has sent back more than 40,000 Salvadorans to El Salvador since 1980.

Our ex-Ambassador to El Salvador, Robert White, testified that people who are returned by the United States to El Salvador are in a great deal of danger because the government of El Salvador presumes these returnees are leftists or are guerrillas or sympathetic to them. Mr. White said that our government has the policy of giving the Salvadoran government the names and addresses of the people who are being returned. Recently both the archbishop of San Salvador and his auxiliary bishop spoke of the fact that there are numerous cases of returned refugees who have suffered torture and death on being returned there.

A law that is ignored by our own government is the Refugee Act of 1980. This law was adopted in conformity with international obligations of the United States under the 1967 protocol relating to the status of refugees. The act defines a refugee as "any person who is outside any country of such person's nationality . . . and who is unable or unwilling to return to . . . that country because of persecution or a well-founded fear of persecution on account of race, religion, nationality, membership in a particular social group or political opinion." Refugees from persecution have a right not to be returned to a country where they are in danger.

All these things are perfectly in keeping with the obligations of the Christian community, that strangers fleeing persecution and death should find safety as well as open hearts and homes in our midst. Our moral principles, moreover, call upon us to protect and shelter citizens of other nations who have been deprived of their homeland by threats of violence or terror or war. We simply cannot in faith allow our compassion to be limited by national origins or territorial boundaries.

In September 1981 the American bishops urged that a moratorium be placed on all deportations to El Salvador until such time as the government in power there were in a position to give reasonable assurance of the safety of its citizens. That same year the U.S. Congress admonished the administration to recognize and take into full account the civil strife in El Salvador.

In 1981 the Office of the United Nations High Commissioner for Refugees reviewed United States treatment of Salvadorans and reported that the United States was violating its legal obligations toward those refugees. The office recommended that it should

> continue to express concern to the United States government, that its apparent failure to grant asylum to any significant number of Salvadorans, coupled with continuing large-scale forceable and voluntary return to El Salvador, would appear to represent a negation of its responsibilities upon its adherence to the protocol on refugees.

We must not conclude, however, that all refugees allowed to remain temporarily will be allowed to remain here permanently.

The refusal to allow extended voluntary departure to Salvadorans is based upon the political support of the United States for the government of El Salvador, a factor that is irrelevant under and indeed violative of the applicable treaties and other international laws governing the rights of persons fleeing war and human-rights violations.

But despite all this fine tradition and international treaties, we Americans have only one thing to offer those who walk these 1,500 miles to our shores: apprehension, jail, and deportation. So they are sent back to face a most uncertain future, afraid that they will face the same assaults and torture that have threatened the lives of Salvadorans for the last five or six years.

Moreover, these Salvadorans were not merely apprehended on our streets; they were taken in tow the very moment they stood, hat in hand, at our immigration desk pleading for asylum.

Let me add something here about conditions in El Salvador. The deplorable human-rights violations have been widely publicized. Up to 1 million Salvadorans (20 percent) have been displaced, that is, forced to move from their homes and to locate in other parts of the country. Over 40,000 (some say over 50,000) have been killed. Tens of thousands of others have been kidnapped, tortured, raped. Military forces and government death squads carried out the torture and death of doctors, students, labor and religious leaders, teachers and peasant leaders. Moreover, there have been indiscriminate and intentional bombings of civilian targets by the Salvadoran air force as well as mass killings of non-combatants by the army. There has also been the use of fragmentation bombs and incendiary weapons against the civilian population. As recently as July 14, 1984, the U.S. State Department admitted that political slayings in El Salvador had occurred at an average rate of ninety-three per month for the past five months in 1984.

So these refugees came to us by the tens of thousands. And they were sent back to El Salvador as rapidly as they came. In 1981 only 67 of some 1,100 received asylum. At the same time 11,637 were deported. In 1982, of 23,000 applicants only 2 percent were granted permission to remain here. Things were so bad there that even El Salvador's President, José Napoleon Duarte, in 1981 asked that the Salvadorans then being deported in the United States "be allowed to remain in the United States until the turmoil is settled." While our government refuses to admit that there is political turmoil in El Salvador and thus attempts to justify its refusal to allow refugees to come here as political refugees, even the president of El Salvador admits it and asks forbearance and some humanitarianism.

Let me tell you now briefly about the Sanctuary Movement, a direct result of our government's position and attitude. It was born in 1981 in Arizona, where a group of Church people from many denominations assist, feed, and house refugees fleeing from El Salvador and Guatemala. These learned for the first time that large numbers of refugees were being held in jails and camps by the U.S. Immigration and Naturalization Service, processed for deportation back to their country to face possible persecution and death. The U.S. Government was calling these refugees "economic migrants" and was shipping them back.

Parenthetically let me say that it is rather foolish on the part of the U.S. Government to speak of the Salvadoran refugees as only economic refugees when it is rather clear that there is a civil war going on that is supported by U.S. dollars and military aid. The Arms Control and Foreign Policy Caucus reported only two months ago that

> the United States has provided $1.7 billion to the government, Central Bank and Armed Forces of El Salvador since the outbreak of the civil war in 1980. Over these five years, the United States funding for El Salvador has grown dramatically—increasing nearly tenfold between fiscal years 1980 and 1984. It now stands at over half a billion dollars a year and the Administration expected to request similar or larger amounts in the future.

How can the U.S. Government claim that these refugees are merely economic refugees when we are paying for a civil war that makes political refugees?

Moreover, the U.S. troops help maintain and promote the use of military equipment, some of which is quite sophisticated. And, of course, our fifty-five military experts are often many more than that!

On February 2, 1985, *The New York Times* reported that El Salvador received an increase of 15 percent in the aid the United States gave it in 1985 over 1984: $200 million in military aid and $426 million in other aid. Who is kidding whom that there is no civil war in El Salvador from which the people are fleeing? If there is no war, but just poor economic conditions, why all this U.S. military help?

But back for a moment to the Sanctuary Movement.

On March 24, 1984, a number of churches in California and Arizona simultaneously announced that they would henceforth provide sanctuary for undocumented aliens from Central America. The movement rapidly spread to other churches. Today there are many hundreds of congregations throughout the United States that have endorsed sanctuary activity. Moreover, countless individuals and organizations participate in a nationwide "underground railroad," much like that which moved slaves North to free territory during the Civil War. Sanctuary is not primarily a place but a pledge of support, of shelter, of food, medical care, job and legal help, and, if need be, the readiness of Church members to accept a jail sentence for such activities.

The Diocese of Brownsville, where most of the refugees come before attempting to find refuge in other parts of the States and Canada, opened Casa Oscar Romero about three years ago for the same purpose. It was named for the martyred archbishop of San Salvador. Many thousands have gone through it. For many it is the first and last American place that shows any compassion or gives any hope. Many refugees, unable to maneuver around immigration checkpoints, are picked up, jailed in the Corralon (the detention center in Bayview, Texas), and deported. I hope that they will forever be spared seeing a photograph of the Statue of Liberty and its message, "Give me your huddled masses yearning to breathe free."

Then our small Casa Romero staff was singled out for persecution, tried, and found guilty of conspiracy and illegal transportation and fined. It was my privilege to bail both Jack Elder and Stacey Merkt out of jail pending their trials. They were not allowed to plead that they were helping refugees who were here under the Refugee Act of 1980, only that they had broken a law— not even made by the U.S. Congress—but made by an agency of the executive branch, the INS, which apparently can disregard American laws, whereas U.S. citizens cannot. Apparently Americans are not allowed to run their own lives under the protection of the First Amendment of the Constitution, which protects them in the free exercise of their religion. Our staff members thought that to give a ride in a car five or six miles to a bus station, located much nearer to the INS center, a bus station that was always patrolled by the border patrol, would be both American and Christian. More recently others have been arrested in Arizona on the same charges.

And, of course, they and members of the Sanctuary Movement have had to suffer their share of untrue statements and misrepresentation. Some opponents state that the Sanctuary Movement claims that *all* young men deported from the Untied States to El Salvador are killed. No one ever claimed that. Another charge is that the Sanctuary Movement is using refugees as pawns in their efforts to change American foreign policy. Such a charge is unworthy of both the members of the movement and of those who make it.

The Center for Constitutional Rights in New York has stated our position very well.

We believe that international law mandates the U.S. to protect people fleeing war crimes, human-rights violations, persecution. If the U.S. were performing its obligations under the principles recognized in the Geneva Conventions or international humanitarian law, the refugee would not be here illegally. The charge of abetting an illegal presence in the United States is at the heart of the prosecution of sanctuary workers. Since we reject that charge of illegality, we believe that the indictments against sanctuary workers should be dismissed on that ground alone. Moreover, we believe religious sanctuary workers such as Elder are protected by the First Amendment which supports the free exercise of religion. In providing sanctuary they are acting in accordance with religious doctrines which do not conflict with U.S. laws.

While the government seems adamant in its seemingly untenable position, somebody is trying to do something about the un-American posture of our government vis-à-vis real refugees from oppression and war. A year and a half ago the De Concini-Moakley bill was introduced in both the Senate and the House that would do what the administration declines to do—temporarily suspend the deportation of Salvadorans from the United States. It provides for the temporary suspension of deportation for certain nationals of El Salvador for a period of two years, mandates a presidential study of the living conditions of displaced Salvadorans in their own country and in neighboring countries, and directs a congressional review of possible steps to improve the conditions described in the presidential report. This bill does not grant amnesty to all Salvadorans in the United States. It gives temporary relief from the fear of involuntary expulsion from the United States.

Those of us who are Christian or American or both must decide very soon whether we are committed to the moral obligations imposed upon us either by Christ or by our American legal system. The blood being shed in El Salvador is blood on our hands. We are fostering and paying for their civil war. We have taken sides—for that government and against that people. Our refusal to accept Salvadoran refugees as refugees and our sending them back to be fodder in that civil war is another page of shame in our American history.

17

Apartheid: Nightmare for South Africa— Challenge to the United States

DANIEL P. REILLY
Bishop of Norwich

I am happy to have this opportunity to address so important a subject. It is both a special privilege and a great responsibility. First of all, however, I would like to set the context of my presentation. I am not, nor do I pretend to be, an expert on South Africa and especially South African politics. I have visited there, spoken to many important people and groups involved in South African problems, and try to keep myself informed about developments there from day to day. So I write rather as a brother of those suffering in South Africa, as a Christian concerned about their human dignity, as an American citizen disturbed by the seeming indifference of our government in this matter, and as a teacher in the Church who must condemn the immorality of apartheid.

At the invitation of the South African Bishops' Conference and on behalf of the National Conference of Catholic Bishops, I recently visited South Africa to learn firsthand something about the actual situation of this racially divided country. I would like to share with you some of the things I learned so that you might have a greater awareness of the problems of South Africa in which the United States as a nation is involved and about which we as Christians and fellow human beings must have concern.

Delivered at the Cathedral-Basilica of St. James in Brooklyn on May 5, 1985.

191

Political Situation

Since 1652, when whites first entered South Africa, they have inflicted racial oppression on the blacks living there. The whites are comprised of two main groups: the Afrikaners (those of Dutch ancestry) and the English (those of British ancestry). Because of their superior weapons, the Europeans were able to win the continual wars they waged against the African population. The whites stripped the blacks of their land and livelihood. From the beginning the black resistance was brutally crushed, and the blacks were forced to submit to laws established and controlled by whites. In 1948, the National Party, dominated by the Afrikaners, was elected to power by the white majority on a platform of further strengthening white supremacy. Under this government, South Africa has institutionalized its oppressive apartheid policies.

"Apartheid," a word meaning "apart" or "separate," is the system of legalized racism in the Republic of South Africa guaranteeing the domination of a white minority over the black majority. At the present time in a population of some 29 million there are 4.5 million whites (15 percent of the population), 21 million African blacks (73 percent), 2.6 million "so-called" colored (mixed race, 9 percent), and 820,000 Asians (Indians, 3 percent).

The apartheid laws have become increasingly tyrannical with the passage of time and today are being fiercely challenged by black South Africans and many countries of Africa and the world. For decades black leaders in South Africa (e.g., African National Congress) believed that passive resistance would ultimately gain their freedom. But as the jailing and the killing of black leaders and activists continue to mount, momentum has been building in the black community for agitation and more aggressive resistance to unjust laws. Rioting, protest marches, and mob attacks that have left hundreds of people dead have occurred in the black townships and have spread to the nearby mixed race or colored areas. Thousands have been arrested without charges brought against them, and 250,000 blacks have been detained for traveling in areas denied to them in their own country.

The black majority is without political power. In 1984 a constitutional agreement was made whereby the colored and the Indians have separate Parliaments, but both are dominated by the white-majority Parliament. Although a majority of coloreds and Indians, perceiving this as a further entrenchment of apartheid, rejected the arrangement, the government went ahead with it. The entire political system is based on skin color. No other criterion—economic, educational, or other—has any relevance.

Under apartheid blacks are denied all political, economic, and social rights. By law, they are denied the right to vote, to receive decent education, or to have decent employment. They are forced to live in inferior housing and have inferior hospitals. They are told where they may live, the race of people whom they marry, on what buses they may ride, and what churches to attend. The white government controls every black person through a sophisticated computer network requiring all blacks over the age of sixteen to carry a "passbook" at all times. The passbook contains fingerprints, a photograph, and employment records. If it is not produced upon demand, blacks can be jailed and fined. More than 13 million incidents of Africans being convicted of pass-law offenses have taken place since the National Party came to power in 1948—almost 1,000 every day.

Economic Situation

The whites gained control over blacks in South Africa by taking their land. Today under apartheid the most fertile and mineral-rich land (87 percent of the country) is set aside for the white minority, while 13 percent of the land, the poorest in South Africa, is left for the black majority. Under apartheid laws no black is allowed to own land in areas restricted for whites only. Some blacks are allowed to live in black townships near the urban areas, but they are not allowed to purchase land. Blacks who have purchased land that is later designated a "black spot" in a "white area" are stripped of their ownership and forcibly removed to designated areas for Africans. Their communities are bulldozed or burned.

The areas designated for Africans have been divided into ten barren reservations, pockets of land scattered throughout the country called *bantustans* or homelands. These *bantustans* are in remote rural areas where there are no cities, no jobs, no access to health or recreational facilities. and the land cannot support even minimal farming. At present approximately 50 percent of the

African population lives in the *bantustans*. Over 3 million black South Africans have been forcibly removed from their homes and literally dumped on this barren land. Of the ten *bantustans*, the apartheid government has declared a phony "independence" for four of them, thus stripping blacks of rights to citizenship in their own country

Since the land that was their livelihood was taken, the blacks have been forced to work in an economy geared only toward white profit. The apartheid economy could not run without cheap black labor, but the blacks receive no benefits from that economy. Black workers are paid less than one-third of what whites are paid for doing the same job. Over 60 percent of urban black families earn less than the white government says is necessary to survive. Rural blacks are even worse off. Since there is little work in the *bantustans*, Africans are forced to leave their families and look for work in the mines, factories, farms, and homes of white South Africa, while living outside "white areas" in single-sex dormitories. These migratory workers often work for eleven months out of the year and see their families for only one month. Apartheid is destroying black family life in South Africa.

Blacks who do find jobs often work under very unsafe conditions and are not allowed to supervise whites. Yet, blacks have not had the means to work for better conditions. Independent black trade unions have forced some government concessions, but strikes and boycotts are still often suppressed by force. Labor leaders are harassed, detained, and sometimes tortured or killed while in detention by South African police.

The vast majority of South Africans, then, is denied the right to vote, the right to live together as families, and the right to earn an adequate education, indeed the right to a truly human existence.

The Churches and Apartheid

The majority Church in South Africa is the Dutch Reformed Church that supports racial separation, and has even built a theology to support it. South Africa for them is the Promised Land and they are the Chosen People. There have, however, been some dissenters in recent years, and the Dutch Reformed Church internationally has condemned apartheid as heresy.

The Catholic Church has a minority of approximately 10 percent of the population; 80 percent of the South African Catholics are black. Most Catholic clergy, however, are white. There is one black archbishop in Capetown and several other black bishops.

The Catholic Church, as well as Episcopalians, Lutherans, and Methodists, has opposed the apartheid system for years. The Lutheran World Federation in 1977 and the World Alliance of Reformed Churches in 1982 have officially declared apartheid in South African a *status confessionis* issue. This commits these churches to a public and unequivocal rejection of apartheid as a matter of faith. Major American denominations have also adopted such a position. This Church opposition to apartheid is doubly important since the South African Government contends that apartheid is based on Christian principles.

The best-known religious leader in the struggle against apartheid is Anglican Archbishop Desmond Tutu of Johannesburg, the 1984 winner of the Nobel Peace Prize. On numerous occasions, Archbishop Tutu has called upon the world Christian community and the governments of the West to use every means available, political and financial, to press for a change in South Africa. He has stated that the present situation is our last chance for a peaceful change.

At Wesleyan University in my diocese in March of 1984 Archbishop Tutu explained persuasively why apartheid is heresy:

Apartheid is a system that says the value of human beings resides in a biological irrelevance, the color of their skin. We who are Christians say our value is something that resides in us and is intrinsic to who we are because we are created in the image of God. Apartheid denies that! Apartheid says we are made for separation, for disunity, for alienation, for enmity. And the Gospel of Our Lord Jesus Christ says "no" we are made for fellowship, for togetherness, for reconciliation, for compassion, for caring, for loving. Apartheid says: people of different races and background are ultimately irreconcilable. But the Gospel of Our Lord Jesus Christ says "no"—God was made in Christ reconciling the world to himself. The central thing that Jesus Christ has done is to reconcile not only us with God but with one another. That means that in Christ there can never be distinctions that are significant for separa-

tion. Apartheid denies the central core of the Christian faith.
So apartheid is heretical.

Archbishop Tutu has strong support for this judgment. In his
remarks to the special committee against apartheid in July 1984
Pope John Paul II declared: "Every form of discrimination based
on race, whether occasionally, or systemically practiced, and
whether it is aimed at individuals or whole racial groups, is absolutely unacceptable."

This condemnation followed a strong statement by his prede-
cessor, Pope Paul VI, to the same committee in May of 1974:

> We unhesitatingly proclaim once again the dignity of the
> human person . . . [taking] into account the common origin,
> nature and density of all members of the human family and
> the equality of their fundamental rights. This equality de-
> mands an ever more explicit recognition in civil society of
> every human being's essential rights and consequently the
> aspirations of all . . . desiring to enjoy those rights which flow
> from their dignity as human persons are wholly legitimate."

Archbishop Dennis Hurley of Durban, a bishop for thirty-six
years and the president of the South African Catholic Bishops Conference, has been an outspoken and courageous champion of these
rights. He was accused of treachery against South Africa and summoned to trial last February for condemning South African military atrocities against the people in illegally occupied Namibia in
1983 (SACBC report on that country).

Archbishop Hurley was threatened with up to eight years in
prison and a $12,000 fine. The planned trial attracted wide at-
tention in the West, but on the day of the trial Archbishop Hurley
was told that the case against him had been dropped! He is joined
by his brother Catholic bishops in solid opposition to and in protest
against apartheid. The Catholic Church is coming more blatantly
under fire from the government in a decided campaign to silence its
dissent. The government also threatened to charge the Rev. Allan
Boesak, president of the World Alliance of Reformed Churches,
for criticizing the police. The South African Council of Churches,
once headed by Archbishop Tutu and presently by the former

Reformed Dutch minister Dr. Byers Naude, who was banned from 1977 to 1984, is constantly harassed and intimidated.

Repression such as "banning," detention, and harassment of church leaders is intended by the South African Government to put more pressure on the churches in South Africa to desist from their attacks on apartheid.

Prime Minister Peter W. Botha warned in 1981 that the churches should "keep themselves busy preaching the Gospel" and avoid confrontation with the government. The South African Council of Churches in its 1984 National Conference responded to that warning by saying that "when peace is broken or threatened by injustice, the Christian has a responsibility to work for peace, to work for righteousness by striving to rectify what is unrighteous and unjust."

The churchmen are aware of the danger of this situation. Archbishop Hurley has said, "a new state of war is developing between the police and the people." In February 1984 Bishop Tutu made the same evaluation and followed it up with a word of hope, "Humanly speaking, we are going to have a blood bath in South Africa. But I am a Christian, and I believe all Christians must be prisoners of hope. No Christian can ever be anything but an optimist."

Recent Events

The current wave of repression is only the latest excess of a system of institutional racism that affects the daily lives of the overwhelming majority of South Africans. There is black unrest all over the country—violence is commonplace, labor strikes and student strikes, ghetto uprisings and attacks on blacks working with the system are frequent. The killing of eighteen (or more) blacks in Uotenhage on March 21 of 1985 by South African police highlighted the crisis to fever pitch. Over the past few months more than 200 people have been killed. Just recently President P. W. Botha told Parliament that there "had been a drastic escalation of the revolutionary climate in the country." Botha told Parliament that "the potential for extensive country-wide violent disturbances has increased markedly." He accused major religious and political opposition groups of seeking "the destruction of our system of government and civilized values."

In his speech, Botha offered to negotiate with black leaders who reject violence. In addition, in what appeared to be a major concession to long-standing black demands, he also said that freehold rights would be granted to certain black residents of South African cities.

But the main thrust of Botha's speech was an attack on groups that have been sharply critical of apartheid. He said the United Democratic Front, a coalition of several hundred anti-apartheid groups claiming more than 2 million members, was responsible for the present unrest.

Despite this harsh reality, the Reagan administration for the last four years has followed a policy of what it calls "constructive engagement" toward South Africa in the belief that "quiet diplomacy" and "friendly persuasion" will convince the white-minority regime to abandon apartheid by making changes internally and moving toward the independence of Namibia. Given the increased violence and oppression noted previously, it seems abundantly clear that such a policy is not working and is even aiding and abetting apartheid.

Both President Reagan and Secretary of State Schultz have condemned apartheid, but their refusal to invoke sanctions against South Africa weakens their condemnation. Because of this, black South Africa and independent African states see the United States as a supporter of apartheid.

In the words of Archbishop Tutu, "Constructive engagement has only assisted in making the South African government more intransigent." It is time to recognize the failure of this policy and to adopt a new one.

What Can We Do?

Certainly we must pray for the persecuted and the persecutors. We must stay in contact with the Church in South Africa in any way possible. We should communicate our indignation to our representatives in Congress, to the State Department, and to the President.

We must send a signal to our elected officials that the American people wish them to forge a fresh approach to South Africa and that the United States should give strong moral leadership in that area. This means that the United States must address the reality that the system of apartheid is strengthened by investments, loans, and other assistance, including nuclear cooperation, coming from our country. Total United States investment in South Africa is now $14.6 billion. This certainly gives our government great leverage in seeking a solution.

We should call upon our government, our churches, and our people to use any and every peaceful means available to bring pressure upon the South African Government to end this evil system. In doing so, we are acting as the people of God charged to safeguard, in the words of Pope John Paul II, "the dignity of the human person and the well-being of all mankind."

18

The Bishops' Peace Pastoral

THOMAS J. GUMBLETON
Auxiliary Bishop of Detroit

In November 1980, during the annual meeting of the National Conference of Catholic Bishops, Archbishop John Roach made a statement in his presidential address to the bishops that I think really set the stage for the development of our peace pastoral letter. He said that on a global scale *the most dangerous moral issue in the public order today* is the nuclear-arms race. And he went on to challenge us as pastoral leaders and teachers in the Catholic Church of the United States to address this most dangerous moral issue.

He also emphasized that Pope John Paul II had said that the American Church had a special responsibility to address this issue. The pope said that when he was at the White House in November of 1979.

During the course of the development of the peace pastoral many things happened that impressed upon me in an ever-deeper way how true it is that we are confronting the most dangerous moral issue in the public order. One of the people who met with our committee during the first ten months of the development of the letter, when we were interviewing, discussing, and carrying on conversations with a wide variety of people in order to deepen our own understanding of all the complexities of this issue, was Admiral Noel Gayler, a man who had just recently retired from his high-level policymaking position in the Pentagon. Admiral Gayler came into the room where we were meeting, sat down, and said:

Delivered at the Cathedral-Basilica of St. James in Brooklyn on May 23, 1980.

If there is one thing I can impress upon you and that you will not forget as you try to develop your letter, it is this: When we are talking about nuclear weapons, we are talking about weapons that are qualitatively different from any other weapons the world has ever known. I'm saying this to you as a military person.

He reminded us he had spent forty-six years in the military service of the United States and was someone who had been engaged in battle—who had had to use weapons. (He'd gone into the service when he was just a youth, at seventeen.)

I've commanded people serving under me to go into battle and so I know what that means. In every battle situation in which I've ever been there was always at least some kind of reasonable relationship between the weapons we were using and the outcome we hoped to achieve. But with nuclear weapons that is not the case. There is no political or military purpose worth the risk of a nuclear war because these weapons can never be used in any rational way. Don't let anybody fool you that, when they're talking about so-called battlefield weapons, they are tactical nuclear weapons. You must realize that among those weapons, some that are in place in Europe right now, these so-called tactical weapons have more destructive capability than a Hiroshima bomb.

His point was clear. There is no way such weapons can ever be used rationally. Even if you believe in war, you must have some sense that the weapon you are using can be controlled, that it can achieve a definite purpose. These weapons, he said, are qualitatively different because they do not have any reasonable purpose. Admiral Gayler left me with a deep conviction that these weapons are qualitatively different and that, in fact, when we are confronting the question about their use, we are indeed confronting the most dangerous moral question in the public order today—dangerous because we know that when these weapons are used the very world in which we live will be totally in danger.

A nuclear war threatens the fate of the earth. That is what is at stake. For the first time in all of history, scientists point out to us, we humans have the capacity to destroy the world as we know it. That's the danger that we confront.

But it is not just the physically dangerous price that we are concerned with in the pastoral letter. As believers, disciples of Jesus, we are even more concerned about the moral dangers, about what we might do to ourselves spiritually unless we make a very significant change in the direction in which we are going.

Yes, the danger to the earth is something that terrifies all of us. But what does it profit anyone to gain the whole world and suffer the loss of their soul? Even if we could use these weapons and win somehow according to someone's definition of nuclear war, what would we have gained if we have destroyed ourselves spiritually? And it is because there is so much at stake spiritually and morally, it's because of that, above all, that the Catholic bishops have proposed for the whole Catholic community of the United States our pastoral letter.

As set forth in that letter, we have two purposes for which we are addressing the Catholic community and any others who are willing to read, reflect, and pray over our pastoral. The first purpose is our hope that it will help individual Catholic people to form their consciences. We want this letter to be a means by which each one of us can know and choose a truly moral course.

We also intend that the letter will do something beyond that. We say this very explicitly in the letter. We hope that it will be a means by which the whole Catholic community will become deeply engaged in the most important public-policy debate our nation has ever faced, influence that debate, and help to determine its outcome, so that we choose as a people a moral course. In order for these two purposes to be achieved we have developed a pastoral letter that has four main parts to it.

The first part is the section we called "Religious Principles and Perspectives." Here we try to set forth what is a truly comprehensive, even though succinct, as well as very accurate statement of what Catholic theology about war and peace truly is.

We start with our scriptural roots, going back into the Hebrew Scriptures and developing the teachings we discovered there within the light that comes to us from the Gospels of Jesus and the letters of the first disciples. And we bring together in this first part of the letter the theological reflection that has gone on in the Catholic community for 2,000 years.

We set forth there a theology about war and about peace that is a challenging theology, a difficult theology, if we begin to study it carefully and react to it with sincerity and integrity. It's a theology that reminds us that in the Catholic tradition there are two options Christians have determined they might follow in trying to achieve justice that can be the foundation for peace in the world.

One of these options, much neglected in the Catholic community, is part of our 2,000-year history, from the very beginning of that first community of the disciples of Jesus. It is a theology that says that a Christian will never use violence, never go to war, but will choose instead the pacifism that Jesus himself always followed in his own life.

We set this forth as a genuine option for Christians today in the face of the most horrendous weapons systems that have ever been developed. And perhaps today (maybe even more than ever before) the option of nonviolence, of Christian pacifism, is the only option that truly makes sense—in the way that God's foolishness is wiser than human wisdom and God's weakness is stronger than human strength.

At the same time we developed in our pastoral the other option that many, many Christians have come to choose, because in their understanding the only way certain kinds of injustices, oppression, tyranny can be overcome is by using force, even lethal force. But we insist—and this is a very important part of the teaching of the letter—that both of these options flow from the same fundamental premise—the premise that for the Christian the presumption always is against the use of violence.

That is the premise, because Jesus in his own life always rejected violence for any reason whatsoever, and so the disciple of Jesus must start with that presumption. If I am to be faithful to Jesus, I must presume that I will not use violence. The Christian pacifist will work to achieve justice, to bring peace into the world by saying, never, never will I use violence as I struggle for justice and for peace. I will find other means to overcome evil, to overcome injustice, even tyranny of the worst kind.

The person who follows the option of a just war starts with the presumption against violence, but concludes that in certain circumstances, when conditions that are very rigid and strict are present, the presumption against violence can be overridden and one may be morally justified in using force to achieve justice.

There are many conditions, however, that must be present, and our pastoral letter stresses this and insists that the just-war theology is not simply an easy excuse to go to war. It is a theology that was elaborated by Augustine and Thomas Aquinas and Suarez and others to prevent war, to try to prevent human persons from going to war, and if war happens nevertheless, to put very strict moral limits on what one may choose to do in war. And those conditions must be present and continue to be present if the presumption against violence is to be overridden.

Two of those conditions become supremely important. When we are confronted with the question of modern warfare (and I emphasize "modern warfare"—not simply nuclear warfare— because it isn't just the use of nuclear arms that so quickly exceeds the limits of a just-war theology), so much is involved that would make it impossible to wage war within the limits of this theology.

Pope John Paul II made this clear when he spoke at Coventry on his visit to England. He pleaded in his homily that we make war something out of the tragic past of human history. And he said: "I mean not just nuclear war, but modern war. It must be something out of the past of human history, that tragic past."

The two conditions that make modern warfare so much of a moral problem for followers of Jesus are these: the condition that we call the principle of discrimination or the principle of noncombatant immunity. It is something that has been part of the theology about war since the very beginning and must continue to be part of the theology of war, and that is that noncombatants may never be deliberately killed or crippled or maimed or left with radiation sickness.

Noncombatants must be protected. There must be the possibility of discriminating between combatants and noncombatants. That's what makes Admiral Gayler's testimony so important. He pointed out that today's battlefield weapons have a destructive capacity that exceeds a Hiroshima bomb. How could such a weapon ever be used, especially when you consider *where* they're thinking of using it in battle? Those are not battlefields. They are cities of Europe. There would be no way to discriminate between the combatants and the noncombatants when weapons such as these would be used.

The principle of discrimination is a very important condition that we must consider when we are talking about modern warfare. Yet another principle that also becomes vitally important is the principle of proportionality. This is the principle which insists that, if we are to engage in war in any kind of moral way, the good we hope to achieve must surpass the evil we know will happen.

One of the other people who spoke to us during the course of our conversations before we began writing the letter was Roger Molander. Probably many of you recognize the name. Roger Molander has started an organization called Ground Zero. It is an organization that tries to help people focus on what will be needed when a nuclear device is exploded over the city in which they live.

We spoke to Roger Molander not because he was the founder of this organization, but rather because he had only recently been on the staff at the National Security Council of the United States Government. We spoke to him as one of the experts in defense strategies and defense policies of the United States.

He shared with us an incident in his own life that had been very decisive in convincing him that he had to change, dramatically change his life, leave the work he was doing, and give up his promising career in the government. He said he had been at the Pentagon for a meeting, and before it started he was chatting with a Navy captain who was expressing a lot of anger. The captain was upset because people in the tens of thousands were demonstrating, especially in Europe, at that time. But people were also beginning to demonstrate in large numbers in the United States, and the Navy captain felt these people were unpatriotic, that they didn't love our country, and he was angry about that.

He was also angry because he said these people exaggerate the problem. He said if you listened to them you would think a nuclear war would mean the end of the world, whereas it would mean only 500 million people killed. Roger Molander said he was stunned when he heard that. He said, "I couldn't even respond. I just sat there and said to myself 'five hundred million people.'" Five hundred million people! One-eighth of the world's population immediately destroyed in a nuclear war. And that's not even to begin to measure, if it could be measured, the rest of the destruction and devastation that would happen.

Millions of people left with crippling diseases, radiation sickness. Large areas of the earth uninhabitable for centuries. What good could we ever hope to achieve that would be proportionate to that evil? I think there is clearly no good that could ever—whatever it might be—be proportionate to the evil of nuclear war.

Because of this teaching of Catholic theology coming out of our scriptural and theological roots, the American Catholic bishops have made four very precise judgments about nuclear war. We have tried to apply this teaching to the current situation in those specific ways—something for which we were criticized a great deal by many who wanted us to change the letter. The criticism came from various sources: government, other Church leaders, other conferences of bishops who thought we should never have become that specific. But we felt that unless we began to make specific judgments our letter would not be much help to others in forming their consciences, and so we have identified four judgments that in conscience we must state and follow ourselves as we call our people to reflect on the Catholic teaching that's in this letter and apply it to these situations.

The first judgment is this: We declare that any counter-population warfare, any counter-city warfare, can never be morally justified. This involves the weapons we have in place right now that will destroy whole cities in the Soviet Union. These weapons cannot be used morally. They may not be targeted morally in the way that they are. And we insist on this too, and it's a part of the judgment that I know many people find very difficult to accept. Suppose one of our own cities had been attacked with nuclear weapons and had been destroyed? Surely we could respond and destroy their cities too.

The answer is "no." No, not even in response to a nuclear attack against our own cities would it ever be justified to attack any city in the Soviet Union or anywhere else in the world. Counter-population warfare simply cannot be morally justified. That is a clear judgment we make about the use of nuclear weapons.

A second judgment is this: We talk about what is currently the public policy of the United States. In a situation in Europe where our forces would be under attack, the U.S. retains what is called the option of a flexible response, which includes a determination to use nuclear weapons first. This is currently the policy of our own government, of our military forces in the European theater.

We are committed to use nuclear weapons first. We tried to

examine that question very carefully from a moral point of view. Our judgment on this point is, again, a clear "no." It can never be morally justified to initiate nuclear war. We reached that conclusion because everyone who spoke to us about what would happen once nuclear weapons began to be used (and when I say everyone who spoke to us, I mean people from the military, like Admiral Gayler and General George Segnious and General Edwin Rowney; people from the defense establishment, like Mr. Caspar Weinberger and Dr. Harold Brown and Dr. James Schlesinger; people from the Arms Control Agency; and people who have studied what will happen when a nuclear war breaks out) told us, without exception, that once such weapons are used there would not be any real possibility of maintaining what the military call communication, command, and control. In a short time control would be lost and the use of weapons would escalate until we would have an all-out nuclear exchange. The side that initiated nuclear war would have implicitly chosen to bring about an all-out nuclear exchange. So our judgment is that the initiation of nuclear war can never be morally justified.

We went on then to discuss *limited* nuclear war. Can we make a judgment about that? This might seem in some ways to be the same question, but it isn't quite the same. Here we are talking about the whole strategy that our nation is developing right now under the Policy Guidance Plan that our Secretary of Defense has given to the President.

The President has approved spending $1.6 trillion in five years to build up what he calls a war-making capability. If we are attacked with nuclear weapons, we could carry on what he calls a limited nuclear war that might be protracted for six months; it would be limited to a battlefield situation in which he claims we would prevail. He doesn't say win anymore, but he says prevail.

We looked at that question carefully. Fundamentally, it is a question about whether we can really even possess nuclear weapons for any purpose. In trying to be very, very honest in applying the teaching as carefully as we could, we ask in our letter: Theoretically, if one side is under attack and the other side is using nuclear weapons, would it be justified within the framework of a just war to respond proportionately with nuclear weapons? Theoretically, we say "yes." You have not initiated it, so you have not taken that risk. You are trying to respond in a proportionate way to weapons that are being used against you. So, theoretically, you could justify it. But we say we are not dealing in theory. We are not dealing in abstractions and so we have to ask ourselves questions. What will really happen? In the real world, what will happen when we begin to respond with nuclear weapons? Will we be able to keep the effects of those weapons limited? Will we be able to strike military targets only? Will we be able to prevent all-out escalation?

We conclude by saying we are highly skeptical. We do not believe it can be done. We remind ourselves and others who are reflecting on our letter and trying to form their consciences that the burden of proof is on anyone who would choose to respond in that way. That is because the presumption for a follower of Jesus—for someone who is trying to wage war within the limits of this theology—is that you may not use violence unless you are sure the moral conditions for it can and will be fulfilled. So in effect we are saying in the real world such use of nuclear weapons will not be morally justified.

Finally we come to the question of deterrence, the most difficult moral question that we confront in the letter. It truly is a very difficult moral question. For pacifists, of course, it is easy. I am sure that some of us believe in nonviolence and so, in some ways, this whole thing seems unnecessary. But at the same time, even if we do believe in nonviolence and are committed to that, we should try to understand what is truly a moral dilemma for many Christians who seek the way to bring peace into the world.

For thirty-eight years, we have had a strategy of deterrence. Many people will say that this strategy of deterrence has prevented nuclear war. If it were not for the balance of power or balance of terror—call it that if you want—on both sides, there would have been a nuclear attack from one side or the other.

A strategy of deterrence is intended. That is its purpose: to prevent nuclear war, to prevent tyranny and aggression, to prevent totalitarian attack. It is intended to safeguard the things we cherish: our freedom, our ability to love and serve God as we choose—values that are most important to us. The strategy of deterrence has had as its purpose to protect those values—to prevent nuclear war. At the same time (and this is why it becomes such a difficult moral dilemma) the strategy of deterrence is very,

very seriously flawed morally. That is clear when you begin to consider what the strategy of deterrence means. It is defective from a moral point of view.

Deterrence means, for one thing, that we must be engaged in an arms race constantly, because as we build certain new weapons, so do they, and vice versa. This arms race has been going on now for thirty-eight years. It keeps increasing in quantity the number of weapons. But the qualitative development of the arms race also escalates. We are engaged in an arms race that is exhausting our resources, or at least using them in an extraordinary way for the development of arsenals of death and destruction.

The reason deterrence becomes a moral problem especially is that the resources of the world are needed so that people can eat every day. We live in a world where 800 million people right now are living in absolute poverty. Forty thousand children die every day. Right now, in a world where we have more than enough resources so everyone could have a full human life, 40,000 children die of hunger or hunger-related causes every day—that is 15 children every minute.

But this nation spends $650 billion a year to develop "arsenals of death and destruction." In the 1950's, when the amount was much smaller, President Eisenhower said that was theft from the poor. Pope John Paul in his first encyclical letter said we all know well that the areas of misery and hunger in our globe could have been made fertile in a short time if those vast expenditures for arsenals of death and destruction had been changed into investments for food and the service of life. We all know well that we could feed every person on the earth, and yet we continue to choose to build up arsenals of death and destruction. This is a serious moral problem.

This strategy of deterrence is also morally flawed because it contains within it a clear intent to do evil on a scale that exceeds anything the world has ever known. We know that our understanding of sin clearly is this: We turn away from God. We sin when we have formed the intention to do evil in spite of knowing better. Freely choosing to do evil, that is when we sin.

I remember when we were discussing this strategy of deterrence with three or four people among whom was Ambassador Gerard Smith. Ambassador Smith was with the Arms Control Agency for almost forty years. He was the ambassador-at-large for the development of the Salt II Treaty. We talked about the strategy of deterrence. Dr. Schlessinger and General Segnious were there that day, too. And I hoped, although I knew it was a vain hope, that one of them might say: "Of course, we have to keep on saying we're going to use those weapons. We have to keep on terrifying the Soviet Union so that they won't attack here or there or use their weapons against us. We have to say that. But what President could ever really push the button? Who would do it? So we say it, but the President will never do it."

I half hoped that somebody might say that, but no one did. In fact, Ambassador Smith said just the opposite. In a very clear and forceful way he said there is no such thing as a deterrence strategy without the clear intent to use the weapons. He made this very concrete. He said the President and every person in the military chain of command has the clear intent to do it. They are not pretending. They intend to do it.

Of course, they say we hope we never have to. But we will. What makes that even more clear for me is the realization that every day some places in the world go on alert (people on Strategic Air Command bases, people on Trident submarines). They begin the steps that are necessary to unleash the weapons. It is only after they are two or three or four steps into the procedure that they are given a signal to stop. This is only a practice.

They have started with the clear intent to destroy whole cities of people. That is a terrible sin. It is happening now. But we cannot put all the blame on the people in the military. Everyone of us is implicated in that evil, too. We are part of the nation that has a strategy of deterrence as our public policy. We pay taxes to support it. We vote for people who develop it and support it. We live in a country where we have a privilege and a responsibility to help shape our public policy. When a public policy is morally defective, we have some responsibility for it.

So we are caught up in a terrible evil. What do we do now? What kind of a judgment can we make when we are trapped in this sort of a situation? We say the strategy of deterrence is preventing nuclear war. Maybe it really would be irresponsible to disarm immediately and, as many say, risk evoking that terrible holocaust we dread even to think about. But at the same time, when the position is so morally flawed, what do we do then? Our judgment in the pastoral letter is not totally satisfactory. In this kind of a moral dilemma, it is hard to come up with a clear answer. We say that in the present situation with the current balance of terror, call it what it is, a strategy of deterrence can be judged morally acceptable. *But only in strictly conditioned ways.* Two conditions are necessary. The first is that it may not be a long-term strategy. Because it is morally flawed, we have to set the determination that we are going to move away from it. We have to be moving in a different direction, turning our policy around. Then, the second condition follows directly from the first: that the strategy of deterrence must be used as a step toward progressive disarmament. We must reverse what has been happening for thirty-eight years. We must be moving toward progressive disarmament.

Only when these two conditions are fulfilled can we then say that we judge the strategy of deterrence to be morally acceptable.

Those are the four judgments, then, that we make in our pastoral letter. We invite everyone who reads the letter, studies it, and prays over it to examine the Catholic teaching set forth so clearly in the first part and then to apply it. Each of us then can form our own decisions of conscience, decisions about those public policies and what we must do about them.

In the third part of the letter we develop a section called "Promoting Peace." There, too, we try to take Catholic teaching about war and peace and set it forth in very concrete terms. We describe a way we think peace could be built, promoted in our world.

That third section of the letter has many important parts to it. It will not be enough to prevent the deployment of the Pershing II missiles or the cruise missiles. We urge that each of us has to start by looking at the attitude in our own hearts, think of the people and leaders of the Soviet Union as our brothers and sisters, created by the same God who made you and me, called to live in the life of Jesus just as we are, as brothers and sisters. We forget this. Many of them are even brothers and sisters in the faith. There are many, many people in the Soviet Union who are deeply believing people. But all of them, as God's creation in the human family, are our brothers and sisters and we must begin to think of them in that way. That would be at least the beginning for each of us toward helping our nation to develop a whole new relationship with the

Soviet Union. That would be an important part of promoting peace.

The fourth part of the pastoral letter is what we call a "Pastoral Challenge." All of us are called to ask ourselves who are we? How could we describe ourselves best? We say we are the community of the disciples of Jesus. That is what the Church is today, just as it was in the beginning, the community of the disciples of Jesus. If we understand ourselves in this way, we can quickly begin to understand that, as the pastoral letter suggests, we ought not to be surprised if we must choose a course that is not always popular.

The community of the disciples of Jesus might not be in step with the world around it. We even suggest in the letter that maybe we have to begin to understand once more that martyrdom is normal for the disciple of Jesus. These are hard things to reflect on. If we are going to be truly faithful to who Jesus is and to what his community of disciples is called to be, we are going to have to make some hard choices, some difficult decisions.

And so in the fourth part of the letter we call ourselves to prayer —eucharistic prayer above all—to unite ourselves often with Jesus in his death and resurrection around the altar. We recommend prayer to our Blessed Lady, Queen of Peace. We call ourselves to penance because without penance we will not have the deep insight we need to discover the truth. Penance helps to clear our minds and our hearts, helps us to know deeply what God is asking. We also call ourselves to penance because we insist we have to begin to awaken within ourselves and within our nation a sense of sorrow for the terrible evils that we—yes, we—have done before.

Finally, we call ourselves in that part of the letter to a very careful formation of conscience, each of us trying to respond as faithfully as we can to what Jesus is asking of us.

We conclude the letter, then, with a message of hope. We know that it terrifies us to think about the arms that are already in place, and that are going to be in place in ever-greater numbers, with greater accuracy and greater destructive capability. That fear could paralyze us. It could cause us to not act. It could prevent us from acting.

But we think—and this is something I hope all of us can truly grasp and make our own—that for the Christian, there can never be any kind of paralysis from fear because we are people who can hope. We have a firm foundation for hope. We are the people who know what God has done in Jesus: how the power of God, which is a power that can bring justice and peace into our human community, lived in Jesus to overcome evil, to overcome sin, to overcome death, to raise Jesus to new life as Lord and Son of God in power. That is what we hope in: a God who can do, in a powerful way, what God did in Jesus. That God can work in and through us, too. If we are responsive to what God asks of us and to the way God leads us, we can have well-founded hope. We can be the community of the disciples of Jesus and overcome the terrible evil of the nuclear arms race.

The community of the disciples of Jesus with God's power working can become the peacemakers our world needs now. With that power of God, we can be confident that we will bring His peace and His justice to our world.

Contributors

JOSEPH CARDINAL BERNARDIN, D.D.
Archbishop of Chicago

Joseph Cardinal Bernardin was ordained for his native Diocese of Charleston, South Carolina, in April 1952. During fourteen years there, he served under four bishops in many capacities including the offices of chancellor, vicar general, diocesan consultor, and administrator of the diocese during a period when the see was vacant. Named auxiliary bishop of Atlanta in 1966, he served as vicar general, rector of the Cathedral of Christ the King, and, after the death of Archbishop Hallinan, as administrator of the archdiocese.

In 1968, Bishop Bernardin was elected general secretary of the National Conference of Catholic Bishops and the United States Catholic Conference. As general secretary, he helped reorganize the conference according to the norms recommended by the Second Vatican Council. In November 1972, Pope Paul VI appointed him as archbishop of Cincinnati, and from 1974 to 1977 he served as president of the NCCB and USCC. After almost ten years in the Ohio metropolitan see, he was named archbishop of Chicago by Pope John Paul II in 1982, and he was designated a member of the College of Cardinals in January 1983.

Cardinal Bernardin most recently served as chairman of the NCCB ad hoc Committee on War and Peace during which time he supervised the preparation of the bishops' historic pastoral letter *The Challenge of Peace: God's Promise and Our Response*, which was approved by the conference of bishops in May 1983. Currently, he chairs the NCCB Committee for Pro-Life Activities.

JOHN S. CUMMINS, D.D.
Bishop of Oakland

Born in Oakland, California, raised and educated in Berkeley, John S. Cummins was ordained for the Archdiocese of San Francisco in 1953. He became chancellor of the newly established Diocese of Oakland in 1962, and was secretary to Bishop Floyd Begin at the Second Vatican Council. As chancellor, Bishop Cummins worked with Catholic and Protestant theologians in developing the Graduate Theological Union at Berkeley. Active also in the formation of the California Catholic Conference as the coordinating instrument for interdiocesan pastoral interests, he served as its first executive director for six years. Named auxiliary bishop for the Diocese of Sacramento in 1974, he was installed as the second bishop of Oakland in 1977.

Stressing strong consultative processes in his own diocese, Bishop Cummins has brought this approach to the Education, Family Life, and Youth Ministry committees of the United States Catholic Conference, as well as the chairmanship of the NCCB Committee on Liturgy.

CARROLL T. DOZIER, D.D.
Retired Bishop of Memphis

Best known nationally and internationally for the bold pastoral initiative of two diocesan-wide reconciliation services held in Memphis and Jackson, Tennessee, in December of 1976 and attended by more than 12,000 people, Carroll T. Dozier was ordained as the first bishop of the newly created Diocese of Memphis on January 6, 1971. A native of Richmond, Virginia, Bishop Dozier is an alumnus of Holy Cross College in Worcester, Massachusetts, and holds a degree in philosophy and sacred theology from the Gregorian University in Rome.

Recognized as an ardent advocate of racial justice and a tireless peace activist, Bishop Dozier was an organizer and co-moderator of Pax Christi–U.S.A., and has worked diligently in the field of ecumenism. His writings, particularly widely publicized pastoral letters, include *Peace: Gift and Task*, stressing the Christian mandate to become peacemakers; *Justice: God's Vision—Man's Discipleship*, concerning the obligation to deal justly with all people everywhere; and *Woman: Intrepid and Loving*, regarding the injustices that have been imposed on women throughout history.

In 1980, Bishop Dozier inaugurated St. James Cathedral's *Shepherds Speak* series, and in June of 1982, shortly before his retirement as the bishop of Memphis, he became the first recipient of the cathedral's annual Compostela Award. Bishop Dozier died December 6, 1985.

JOHN J. FITZPATRICK, D.D.
Bishop of Brownsville

John J. Fitzpatrick was born in Trenton, Ontario, in October 1918. Originally ordained for the Diocese of Buffalo, Bishop Fitzpatrick studied theology in Italy and the United States. He subsequently transferred to the Diocese of St. Augustine, Florida, where he served as the director of the Center for Latin Americans and editor of the diocesan newspaper, *The Florida Catholic*. He was ordained auxiliary bishop of Miami in 1968, and three years later, he was appointed the bishop of Brownsville, Texas.

A member of various NCCB committees (Church in Latin America, Hispanic Affairs, Social Development, and World Peace), Bishop Fitzpatrick also served as president of the Texas Conference of Churches and is a board member of the Texas Catholic Conference. Long active in the struggles of migrant workers, the Diocese of Brownsville has most recently become the focus of national attention as a center of the Sanctuary Movement for Latin-American refugees.

JOSEPH A. FRANCIS, S.V.D., D.D.
Auxiliary Bishop of Newark

Joseph Abel Francis is a native of Louisiana and was ordained for the Society of the Divine Word in October 1950. After graduate studies in education at The Catholic University of America, Bishop Francis served his religious community as a teacher, school administrator and principal, and as provincial superior in Missouri, Texas, and California. This national experience led to leadership roles in the Black Priests Caucus, the Conference of Major Superiors of Men, the National Office for Black Catholics, and the National Catholic Conference of Interracial Justice.

Ordained auxiliary bishop for the Archdiocese of Newark in June 1976, Bishop Francis was a drafter of the historic document from the U.S. bishops on racism, *Brothers and Sisters to Us*. A member of the Board of Overseers for Harvard Divinity School and recipient of honorary degrees from Holy Cross College, Catholic Theological Union in Chicago, and Seton Hall University, Bishop Francis was the fourth black American to be ordained a Roman Catholic bishop in this century.

RENE H. GRACIDA, D.D.
Bishop of Corpus Christi

Rene Gracida has had careers in the Air Force during the Second World War—flying thirty-two missions between 1943 and 1945 —and in business as an architect and instructor in architecture. Ordained to the priesthood at thirty-six for the Archdiocese of Miami, Bishop Gracida served ten parishes throughout Florida and held positions as chancellor, vicar general, superintendent of education, and auxiliary bishop of Miami between 1961 and 1975. He was named the first bishop of Pensacola-Tallahassee in October 1975.

Active in liturgical and architectural commissions and societies, Bishop Gracida was a member and chairman of the NCCB Committee for Liturgy, and has also served as chairman of the bishops' ad hoc Committee on Migration and Tourism. A member of the Committee for the Spanish Speaking and consultor to the Pontifical Commission for the Pastoral Care of Migrants and Tourists, he was appointed bishop of Corpus Christi, Texas, by Pope John Paul II in 1983.

THOMAS J. GUMBLETON, D.D.
Auxiliary Bishop of Detroit

Holding a doctorate in canon law from the Pontifical Lateran University in Rome, Bishop Thomas Gumbleton has been the assistant vice-chancellor, vicar general, and since 1968, auxiliary bishop in his home Diocese of Detroit, Michigan. Born in 1930, Thomas Gumbleton has become almost synonymous with the major social-justice movements of our time. As president of Bread for the World and Pax Christi–U.S.A., he has championed the causes of disarmament, nonviolence, and equitable food distribution throughout the world.

In 1979, as a representative of the United States bishops, he visited the American hostages in Iran. In 1982–1983, Bishop Gumbleton served as a principal shaper of the U.S. bishops' landmark pastoral *The Challenge of Peace: God's Promise and Our Response*. Of the forty-two bishops who have participated in the *Shepherds Speak* series, Thomas Gumbleton is the one bishop who has spoken at St. James Cathedral on three separate occasions.

THOMAS C. KELLY, O.P., D.D.
Archbishop of Louisville

Thomas Cajetan Kelly has been a member of the Order of Preachers (Dominicans) for thirty-five years. A native of New York State, Archbishop Kelly holds degrees from Providence College, the Dominican House of Studies in Washington, D.C., and the Angelicum in Rome. Over a period of nearly twenty years, he worked in the nation's capital as secretary to the Dominican Fathers' provincial, secretary to the Apostolic Delegation, associate secretary to the Catholic Bishops' Conference, general secretary of the USCC/NCCB, and as auxiliary bishop of the Archdiocese of Washington.

Appointed archbishop of Louisville, Kentucky, in 1981, he is a member of the bishops' Committee for Liaison with the Conference of Major Superiors of Men, on the board of directors of the Catholic Health Association, and a member of the Pontifical Commission for Religious in the U.S.A. Archbishop Kelly has also co-authored with the bishops of Kentucky a pastoral letter, *Choose Life: Reflections on the Death Penalty.*

RAYMOND A. LUCKER, S.T.D.
Bishop of New Ulm

Installed as the second bishop of New Ulm, Minnesota, in February 1976, Raymond A. Lucker holds a doctorate in theology from the University of St. Thomas in Rome and a doctorate in education from the University of Minnesota. It is in the fields of religious education, catechetics, and evangelization that Bishop Lucker has worked for over thirty years. He became the director of the Department of Education for the United States Catholic Conference in Washington, D.C., in 1969.

A native of St. Paul, Minnesota, he served his home diocese as a pastor, seminary professor, superintendent of schools, and auxiliary bishop of the Archdiocese of St. Paul–Minneapolis. He is active at the national level on NCCB committees regarding the Catechetical Directory, Laity, the Permanent Diaconate, and the Charismatic Renewal.

WILLIAM E. McMANUS, D.D.
Retired Bishop of Fort Wayne–South Bend

William McManus was ordained for the Archdiocese of Chicago in 1939 and a year later began a long and distinguished career in Catholic education by devoting two years to graduate studies at The Catholic University of America. In 1945 he became assistant director of the Department of Education for the National Catholic Welfare Conference (the forerunner of the National Conference of Catholic Bishops), and after more than a decade in Washington, D.C., he returned to Chicago to become the superintendent of Catholic Schools for the archdiocese—a position he held for eleven years.

Ordained as auxiliary bishop of Chicago by the late John Cardinal Cody in 1967, Bishop McManus continued his involvement in education by serving as secretary of Catholic education in Chicago until 1976 when he was appointed the seventh bishop of Fort Wayne–South Bend by Pope Paul VI. He retired as Ordinary of the diocese in the spring of 1985.

ROGER M. MAHONY, D.D.
Archbishop of Los Angeles

Ordained to the priesthood for the Diocese of Fresno, California, in 1962, Roger Mahony obtained an M.S.W. from The Catholic University of America and subsequently served as diocesan director of Catholic Charities and Social Services in Fresno from 1964 to 1970. During that same period he was also the chairman of the California Association of Catholic Charities Directors and a member of the board of directors for the West Coast regional office of the Bishops Committee for the Spanish-Speaking. From 1970 to 1975 he was secretary of the U.S. Catholic bishops ad hoc Committee on Farm Labor, and in 1975 he was appointed as auxiliary bishop of Fresno.

Installed as the third bishop of Stockton in 1980, Bishop Mahony also serves as chairman of the NCCB Committee on Conciliation and Arbitration, as well as the ad hoc Committee on Farm Labor. In 1984 he was named to the Pontifical Commission on Justice and Peace, and one year later was appointed as archbishop of Los Angeles.

JAMES W. MALONE, D.D.
Bishop of Youngstown

Current president of the National Conference of Catholic Bishops/United States Catholic Conference, Bishop James Malone has served his native city and Diocese of Youngstown, Ohio, since priestly ordination on May 25, 1945. Holding a Ph.D. from The Catholic University of America, Bishop Malone administered the

Catholic school system of Youngstown for thirteen years. After tenure as auxiliary bishop, vicar general, and apostolic administrator of his diocese, he was installed as the bishop of Youngstown in 1968. Bishop Malone has been active in the NCCB on both the Administrative and Executive committees, as well as serving a term as its vice president. Among the youngest American bishops to attend the Second Vatican Council, Bishop Malone chaired the National Planning Committee for the Bishops' Assembly for Prayer and Reflection on Episcopal Ministry held at Collegeville, Minnesota, in June 1982.

P. FRANCIS MURPHY, D.D.
Auxiliary Bishop of Baltimore

Ordained in Rome in 1958, after studies at the North American College, P. "Frank" Murphy continued theological studies there while serving on the faculty of the North American College, of which he became assistant vice-rector. In July of 1965, he returned to his native Diocese of Baltimore and became secretary to Lawrence Cardinal Sheehan. As an advisor to the cardinal-archbishop, his primary areas of concern were the renewal following Vatican II, personnel and ministry assignments, and outreach to resigned priests.

After terms of vicar for personnel and chancellor for pastoral concerns, he was ordained an auxiliary bishop for the Archdiocese of Baltimore in February of 1976. Bishop Murphy has served on NCCB committees on Doctrine, Priestly Life and Ministry, Pastoral Research, and Women in Society and in the Church.

DANIEL P. REILLY, D.D.
Bishop of Norwich

Daniel P. Reilly was ordained for his native city and Diocese of Providence, Rhode Island, in 1953. He served there for twenty-two years as an associate pastor, assistant and secretary to the bishop, chancellor, vicar general, and administrator of the diocese. In June 1975, he was appointed the third bishop of the Diocese of Norwich, Connecticut. Bishop Reilly serves on the NCCB Committee on Budget and Finance, and as chairman of the Catholic Relief Services he has traveled extensively, overseeing the emergency work of this world-wide aid and development agency of the Catholic Church in the United States. Having most recently traveled to Lebanon, Ethiopia, Poland, and South Africa, Bishop Reilly's observations from his journey to the latter country formed the basis of his *Shepherds Speak* paper.

JOHN R. ROACH, D.D.
Archbishop of St. Paul–Minneapolis

John R. Roach, a native of Minnesota, has been a priest of his home Diocese of St. Paul and Minneapolis for forty years. During this time, he has served as teacher, seminary rector, parochial pastor, auxiliary bishop, and since 1975, archbishop. During his tenure as vice-president (1977–1980) and president (1980–1983) of the National Conference of Catholic Bishops, he helped guide the formulation of the most significant document yet produced by the American Catholic hierarchy—the peace pastoral, *The Challenge of Peace: God's Promise and Our Response.*

Chairman of the NCCB Committee on Priestly Formation and active on the Administrative Committees and Priorities and Plans Committees of both the NCCB and the USCC, Archbishop Roach also is chairman of the board of directors of the National Catholic Educational Association.

RICHARD J. SKLBA, D.D.
Auxiliary Bishop of Milwaukee

Prior to his 1979 ordination as auxiliary bishop of Milwaukee, Richard J. Sklba had begun a distinguished career as a scripture scholar and professor of biblical studies. Holding degrees from the

Gregorian University, the Angelicum, and the Pontifical Biblical Institute in Rome, Bishop Sklba is past president of the Catholic Biblical Association and the Midwest Association of Theological Schools. His articles have appeared in *The Catholic Biblical Quarterly* and *The Bible Today*. Long active in the Catholic Theological Society of America and the Chicago Society for Biblical Research, he also serves in the National Conference of Catholic Bishops on the Liturgy, Sacraments and Ministry, Permanent Diaconate, and Learned Societies committees. Besides his work as a parish priest, college professor, and seminary rector, Bishop Sklba is currently vicar general of the Archdiocese of Milwaukee and episcopal delegate for Parish and Pastoral Concerns.

J. FRANCIS STAFFORD, D.D.
Bishop of Memphis

After twenty-five years of pastoral service in his native city of Baltimore, J. Francis Stafford was named the second bishop of Memphis, Tennessee, in January 1982. Formally trained in theology at the Gregorian University in Rome and in social work at The Catholic University of America in Washington, D.C., Bishop Stafford has had extensive experience with the problems of the urban poor as auxiliary bishop of the Archdiocese of Baltimore for six years. His priestly work centered in Catholic Charities and social-welfare administration. These fields prepared Bishop Stafford for his present episcopal responsibilities in a see that covers the western third of Tennessee. He has established in Memphis a commission with the Diocese of Nashville that works jointly with government and civic organizations on public-policy issues, and one specific consequence of this interdiocesan effort was a pastoral letter on capital punishment that Bishop Stafford wrote in cooperation with the Most Reverend James D. Niedergeses, Bishop of Nashville.

Bishop Stafford is internationally active as an ecumenist. He is a member of the Oriental Orthodox/Roman Catholic Consultation of the NCCB and is co-chairman of the Roman Catholic/World Methodist Council Bilateral Dialogue and the Roman Catholic/

Lutheran Dialogue. For seven years he has worked in the area of marriage and family life for the United States Catholic Conference.

REMBERT G. WEAKLAND, O.S.B., D.D.
Archbishop of Milwaukee

Milwaukee's ninth archbishop, Rembert Weakland has served the Church internationally for over thirty years. A Benedictine monk since 1945, Archbishop Weakland has pursued graduate theological and musical studies in the United States and Europe—particularly at Sant'Anselmo in Rome and the Juilliard School of Music in New York.

A native of Pennsylvania, Rembert George Weakland was elected archabbot of St. Vincent Archabbey in 1963, and in 1967 was elected abbot primate of the International Benedictine Confederation. He served as a member of the Vatican Liturgical Commission, as well as in the synods of bishops from 1967 to 1977 representing the Union of Male Religious Superiors.

Appointed archbishop of Milwaukee in 1977 by Pope Paul VI, he currently serves as the chairperson of the National Conference of Catholic Bishops' ad hoc Committee on Catholic Social Teaching and the U.S. Economy, and is co-chairperson of the consultation between the Roman Catholic and Eastern Orthodox Churches.